Where do I go for answers to my travel questions?

What's the best and easiest way to plan and book my trip?

frommers.travelocity.com

Frommer's, the travel guide leader, has teamed up with **Travelocity.com**, the leader in online travel, to bring you an in-depth, easy-to-use resource designed to help you plan and book your trip online.

At **frommers.travelocity.com**, you'll find free online updates about your destination from the experts at Frommer's plus the outstanding travel planning and purchasing features of Travelocity.com. Travelocity.com provides reservations capabilities for 95 percent of all airline seats sold, more than 47,000 hotels, and over 50 car rental companies. In addition, Travelocity.com offers more than 2,000 exciting vacation and cruise packages. Travelocity.com puts you in complete control of your travel planning with these and other great features:

> **Expert travel guidance from Frommer's** - over 150 writers reporting from around the world!
>
> **Best Fare Finder** - an interactive calendar tells you when to travel to get the best airfare
>
> **Fare Watcher** - we'll track airfare changes to your favorite destinations
>
> **Dream Maps** - a mapping feature that suggests travel opportunities based on your budget
>
> **Shop Safe Guarantee** - 24 hours a day / 7 days a week live customer service, and more!

Whether traveling on a tight budget, looking for a quick weekend getaway, or planning the trip of a lifetime, Frommer's guides and Travelocity.com will make your travel dreams a reality. You've bought the book, now book the trip!

Travelocity.com
A Sabre Company

Frommer's

Here's what the critics say about Frommer's:

"Amazingly easy to use. Very portable, very complete."

—*Booklist*

♦

"The only mainstream guide to list specific prices. The Walter Cronkite of guidebooks— with all that implies."

—*Travel & Leisure*

♦

"Complete, concise, and filled with useful information."

—*New York Daily News*

♦

"Hotel information is close to encyclopedic."
—*Des Moines Sunday Register*

♦

"Detailed, accurate and easy-to-read information for all price ranges."

—*Glamour*

P O R T A B L E

Maine Coast
3rd Edition

by Wayne Curtis

HUNGRY MINDS, INC.

New York, NY • Indianapolis, IN

ABOUT THE AUTHOR

Wayne Curtis is a travel writer who lives in Eastport, Maine. His stories have appeared in numerous magazines and newspapers, including *The New York Times, Yankee, House Beautiful,* and *Discovery Channel Online.* He's also the author of *Frommer's Guide to Atlantic Canada,* and *Maine: Off the Beaten Path* (Globe Pequot).

Published by:

HUNGRY MINDS, INC.

909 Third Avenue
New York, NY 10022
www.frommers.com

ISBN 0-7645-6343-2
ISSN 1093-0221

Editor: Amy Lyons
Production Editor: Cara L. Buitron
Photo Editor: Richard Fox
Design by Michele Laseau
Cartographer: Elizabeth Puhl
Production by Hungry Minds Indianapolis Production Services
Cover Photo: Pemaquid Lighthouse in Pemaquid Point, Maine

SPECIAL SALES

For general information on Hungry Minds' products and services, please contact our Customer Care department; within the U.S. at 800-762-2974, outside the U.S. at 317-572-3993 or fax 317-572-4002. For sales inquiries and reseller information, including discounts, bulk sales, customized editions, and premium sales, please contact our Customer Care department at 800-434-3422.

Manufactured in the United States of America

5   4   3   2   1

Contents

List of Maps

AN INVITATION TO THE READER

In researching this book we have discovered many wonderful places—hotels, restaurants, shops, and more. We're sure you'll find others. Please tell us about them, so that we can share the information with your fellow travelers in upcoming editions. If you were disappointed with a recommendation, we'd love to know that, too. Please write to:

Frommer's Portable Maine Coast, 3rd Edition

Hungry Minds, Inc.

909 Third Avenue

New York, NY 10022

AN ADDITIONAL NOTE

Please be advised that travel information is subject to change at any time, and this is especially true of prices. We, therefore, suggest that you write or call ahead for confirmation when making your travel plans. The authors, editors, and publishers cannot be held responsible for the experiences of readers while traveling. Your safety is important to us, however, so we encourage you to stay alert and be aware of your surroundings. Keep a close eye on cameras, purses, and wallets all favorite targets of thieves and pickpockets.

WHAT THE SYMBOLS MEAN

✪ Frommer's Favorites

Our favorite places and experiences—outstanding for quality, value, or both.

The following abbreviations are used for credit cards:

AE	American Express	EC	Eurocard
CB	Carte Blanche	JCB	Japan Credit Bank
DC	Diners Club	MC	MasterCard
DISC	Discover	V	Visa
ER	EnRoute		

FIND FROMMER'S ONLINE

www.frommers.com offers up-to-the-minute listings on almost 200 cities around the globe including the latest bargains and candid, personal articles updated daily by Arthur Frommer himself. No other Web site offers such comprehensive and timely coverage of the world of travel.

Planning a Trip to the Maine Coast

*H*umorist Dave Barry once wryly suggested that Maine's state motto should be "Cold, but damp."

Cute, but true. There's spring, which tends to last a few blustery, rain-soaked days. There's November, in which Arctic winds alternate with gray sheets of rain. And then winter brings a character-building mix of blizzards and ice storms to the fabled coast.

Ah, but then there's summer. Summer in Maine brings ospreys diving for fish off wooded points; gleaming cumulus clouds building over the rounded peaks of Acadia, and the haunting whoop of loons echoing off the dense forest walls bordering the lakes. It brings languorous days when the sun rises before most visitors and it seems like noontime at 8am. Maine summers bring a measure of gracious tranquility, and a placid stay in the right spot can rejuvenate even the most jangled nerves.

The trick comes in finding that right spot. Those who arrive here without a clear plan may find themselves cursing their travel decision. Maine's Route 1 along the coast has its moments, but for the most part it's rather charmless—an amalgam of convenience stores, tourist boutiques, and restaurants catering to bus tours. Acadia National Park, for all its vaunted ocean vistas, also has world-class congestion along some of the byways in and around the park. In this it's no different than other national parks of its stature—whether Yosemite or Yellowstone. You need strategy to avoid the worst moments.

Fortunately, Maine's size works to the traveler's advantage. Maine is nearly as large as the other five New England states combined. Straighten out the state's convoluted coast and you'll discover you've got more than a continent's worth of exploring—some 4,500 miles of mainland shoreline. Add to that some 4,600 coastal islands, and you'll realize that with a little planning, you should easily be able to find your piece of Maine away from the bustle and crowds.

This chapter is designed to provide most of the nuts-and-bolts travel information you'll need before setting off to explore coastal Maine. Browse through the following sections before you hit the road to ensure you've touched all the bases.

1 Visitor Information & Money

VISITOR INFORMATION

For a comprehensive overview of what's what in the state contact the **Maine Tourism Association** (☎ 207/623-0363; www.mainetourism.com), which publishes a stout "official" travel guide entitled "Maine Invites You" (also available free at official information centers; you often have to ask for it). The state's department of tourism (☎ 800/533-9595; www.visitmaine.com) is also helpful. For local and regional information, chambers of commerce addresses and phone numbers are provided for each region in the chapters that follow.

MONEY

Budget travelers accustomed to turning up basic motels for $30 or $35 in other parts of the country are in for a bit of a shock in Maine, at least during the summer. During the height of the tourist season, there's virtually no such thing as a cheap motel along the Maine Coast. Motels where you might reasonably expect to pay $40 per night will command $90 on a Saturday in August. (To be fair, many of the innkeepers in these northern latitudes must make all their profit in what amounts to a 2- or 3-month season.)

What are the alternatives?

- **Travel in the off-season.** Inexpensive rooms are often available in April or May. If that's a little too bleak (trees often aren't in full leaf until late May), consider traveling between Memorial Day and July 4th, when you can often get room discounts and good deals on packages as innkeepers get ready for the crowds of high summer. The best off-season period to my mind is September. The weather is good, and many inns and hotels cut their prices for two or three weeks between the summer and foliage periods.

Maine

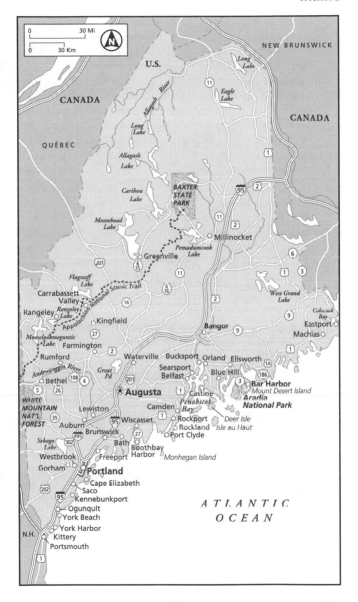

- **Commute from lower-priced areas.** If you're willing to drive a half-hour to an hour to reach prime destinations, you can often find cheaper lodging—including chain motels—in less glamorous locations inland.
- **Camp.** Maine's coast isn't so congested that campgrounds have been driven out to make room for condominiums. You should be able to find great camping at both public and private campgrounds, with prices ranging from $8 to $28 per night. Be aware that coastal campgrounds south of Portland tend to be fewer in number, a bit more crowded, and more expensive; northward, the opportunities expand and the prices tend to fall.

Traveler's checks are commonly accepted everywhere, although some shops may balk at cashing $100 checks for small purchases. Cash machines (ATMs) are easy to find in the more populated areas and regions that cater to tourists. But don't count on finding machines in the smaller villages in the more remote parts of the region. Stock up on cash when you can. To locate the nearest machine in the **PLUS** network, call ☎ **800/843-7587.** For the **Cirrus** network, call ☎ **800/ 424-7787.**

2 When to Go

THE SEASONS

The well-worn joke about Maine's climate is that it has just two seasons: winter and August. There's a kernel of truth to that, but it's mostly a canard to keep outsiders from moving here, repeated the same way Seattle "celebrates" its 11-month rain festival.

SUMMER

The peak summer season runs from July 4th to Labor Day. Vast crowds surge up the Maine Coast during and between the two holiday weekends, swelling traffic on the turnpike and Route 1, and causing countless motels and inns to hang "No Vacancy" signs. This should be no surprise: Summers are exquisite here. (In Portland, it tops 90 degrees only 4 or 5 days a year on average.) Expect to pay premium prices at hotels and restaurants along the coast in mid-season.

Maine's weather is largely determined by the prevailing winds. Southwest winds bring haze, heat, humidity, and often thunderstorms. The northwest winds bring cool weather and knife-sharp vistas. These systems tend to alternate during the summer, with the heat arriving stealthily and slowly, then getting exiled by stiff, cool winds rising from the north a few days later. (The change from hot to cool will sometimes occur in a matter of minutes.) Along the immediate coast it's often warmest in the late morning, since sea breezes typically kick up around lunchtime, pushing temperatures back down in the afternoons. Rain is rarely far away—some days it's an afternoon thunderstorm, sometimes it's a steady drizzle that brings a 4-day soaking. On average, about 1 day in 3 will bring some rain. Travelers should come prepared for it.

Also be aware that early summer brings out the blackflies and the mosquitoes in great multitude, a state of affairs that has spoiled many camping and hiking trips. While this is especially true in the inland areas, it applies along the coast and offshore islands as well. Outdoors enthusiasts are best off waiting until after July 4 for longer adventures if they want to avoid a fate as human pincushions.

Autumn

Don't be surprised to smell the tang of fall approaching as early as mid-August, a time when you'll also notice a few leaves turned fiery red in otherwise green-leafed maples at the edges of wetlands. Fall comes early to northern New England, puts its feet up on the couch, and stays for some time.

Happily, thanks to the low elevation and moderating influences of the ocean temperatures along the coast, the foliage season tends to run even longer along the coast. Inland mountains can be brown and brittle by mid-October, but coastal foliage is just hitting its stride by then, and the tart colors can linger into the first few days of November.

Keep in mind that fall gets the most intense short-term tourist traffic in New England. Maine's coast attracts fewer leaf peepers than Vermont or New Hampshire, but don't expect to be alone during early October. Hotels are often booked up, and reservations are strongly encouraged.

Winter

Winters along Maine's Coast are like wine—some years are good; some are lousy. During a good season, plenty of light, fluffy snow blankets the dark, rocky coast and offers a profound peace and tranquility. The muffling qualities of fresh snow can bring a thunderous silence to the region, and the hiss and pop of a wood fire at a coastal inn can sound like an overwrought symphony. What's more, the sea is typically at its most turbulent during the winter, and can put on a spectacular show during a heavy blizzard. During these winters, coastal vacations can be unforgettable—nothing beats cross-country skiing on fresh snow at the edge of the pounding surf.

During the other winters, the lousy ones, the wet sea winds bring a nasty mélange of rain and sleet. In 1998 a destructive ice storm wreaked havoc on trees (you'll see broken trunks and branches almost everywhere) and citizens, stranding over half of Maine's homes without power for up to 2 weeks. It's bone-numbing cold, and bleak, bleak, bleak.

Ergo, visiting the coast in the winter can be a high-risk venture. It's best to come prepared for hunkering down with a long book or a jigsaw puzzle at a comfortable inn. If the weather cooperates and provides crisp weather and new-fallen snow, consider it an added bonus.

Where to go? Beach towns like York Beach and Ogunquit and tourist destinations like Boothbay Harbor tend to be shuttered and melancholy in the winter. Intrepid winter travelers are better off heading to places with more substantial year-round communities and a good selection of year-round lodging, like Kennebunkport, Portland, and Camden.

SPRING

Maine's spring seemingly lasts only a weekend or so, often appearing around mid-May but sometimes as late as June. One day the ground is muddy, the trees barren, and gritty snow is still collected in shady hollows. The next day, it's in the 80s, trees are blooming, and kids are jumping off the docks into the ocean. Travelers must be very crafty and alert if they want to experience Maine's spring. This is also known as mud season, and it's a time many innkeepers and restaurateurs close up for a few weeks for repairs or to venture someplace warm.

That said, April and May can offer superb days when a blue sky arches overhead and it's warm in the sun. And this may be the most peaceful time of year—a good season for solitary walks on the beach or to sit on rocky promontories with only seagulls for company. Just be aware that as soon as the sun slips behind a cloud or over the horizon, it'll quickly feel like winter again. Don't leave your parka or gloves behind if you venture here in spring.

THE MAINE COAST CALENDAR OF EVENTS

January

✪ **New Year's Portland.** Ring in the New Year with a smorgasbord of events and entertainment throughout downtown Portland. Events for families are scheduled in the afternoon; adult entertainment including loads of live music kicks off later in the evening at numerous auditoriums, shops, and churches. One admission price buys entrance to all events. Call ☎ **207/ 772-6828.** December 31/January 1.

February

• **U.S. National Toboggan Championship,** Camden. Hundreds of teams from around the country converge at the Camden Snowbowl to try their hand at the 400-foot wooden toboggan chute. Call ☎ **207/236-3438.** Early February.

March

• **Maine Boatbuilders Show,** Portland. More than 200 exhibitors and 9,000 boat aficionados gather as winter fades to make plans for the coming summer. It's a great place to meet boatbuilders and get ideas for your dream craft. Call ☎ **207/774-1067.** Late March.

• **Maine Maple Sunday.** Maple sugarhouses throughout the state open their doors to visitors. Call ☎ **207/287-3491.** Third Sunday in March.

April

• **Boothbay Harbor Fisherman's Festival.** Local fishermen display their talents in fish filleting, clam shucking, and even lobster eating. Enjoy seafood feasts, exhibits, games, and a Blessing of the Fleet on Sunday afternoon. Call ☎ **207/ 633-2353.** Second weekend of April.

June

✪ **Old Port Festival,** Portland. A daylong block party in the heart of Portland's historic district with live music, food vendors, and activities for kids. Call ☎ **207/772-2249** for information. Early June.

• **Great Kennebec Whatever Week,** Augusta. A community celebration to mark the cleaning up of the Kennebec River, culminating in a wacky race involving all manner of watercraft, some more seaworthy than others. Call ☎ **207/623-4559** for details. Late June.

- **Annual Windjammer Days,** Boothbay Harbor. For nearly four decades, windjammers have gathered in Boothbay Harbor to kick off the summer sailing season. Expect music, food, and a parade of magnificent sailboats. Call ☎ **207/633-2353.** Late June.

July

- **Fourth of July Celebrations.** Parades, food, fireworks, and festivities abound along the Maine Coast. Check local newspapers or contact chambers of commerce for details.

- **Summer Performance Series,** Portland. Relax and enjoy 50 free noontime performances in Portland's Downtown Parks. Music includes classical, folk, jazz, rock, country, and children's shows. Call ☎ **207/772-6828** for a complete listing.

August

- **Maine Lobster Festival,** Rockland. Fill up on the local harvest at this event marking the importance and delectability of Maine's favorite crustacean. Enjoy a boiled lobster or two, and take in the ample entertainment during this informal waterfront gala. Call ☎ **207/596-0376** or 800/562-2529. Usually the first weekend in August.

- ✪ **Maine Festival,** Brunswick. A weekend-long festival showcasing Maine-made arts and crafts, music, foods, and performers. Boisterous, fun, and filling. Call ☎ **207/772-9012.** Early August.

- **York Days,** York Village. Enjoy a quintessential coastal Maine celebration complete with crafts, road races, parades, dances, concerts, fireworks, and much more. Call ☎ **207/363-1040.** Early August.

- **Blueberry Festival,** Machias. A festival marking the harvest of the region's wild blueberries. Eat to your heart's content. Call ☎ **207/794-3543.** Mid-August.

- **Blue Hill Fair,** Blue Hill. A classic country fair just outside one of Maine's most elegant villages. Call ☎ **207/374-9976.** Late August.

September

- **Windjammer Weekend,** Camden. Come visit Maine's impressive fleet of old-time sailing ships, which host open houses throughout the weekend at this scenic harbor. Call ☎ 207/236-4404. Early September.

❂ **Common Ground Fair,** Unity. An old-time state fair with a twist: The emphasis is on organic foods, recycling, and wholesome living. Special trains run from Belfast to the fair. Call ☎ **207/623-5515.** Late September.

October

- **Fall Foliage Fair,** Boothbay. More than 100 exhibitors display their arts and crafts at the Railroad Village; plenty of festive foodstuffs and live music too. Call ☎ **207/633-4924.** Early October.
- **Fall Festival,** Camden. This 2-day event includes more than 90 artists and craftsmen, children's activities, food, and entertainment. Call ☎ **207/236-4404.** Early October.

November

- **Victorian Holiday,** Portland. From late November until Christmas, Portland decorates its Old Port in a Victorian Christmas theme. Enjoy the window displays, take a free hayride, and listen to costumed carolers sing. Call ☎ **207/772-6828** for details.

December

- **Christmas Prelude,** Kennebunkport. This scenic coastal village greets Santa's arrival in a lobster boat, and marks the coming of Christmas with street shows, pancake breakfasts, and tours of the town's inns. Call ☎ **207/967-3286.** Early December.
- **York Village Festival of Lights.** This beautiful festival displays an entire York Village and York Beach lit with Christmas lights, carolers, a parade, and much more. Call ☎ **207/363-4422.** Early December.

3 Enjoying the Great Outdoors

The Maine Coast is a fine destination for those who like their coastal vacations seasoned with adventure. While southern Maine has classic beach towns where the smell of salt air mixes with coconut oil and taffy, much of the rest of the Maine Coast is unruly and wild. In parts, it seems to share more in common with Alaska—you can see bald eagles soaring above and whales breaching below. In between these two archetypes, you'll find remote coves perfect for a rowboat jaunt, and isolated offshore islands accessible only by sea kayak.

The best places for coastal adventure are often not the most obvious places—those tend to be crowded and more developed. You'll need to do a bit of homework to find the real treasures. A growing number of specialized guidebooks and outfitters can help point visitors in the right direction; some of the best are mentioned below.

BEACHGOING

Swimming at Maine's ocean beaches is for the foolish and the hardy. The Gulf Stream, which prods warm waters toward the Cape Cod shores to the south, veers toward Iceland south of Maine and leaves the state's 4,600-mile coastline washed by the brisk Nova Scotia current, an offshoot of the Arctic Labrador Current. During the summer months, water temperatures along the south coast can top 60° during an especially warm spell where the water is shallow, but it's usually cooler than that. The average ocean temperature at Bar Harbor in summer is 54°; farther east in Passamaquoddy Bay it's 51°.

Maine's beaches are located mostly between Portland and the New Hampshire border. Northeast of Portland there are a handful of fine beaches—including popular **Reid State Park** and **Popham Beach State Park**—but rocky coast defines this territory for the most part. The southern beaches are beautiful, but rarely isolated. Summer homes occupy the low dunes in most areas; mid-rise condos give **Old Orchard Beach** a "mini-Miami" air. For my money, the best beaches are at **Ogunquit,** which boasts a 3-mile-long sandy strand, some of which has a mildly remote character, and **Long Sands Beach** at York, which has a festive, carnival atmosphere right along Route 1A.

Remember that in Maine, the term "sand beach" is not redundant. It simply distinguishes these from their more common cousins, the "pebble beach" and the "cobblestone beach." These probably don't require further definition, but you should be aware that some hyperbolic innkeepers might refer to a nearby pebble beach where closer examination shows the pebbles range in size from billiard balls to bowling balls.

If you love swimming but aren't especially keen on shivering, head inland to the sandy beaches at Maine's wonderful lakes, where the water is tepid by comparison. A number of state and municipal parks offer access. Among the most accessible to the coast are **Sebago Lake State Park** (☎ 207/ 693-6613), about 20 miles northwest of Portland; the municipal **Pemaquid Beach Park** (☎ 207/677-2754), near Damariscotta; and **Swan Lake State Park** (☎ 207/ 525-4404), 6 miles north of Belfast. Small admission fees are charged at all three.

BICYCLING

Mount Desert Island and **Acadia National Park** are the premier coastal destinations for bikers, especially mountain bikers in search of scenic but easy-riding terrain. The 57 miles of well-maintained carriage roads in the national park offer superb cruising through thick forests and to the tops of rocky knolls with ocean views. No cars are permitted on these grass and gravel roads, so bikers and hikers have them to themselves. Mountain bikes can be rented in Bar Harbor. The Park Loop Road, while often crowded with slow-moving cars, offers one of the more memorable road-biking experiences in the state. The rest of Mount Desert Island is also good for road biking, especially on the quieter western half of the island.

In southern Maine, **Route 103** and **Route 1A** offer pleasant excursions for bikers along the coast. Offshore, bring your bike to the bigger islands for car-free cruising. **Vinalhaven** and **North Haven** in Penobscot Bay, and **Swan's Island** in Blue Hill Bay, are all popular destinations.

BIRD WATCHING

Bird watchers from southern and inland states should be able to lengthen their life lists along the Maine Coast, which attracts migrating birds cruising the Atlantic flyway (it's warbler mania in spring!) and boasts populations of numerous native shorebirds, such as plovers (including the threatened piping plover), whimbrels, sandpipers, and dunlins. Gulls and terns are frequently seen; you'll see a surfeit of herring and great black-backed gull, along with the common tern; less frequently seen are Bonaparte's gull, laughing gull, jaeger, and the arctic tern. Far up the coast near Lubec, look for members of the alcid family, including razorbill and guillemot. Puffins (another alcid) nest on several offshore islands; tour boats to view puffins depart from Boothbay Harbor, Bar Harbor, and Jonesport.

For a recording of recent sightings of rare birds, call ☎ **207/ 781-2332.**

CAMPING

Car campers traveling the Maine Coast have plenty of choices, from well-developed private campgrounds to more basic state parks. **Acadia National Park** tends to be the biggest draw, but there's no shortage of other options on and near the coast.

Among the coastal state parks worthy of an overnight are **Lamoine State Park** (☎ **207/667-4778**), which is convenient to Acadia National Park yet away from the thickest of the crowds, and remote **Cobscook Bay State Park** (☎ **207/ 726-4412**), where most campsites are on the water, offering a great view of the massive 28-foot tides that slosh in and out. For more information about other state parks, contact the **Department of Conservation,** State House Station #22, Augusta, ME 04333 (☎ **207/287-3821**). To make camping reservations at most state park campgrounds, call between January and August (☎ **207/287-3824** or 800/332-1501 in Maine).

Maine also has more than 200 private campgrounds spread throughout the state, many offering full hookups for RVs. For a guide to the private campgrounds, contact the Maine **Campground Owners Association,** 655 Main St., Lewiston, ME 04240 (☎ **888/274-9030** or 207/782-5874; www.campmaine.com). Campsites get booked quickly for summer weekends, so call ahead for reservations.

CANOEING

The state's best canoeing tends to be far inland and deep in the woods, but day paddlers can find good trips at several lakes along the coast, or in some of the protected bays. For a low-key afternoon with a paddle, head to **Long Pond** on Mt. Desert Island, where canoes may be rented by the hour. Two excellent sources for detailed canoeing information statewide are the *AMC River Guide: Maine* and *Quiet Water Canoe Guide: Maine,* both published by the Appalachian Mountain Club, 5 Joy St., Boston, MA 02108.

FISHING

Deep-sea fishing charters are available at many of the harbors along the Maine Coast, with options ranging from inshore fishing expeditions for stripers and bluefish, to offshore voyages in search of shark, cod, and pollack. Prices range from $25 per person for day trips to $395 to charter an offshore boat for the day. Visitor information centers and chambers of commerce listed in this guide will be able to match you up with the right boat to meet your needs.

Saltwater fishing requires no license. For freshwater fishing, nonresident **licenses** are $50 for the season, or $21 for 3 days. Seven- and 15-day licenses are also available. Fees are reduced for juniors (12 to 15); no license is required for those under 12. Licenses are available at many outdoor shops and general stores throughout the state, or by mail from the address below. For a booklet of fishing regulations, contact the Department of **Inland Fisheries and Wildlife,** State House Station #41, Augusta, ME 04333 (☎ **207/287-8000**).

For freshwater fishing not too far from the Downeast coast, **Grand Lake Stream** is a popular and historic destination. Located deep in the woods of Washington County, close to the border with Canada, the area has a rich heritage as a fisherman's settlement, and a number of camps and outfitters cater to the serious angler, especially those in search of landlocked salmon, smallmouth bass, and brook trout. Among the classic fishing lodges in this area are **Weatherby's** (☎ **207/ 796-5558**) and **Indian Rock Camps** (☎ **800/498-2821** or 207/796-2822).

GOLFING

With six of its holes bordering Penobscot Bay, the golf course at the **Samoset Resort** in Rockport (☎ **207/594-2511**) is easily the state's most dramatic. (It's also among the priciest, with greens fees running $95 during peak season—if you can even get a reservation.) Other notable courses along the coast (although not necessarily on the water) are the historic **Kebo Valley Golf Club** (☎ **207/288-3000**) in the rolling hills outside of Bar Harbor; and Kennebunkport's **Cape Arundel Golf Club** (☎ **207/967-3494**), which is favored by a certain ex-president when he's in town.

HIKING

Serious hiking—as opposed to strolling—is limited along the Maine Coast. The most challenging and most rewarding trails are found at Acadia National Park. Although the peaks top out at 1,530 feet, the terrain may be more rugged than you might expect, and often leads to blustery hilltops of granite and blueberry, offering exceptional vistas of islands and sea. Another good destination for hilly coastal hiking is Camden Hills State Park on the west shore of Penobscot Bay.

Less demanding strolls may be found tucked all up and down the coast, with many of these a matter of local knowledge. Two fine pathways skirt the water in York (see chapter 2), and even in Portland (see chapter 3) you can saunter on well-maintained (and heavily used) recreational pathways along about 5 miles of tidal waters. More inveterate explorers should continue eastward along the coast to Washington County. Hikes at Great Wass Island, near Cutler, and at West Quoddy Head (and just over the border on Canada's Campobello Island) provide a measure of remoteness and solitude that has been lost along much of the rest of the Maine Coast.

More detailed information on hiking in the area may be found in John Gibson's fine book, *50 Hikes in Southern and Coastal Maine* (1996, Backcountry Publications). For a coastal walking vacation with all the details taken care of, contact **New England Hiking Holidays,** P.O. Box 1648, North Conway, NH 03860 (☎ **800/869-0949;** www.nehikingholidays.com), which offers excursions to the Maine Coast each summer. Trips typically involve moderate day hiking coupled with nights at comfortable lodges.

SEA KAYAKING

Sea kayakers nationwide migrate to Maine in the summer for world-class voyaging. The 3,500 miles of rocky coastline and the thousands of offshore islands have created a wonderful sea kayaker's playground. Paddlers can explore protected estuaries far from the surf, or test their skills and determination with excursions across choppy, open seas to islands far offshore. It's a sport that can be extremely dangerous (the seas can turn on you in a matter of minutes), but can yield plenty of returns for those with the proper equipment and skills.

The nation's first long-distance "water trail" was created here in 1987 when the **Maine Island Trail** was established. This 325-mile waterway winds along the coast from Portland to Machias, and incorporates some 70 state and privately owned islands along the route. Members of the Maine Island Trail Association, a private nonprofit, are granted permission to visit and camp on these islands, as long as they follow certain restrictions (for example, don't visit designated islands during nesting season). The association seeks to encourage low-impact, responsible use of these natural treasures. A guidebook, published annually, provides descriptions of all the islands in the network and is free with association membership (note that the guide is available only to members). Membership is $40 per year (individual or family); contact the **Maine Island Trail Association,** P.O. Box C, Rockland, ME 04841 (☎ **207/596-6456** or 207/761-8225).

For novices, Maine has a number of kayak outfitters offering guided excursions ranging from an afternoon to a week. Recommended outfitters that offer a wide array of trips in Maine include the **Maine Island Kayak Co.,** 70 Luther St., Peaks Island, ME 04108 (☎ **800/796-2373** or 207/766-2373; www.maineislandkayak.com) and **Maine Sport Outfitters,** P.O. Box 956, Rockport, ME 04856 (☎ **800/722-0826** or 207/236-8797; www.mainesport.com).

WINDJAMMING

An ideal way to combine time in the outdoors with relative luxury and an easy-to-digest education in maritime history is aboard a windjammer cruise on the coast. Maine boasts a sizeable fleet of sailing ships both vintage and modern that offer private cabins, meals, entertainment, and adventure. The ships range in size from 53 to 132 feet, and most are berthed in the region between Boothbay Harbor and Belfast. You choose your adventure: An array of excursions is available, from simple overnights to weeklong expeditions gunkholing among Maine's thousands of scenic islands and coves.

Several windjammer festivals and races are held along the Maine Coast throughout the summer; these are perfect events to shop for a ship on which to spend a few days. Among the more notable events are the **Windjammer Days** in Boothbay Harbor (late June) and the **Camden Windjammer Weekend** in early September. For information on windjamming vacations, contact **Maine Windjammer Association** at ☎ **800/807-9463,** or on the web at www.sailmainecoast.com.

4   Tips for Travelers with Special Needs

FOR TRAVELERS WITH DISABILITIES

Prodded by the Americans with Disabilities Act, a growing number of inns and hotels are retrofitting rooms for people with special needs. Most innkeepers are quite proud of their improvements—when I arrive for a site visit, they're invariably quick to show me their new rooms with barrier-free entrances, wheelchair-accessible showers, and fire alarms equipped with strobe lights. Outdoor-recreation areas, especially on state and federal lands, are also providing more trails and facilities for those who've been effectively barred in the past owing to seemingly small barriers. Accessibility is improving region-wide, but improvements are far from universal. When in doubt, call ahead to ensure that you'll be accommodated.

Travelers with disabilities may also want to consider joining a tour that caters specifically to them. **Wilderness Inquiry,** 808 14th Ave SE, Minneapolis, MN 55414 (☎ 800/ 728-0719 or 612/676-9400; www.wildernessinquiry.org) offers adventure travel packages for travelers with disabilities nationwide, including three lake and river canoe trips in Maine.

Other resources include *A World of Options,* a 658-page book of resources for travelers with disabilities that covers everything from biking trips to scuba outfitters. It costs $35 (postage included) and is available from **Mobility International USA,** P.O. Box 10767, Eugene, OR, 97440 (☎ 541/ 343-1284, voice and TDD; www.miusa.org). For more personal assistance, Moss Rehab in Philadelphia offers a free **Travel Information Service** for people with disabilities. Call ☎ 215/456-5995.

Many of the major car-rental companies now offer hand-controlled cars for drivers with disabilities. **Avis** (☎ 800/ 331-1212) can provide such a vehicle at any of its locations in the U.S. with 48-hour advance notice; **Hertz** (☎ 800/ 654-3131) requires between 24 and 72 hours of advance reservation at most of its locations. **Wheelchair Getaways** (☎ 800/873-4973; www.wheelchairgetaways.com) rents specialized vans with wheelchair lifts and other features for travelers with disabilities in more than 100 cities across the U.S. Delivery can be arranged to Maine.

FOR SENIORS

The Maine Coast is well suited for older travelers, with a wide array of activities for seniors and discounts often available. It's wise to request a discount at hotels or motels when booking the room, not when you arrive. An identification card from the **American Association of Retired Persons (AARP),** 601 E St., NW, Washington, DC 20049 (☎ **202/434-2277;** www.aarp.org) can be invaluable in obtaining discounts.

Excellent programs for seniors are offered by **Elderhostel,** 75 Federal St., Boston, MA 02110 (☎ **617/426-7788;** www.elderhostel.org). These educational programs for people over 55 years old are reasonably priced, and include lodging and meals. Participants can study everything from the art of downhill skiing to the art of autobiography. The locations of these classes are often intriguing and dramatic.

FOR FAMILIES

Families rarely have trouble finding things to do with kids along the Maine Coast. The natural world holds tremendous wonder for the younger set—an afternoon exploring a tide-pool can be a huge adventure. Older kids often like the challenge of learning to paddle a sea kayak in choppy seas, or playing video games at an arcade. And there's always the beach, which is usually good for hours of sunny diversion. Recommended destinations for families include the obvious—**Old Orchard Beach** and **Acadia National Park**—along with less obvious, like **Sebasco Harbor Resort** south of Bath, **Samoset Resort** in Rockport, and the rocky headland and nearby beach of **Pemaquid Point.**

Be aware that many inns cater to couples, and kids aren't exactly welcomed with open arms. Many inns don't allow kids, or strongly prefer only children over a certain age. Innkeepers will let you know when you make your reservation, but you should mention that you're traveling with kids. Anyway, it's often wise to mention that you're a family when booking a room; often you'll get accommodations nearer the game room or the pool, making everyone's life a bit easier.

Several specialized guides offer more detailed information for families on the go. Try *Best Hikes with Children in Vermont, New Hampshire & Maine* by Cynthia and Thomas Lewis (Mountaineers, 2000), *Fun Places to Go With Children in New England* by Pamela Wright and Diane Bair (Chronicle Books,

1998), and *Great Family Vacations North East* by Candyce Stapen (Globe Pequot, 1999).

FOR GAY & LESBIAN TRAVELERS

Ogunquit on the south coast is an historic gay resort, a sort of low-key Provincetown. (Unlike at Provincetown, straight visitors can visit here and not realize that there's a substantial gay population in summer.) Ogunquit features a lively bar-beach scene in the summer; in the winter the scene is decidedly mellower. Several Ogunquit B&Bs are owned by gay entrepreneurs.

Portland, Maine, has the most substantial gay population, attracting many refugees who've fled the crime and congestion of Boston and New York. Portland hosts a sizable gay pride festival early each summer that includes a riotous parade and a dance on the city pier, among other events. Portland's oldest gay club is **The Underground** (☎ 207/773-3315), located at 3 Spring St. near the Old Port. Half of the place is a tidy, friendly bar and hangout; the other half is a dance club with pulsing lights and music. Other places are **Blackstones** (☎ 207/775-2885), at 6 Pine St., which is a low-key neighborhood bar, and **Sisters** (☎ 207/774-1505), 45 Danforth, which is a popular lesbian hangout.

5 Getting There

BY CAR

Arriving from the south, take I-95, which parallels the southern Maine Coast before veering inland near Brunswick. If you're headed to mid-coast Maine, take I-95 to Brunswick and follow Route 1 up to the coast. If you're driving to Camden or Belfast on western Penobscot Bay, you can avoid coastal traffic by taking the turnpike to Augusta, then connecting via Route 17 (to Camden) or Route 3 (to Belfast).

Those heading directly to Acadia National Park will find it most expedient to follow interstates to Bangor, then Route 1A to Ellsworth, where you can connect to Route 3 onward to Mount Desert Island.

BY PLANE

Several commercial carriers serve Portland and Bangor. Airlines most commonly fly to these airports from New York or Boston, although direct connections from other cities, such as

Chicago and Philadelphia, are also available. Many of the scheduled flights to northern New England from Boston are aboard smaller prop planes; ask the airline or your travel agent if this is an issue for you.

Portland is served by regularly scheduled flights on **Air Nova** (☎ 902/873-5000 www.airnova.ca), **American Airlines** (☎ 800/433-7300; www.aa.com), **Delta/Business Express** (☎ 800/638-7333; www.delta-air.com), **Continental** (☎ 800/525-0280; www.flycontinental.com), **US Airways** (☎ 800/428-4322; www.usairways.com), **United** (☎ 800/241-6522; www.ual.com), and **Northwest Airlines** (800/225-2525; www.nwa.com). For general airport information, see www.portlandjetport.org.

Several smaller coastal airports in the region are served by feeder airlines and charter companies, including Rockport and Bar Harbor (actually, it's Trenton, which is just across the causeway from Mount Desert Island). Contact **Colgan Air** (☎ **800/272-5488** or 207/596-7604; www.colganair.com).

Many travelers headed for Maine find they pay less and have a wider choice of flight times by flying into Boston's Logan Airport, or into Manchester, N.H., which is the regional outpost of budget-friendly **Southwest Airlines** (☎ **800/435-9792;** www.iflyswa.com). Boston and Manchester are both about two hours by car from Portland.

BY BUS

Express bus service is well-run if a bit spotty in northern New England. Major cities and tourist destinations are served by bus, along with a handful of intermediate coastal towns and villages. Tickets are about $20 (one-way) from Boston to Portland—and taking the bus requires no advance planning.

Two major bus lines serve coastal Maine: **Vermont Transit Lines** (☎ **800/451-3292** or 800/642-3133), which is affiliated with Greyhound; and **Concord Trailways** (☎ **800/639-3317**). Concord Trailways buses tend to be a bit more luxurious (and a few dollars more expensive) than Vermont Transit, and run videos and offer music piped through headphones en route.

BY TRAIN

Rail service from Boston to Portland and possibly beyond was originally slated to begin in 1994, but wrangling over track upgrades and other issues has severely delayed the process. At press time, train service was slated to begin in early 2001, and this time it looked like it actually might happen. For an update, contact Amtrak at ☎ **800/872-7245;** www.amtrak.com.

6　Getting Around

BY CAR

The Portland and Bangor airports (see "Getting There," above) both host national car-rental chains. Some handy phone numbers are **Avis** (☎ 800/331-1212), **Budget** (☎ 800/527-0700), **Enterprise** (☎ 800/325-8007), **Hertz** (☎ 800/654-3131), **National** (☎ 800/227-7368), **Rent-A-Wreck** (☎ 800/535-1391), and **Thrifty** (☎ 800/367-2277).

Don't underestimate the size of the Maine Coast—Kittery to Eastport (the easternmost city in the United States) is 293 miles. Driving times can be longer than you'd expect due to narrow roads and zigzagging peninsulas, not to mention high-season traffic.

In the summer, I-95 leading from Boston to Maine is often sluggish on Friday afternoons and evenings, and Route 1 along the coast can also bottleneck where two-lane bridges span tidal rivers. To avoid the worst of the tourist traffic, try to stay put on weekends and during big summer holidays; if your schedule allows it, take an extra day off work and head back after the holiday crush. It'll pay handsome dividends in lowered blood pressure.

If you're a connoisseur of back roads and off-the-beaten-track exploring, the **Maine Atlas and Gazetteer,** produced by DeLorme Mapping (☎ **888/227-1656**) in Yarmouth, is an invaluable tool. It offers an extraordinary level of detail, right down to logging roads and canoe launch sites. DeLorme's atlases are available at many local book and convenience stores, or at the company's headquarters and map store in Yarmouth, a few minutes north of Portland (Exit 17 off I-95).

BY PLANE

Contact **Colgan Air** (☎ **800/272-5488** or 207/596-7604) for information on scheduled flights to Rockland and Bar Harbor. **Quoddy Air** (☎ **207/853-0997**), based in Eastport, offers charter service to airports in and around Downeast Maine.

BY BUS

See the "Getting There" section, above, for information about bus lines serving the Maine Coast.

FAST FACTS: The Maine Coast

AAA   The club's Maine headquarters (☎ **207/780-6900**) is in Portland and can help members with trip planning and discount tickets to events and attractions. Call ☎ **800/222-4357** for membership information.

Emergencies   In the event of fire, crime, or medical emergency, dial ☎ **911.**

Liquor Laws   The legal age to consume alcohol in Maine is 21, and hard liquor is sold through state-run stores as well as "agency stores," which are often found as sections in some of the larger supermarkets. Beer and wine are available in grocery and convenience stores. Purchasing is strictly regulated; even those clearly over the age of consent may be asked to show ID.

Maps   Free road maps may be had at official tourist information centers (ask for one at the desk). For more detailed coverage, consider purchasing a DeLorme atlas of the state (see "By Car" under "Getting Around," above).

Newspapers/Magazines   Almost every small town seems to have a daily or weekly newspaper covering events and happenings of the area. These are good sources of information for small-town events and dinner specials at local restaurants—the day-to-day things that slip through the cracks at the tourist bureaus.

The state's two main daily papers are the *Bangor Daily News,* which covers the northern and eastern0 parts of the state, and the *Portland Press Herald,* which covers the rest. The *Press Herald* maintains an active web site (**www.portland.com**), which is handy for getting a sense of the state before you arrive.

Taxes   The sales tax in Maine is 5.5%, but increases to 7% for accommodations and meals.

2

The South Coast

*M*aine's southern coast runs roughly from the state line at Kittery to Portland, and is the destination of the majority of travelers into the state (the numbers are swelled by day trippers from the Boston area). While it will take some doing to find privacy and remoteness here, you'll will turn up at least two excellent reasons for a detour: the long, sandy beaches that are the region's hallmark, and the almost tactile sense of history in the coastal villages.

Thanks to quirks of geography, nearly all of Maine's sandy beaches are located in this 60-mile stretch of coastline. It's not hard to find a relaxing sandy spot, whether you prefer dunes and the lulling sound of the surf or the carnie atmosphere of a festive beach town. The waves are dependent on the weather— during a good Northeast blow they pound the shores and threaten decades-old beach houses. During the balmy days of mid-summer the ocean can be as gentle as a farm pond, with barely audible waves lapping timidly at the shore.

One characteristic all of the beaches have in common: the chilly waters of the Gulf of Maine. Except for those of the very young, who seem immune to blood-chilling temperatures, swimming sessions in these waters tend to be very brief and often accompanied by shrieks, whoops, and agitated hand-waving. The beach season itself is brief yet intense, running from July 4th to Labor Day. Of late it seems to be stretching out into fall at an increasing number of beach towns (Columbus Day usually brings the remaining businesses to a close), but after Labor Day shorefront communities adopt a slower, more somnolent pace.

On foggy or rainy days, plan to search out the South Coast's rich history. More than three centuries ago the early European newcomers first settled here, only to be driven out by hostile Native Americans, who had been pushed to the brink by treaty-breaking British settlers and prodded by the mischievous French. Settlers later reestablished themselves, and by the early 19th century the southern Maine Coast was one of the most prosperous regions in the nation. Shipbuilders constructed brigantines and sloops, and merchants and traders constructed warehouses along the rivers to store their goods. Even today, many handsome and historic homes here can attest to the region's former prosperity.

A second wave of settlers, wealthy city dwellers from Boston and New York, came to Maine's coast in the mid- to late-19th century seeking respite from the summer heat and city congestion. They built shingled estates (which they coyly called "cottages") with views of the Atlantic. At the beginning of the 20th century, aided by trolleys and buses, wealthy rusticators were followed by the emerging middle class, who built bungalows near the shore and congregated at oceanside boarding houses to splash in the waves.

1 Kittery & the Yorks

Driving into Maine from the south, as most visitors do, the first town you'll come to is Kittery. Kittery was once famous nationally for its naval yard (it's still operating), but regionally at least Kittery is now better known for the dozens of factory outlets clustered here. (Why they chose to spring up here and not a couple of miles away in sales-tax-free New Hampshire remains an enduring mystery.) Maine has the second highest number of outlet malls in the nation (only California has more), and Kittery is home to a good many of them.

"The Yorks," just to the north, are comprised of three towns that share a name but little else. In fact, it's rare to find three such well-defined and diverse New England archetypes in such a compact area. York Village is redolent with early American history and architecture. York Harbor reached its zenith during America's late-Victorian era, when wealthy urbanites built rambling cottages at the ocean's edge. York Beach has a turn-of-the-century beach town feel, with amusements, taffy shops, a modest zoo, and small gabled summer homes set in crowded enclaves near the beach.

ESSENTIALS
GETTING THERE

Kittery is accessible from I-95 or Route 1, with exits well marked. The Yorks are reached most easily from Exit 1 of the

Maine Turnpike. From the exit, look for Route 1A just south of the turnpike exit. This route connects all three York towns.

Travelers entering the state on I-95 can stock up on travel information for the region and beyond at the **Kittery Information Center** (☎ 207/439-1319), located at a well-marked rest area. Open 8am to 6pm in summer, 9am to 5:30pm year-round, it's amply stocked with brochures, and the helpful staff can answer most questions.

The **York Chamber of Commerce,** P.O. Box 417, York, ME 03909 (☎ 207/363-4422), operates a helpful information center at 571 Rte. 1, a short distance from the turnpike exit. It's open year-round, daily in summers 9am to 5pm (until 6pm Fridays), limited days and hours in the off-season.

A trackless trolley (a bus retrofitted to look like an old-fashioned trolley) links all three York towns and provides a convenient way to explore without having to be hassled with parking. Hop on the trolley at one of the well-marked stops for a 1-hour narrated tour for $4 or get an all-day pass for $5. Partial trips are $2.

EXPLORING & SHOPPING IN KITTERY

Kittery's consumer mecca is 4 miles south of York on Route 1. Some 120 factory outlets flank the highway, scattered among more than a dozen strip malls. Name-brand retailers include Dansk, Eddie Bauer, Corning Revere, Ann Klein, Coldwater Creek, Le Creuset, Calvin Klein, Crate & Barrel, Donna Karan, Converse, Polo/Ralph Lauren, Tommy Hilfiger, Levi's, Old Navy, Bose, Nautica, and Noritake. The area can be aggravating to navigate during the summer owing to the four lanes of often heavy traffic and capricious restrictions on turns. Information on current outlets is available from the **Kittery Outlet Association.** Call ☎ **888/548-8379,** or visit the web site at www.thekitteryoutlets.com.

Departing from downtown Kittery (south of the outlet zone), a scenic route north to York follows winding Route 103. (It's perfect for a drive, a bit busy and narrow for a bike ride.) The road passes through the historic village of Kittery Point, where homes seem to be located just inches from the roadway, and past two historic forts (both in public parks). Look for the **Lady Pepperell House** on your right at the first left elbow in the road. The handsome cream-colored Georgian

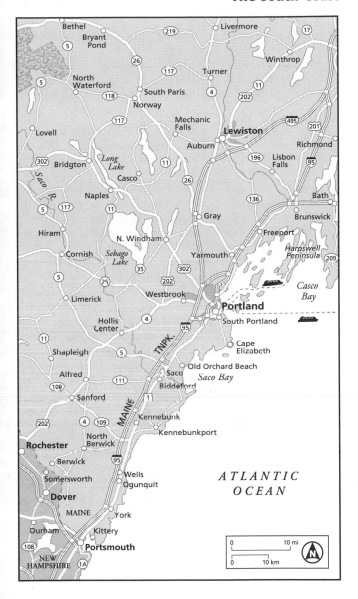

home was built in 1760, and is considered one of the most elegant Georgian-style homes in the nation. However, it is not open to the public.

Just before coming into the village of York, keep an eye on your left near the marshes and tidal inlets for the Wiggly Bridge (see "Walks Along the Water," below).

DISCOVERING LOCAL HISTORY

Old York Historical Society. 5 Lindsay Rd., York. ☎ **207/363-4974.** $7 adults, $3 children 6–16 (includes admission to all buildings). Tues–Sat 10am–5pm; Sun 1–5pm. (Last tour leaves at 4pm.) Closed mid-Oct to mid-June.

John Hancock is famous for his oversized signature on the Declaration of Independence, his tenure as governor of Massachusetts, and the insurance company named after him. What's not so well known is his earlier checkered past as proprietor of Hancock Wharf, a failed enterprise that is but one of the intriguing historic sites in York Village, a fine destination for those curious about early American history.

First settled in 1624, York Village has several early homes open to the public. Tickets are available at any of the properties, but a good place to start is **Jefferds Tavern,** across from the handsome **old burying ground.** Changing exhibits here document various facets of early life. Next door is the **School House,** furnished as it might have been in the last century. A 10-minute walk along lightly traveled Lindsay Road will bring you to **Hancock Wharf,** next door to the **George Marshall Store.** Nearby is the **Elizabeth Perkins House** with its well-preserved Colonial Revival interiors.

The two don't-miss buildings in the society's collection are the intriguing **Old Gaol and the Emerson-Wilcox House. Old Gaol,** with its now-musty dungeons, was built in 1719 as a jail for criminals and debtors. Old Gaol is the oldest surviving public building in the United States. Just down the knoll from the jail is the **Emerson-Wilcox House,** built in the mid-1700s. Added to periodically over the years, it's a virtual catalog of architectural styles and early decorative arts.

WALKS ALONG THE WATER

Two local strolls will allow visitors to stretch their legs and get the cobwebs out of their heads.

York Harbor and York Village are connected by a quiet pathway that follows a river and passes through gently rustling woodlands. **Fisherman's Walk** departs from below Edward's Harborside Inn, near the Stage Neck Inn. (There's limited parking at tiny York Harbor Beach.) Follow the pathway along the river, past lobster shacks and along lawns leading up to grand shingled homes. Cross Route 103 and walk over the **Wiggly Bridge** (said to be, not implausibly, the smallest suspension bridge in the world), then head into the woods. You'll soon connect with a dirt lane; follow this and you'll emerge at Lindsay Road near Hancock Wharf (see above). The entire walk is about a mile, and depending on your pace, will take a half-hour to 45 minutes.

Also departing from near York Harbor Beach is the **Cliff Walk,** a trail that follows rugged terrain along rocky bluffs and offers sweeping views of the open ocean and glimpses of life in some of the town's more grand cottages. The far end of this trail has been destroyed by ocean waves and not rebuilt; you'll have to retrace your steps back to the beach. The pathway remains the subject of recent disputes between the town and landowners seeking to limit access. Check signs for any new restrictions before you set off.

BEACHES

York Beach actually consists of two beaches—**Long Sands Beach** and **Short Sands Beach**—separated by a rocky headland and a small island capped by scenic **Nubble Light.** Both offer plenty of room for sunning and Frisbees when the tide is out. When the tide is in, they're both a bit cramped. Short Sands fronts the town of York Beach with its candlepin bowling and video arcades. It's the better bet for families traveling with kids who have short attention spans. Long Sands runs along Route 1A, across from a profusion of motels, summer homes, and convenience stores. Parking at both beaches is metered (50¢ per hour).

Public restrooms are available at both beaches; other services, including snacks, are provided by local restaurants and vendors.

WHERE TO STAY
IN KITTERY

Inn at Portsmouth Harbor. 6 Water St., Kittery, ME 03904. ☎ **207/439-4040.** Fax 207/438-9286. www.innatportsmouth.com. E-mail: info@innatportsmouth. 6 units. A/C TV TEL. Apr–Oct $135–$175 double; Nov–Mar $135–$155. Rates include full breakfast. 2-night minimum in summer, holidays. AE, MC, V. Children over 16 welcome.

This 1899 home is located just across the river from Portsmouth, N.H.—about a half-mile away across a bridge (it's a pleasant walk). Guests here get a taste of small coastal town life, yet with access to the restaurants and shopping of Portsmouth. The rooms are tastefully restored and furnished with eclectic antiques, although most are on the small side. But, all are boldly furnished and fun—"Valdra" has ruby red walls, attractive antiques, and an above-average sized bathroom with historic accents; "Royal Gorge" is on the third floor and has limited skylight views of the harbor and a cast-iron tub with handheld shower. The whimsically decorated sitting room downstairs has two couches, where you can sprawl and browse through some of the more intriguing and readable books I've seen at any inn. Breakfasts are flat-out great: large and tasty with fresh-squeezed juice and selections like corn pancakes with smoked salmon.

IN THE YORKS

Dockside Guest Quarters. Harris Island (P.O. Box 205), York, ME 03909. ☎ **888/860-7428** or 207/363-2868. Fax 207/363-1977. www.docksidegq.com. E-mail: info@docksidegq.com. 25 units (2 with shared bathrooms). TV. Mid-June–early Sept, $137–$199 double ($78 with shared bathroom); early summer/late fall $100-$140; winter-spring (open weekends only) $85–$115. 2-night minimum July–Sept. DISC, MC, V. Directions: Drive south on Route 103 from Route 1A in York Harbor; after bridge over York River, turn left and follow signs.

David and Harriet Lusty established this quiet retreat in 1954, and recent additions (mostly new cottages) haven't changed the friendly, maritime flavor of the place. Situated on an island connected to the mainland by a small bridge, the inn occupies nicely landscaped grounds shady with maples and white pines. Five of the rooms are in the main house, built in 1885, but the bulk of the accommodations are in small, modern town house–style cottages constructed between 1968 and 1998. These are simply furnished, bright, and airy, and all have private decks that overlook the entrance to York Harbor. (Several rooms also feature wood stoves.)

Dining: The inn operates a locally popular restaurant on the property, serving traditional New England meals such as broiled halibut, baked stuffed lobster, and braised lamb. Entrees are $13 to $17. Breakfast is available for $3.

Amenities: Rowboats, badminton, croquet, ocean swimming. laundry service, bicycle rental, sundeck.

Stage Neck Inn. Stage Neck (P.O. Box 70), York Harbor, ME 03911. ☎ **800/222-3238** or 207/363-3850. www.stageneck.com. E-mail: reserve@stageneck.com. 60 units. A/C TV TEL. June–Labor Day $165–$230 double; early fall $135–$200 double; winter $110–$145 double; spring $135–$165 double. Ask about off-season packages AE, DISC, MC, V. Head north on 1A from Rte. 1; make second right after York Harbor post office.

Since about 1870, a hotel in one form or another has been housing guests on this windswept bluff located between the harbor and the open ocean. The most recent incarnation was constructed in 1972, and furnished with an understated, country-club–like elegance. The hotel, while indisputably up to date, successfully creates a sense of old-fashioned intimacy and avoids the overbearing grandeur to which many modern resorts aspire (often with poor results). Almost every room has a view of the water, and guests enjoy low-key recreational pursuits. York Harbor Beach is only steps away.

Dining: The inn has two dining rooms—Sandpiper Bar and Grille, and Harbor Porches. Both offer three meals daily. Dinner entrees at the more elegant Harbor Porches range from blackened Maine crab cakes to grilled pork medallions with apple-Dijon-garlic glaze ($17 to $24). Less formal fare is served at Sandpiper's.

Amenities: Indoor and outdoor pools, ocean swimming, jacuzzi, tennis courts, fitness room, sauna.

Union Bluff Hotel. Beach St. (at the north end of Short Sands Beach), York Beach, ME 03910. ☎ **207/363-1333** or 800/833-0721 (out of state). www.unionbluff.com. 61 units. A/C TV TEL. Summer $109–$229 double; early fall midweek $59–$189, weekends $79–$189; $68–$88 double; spring and late fall $58–$78 double; winter $48–$68 double. $208 suite in season; $158 off-season. AE, DISC, MC, V.

With its stumpy turrets, dormers, and prominent porches, the Union Bluff has the look of an old-fashioned beach hotel. So it's a bit of a surprise to learn it was built in 1989 (the fifth hotel to rise on this site since the late 1800s). Inside is a generic-modern building; rooms have oak furniture, wall-to-wall carpeting, and small refrigerators. There's a comfortable and quiet deck on the top floor for getting away from it all (alas, no ocean view). Step outside and you're virtually at the beach and the Fun-O-Rama arcade with its candlepin bowling and banks of video games. (It can be noisy in the evening if your room faces this direction.) Twenty-one rooms are located in a motel annex next door, and the rooms here are also simply furnished. Stick to the main inn for better views; the best rooms are the suites on the top floor, which offer beach vistas from sitting areas within the turrets.

Dining: There's a lounge and a restaurant, both of which are open daily during the warmer months (weekends only in the off-season). The restaurant features mostly traditional New England fare, like clam chowder and steamers, along with baked haddock, prime rib, and a number of pasta selections ($9.95 to $15.95).

WHERE TO DINE
IN KITTERY

Bob's Clam Hut. Rte. 1, Kittery. ☎ **207/439-4233.** Reservations not accepted. Sandwiches $1.50–$3.95; dinners $3.95–$18.45. AE, MC, V. Daily Memorial Day–Labor Day 11am–8pm (Sat–Sun until 9pm). Open year-round but closing times vary in off-season; call ahead. Located just north of the Kittery Trading Post. FRIED FISH.

Operating since 1956, Bob's manages to retain an old-fashioned flavor—despite now being surrounded by slick new factory outlet malls—while serving up heaps of fried clams and other diet-busting enticements with great efficiency. (From Bob's brochure: "Our suppliers marvel at the amount of fryolator oil we order.") Order at the front window, get a soda from a vending machine, then stake out a table inside or on the deck (with a Route 1 view) while waiting for your number to be called. The food is surprisingly light, cooked in cholesterol-free vegetable oil; the onion rings are especially good. To ensure that your diet plans have been irrevocably violated, Bob's also offers Ben & Jerry's Ice Cream.

Chauncey Creek Lobster Pier. Chauncey Creek Rd., Kittery Point. ☎ **207/439-1030.** No reservations. Lobsters priced to market; other items $1.50–$8.95. MC, V. Daily 11am–8pm (until 7pm during shoulder seasons); closed Mon after Labor Day. Closed Columbus Day–Mother's Day. Located between Kittery Point and York on Route 103; watch for signs. LOBSTER.

It's not on the wild, open ocean, but Chauncey's remains one of the most scenic lobster pounds in the state, not the least because the Spinney Family, who have been selling lobsters here since the 1950s, takes such pride in their place. You reach the pound by walking down a wooden ramp to a broad deck on a tidal inlet, where some 42 festively painted picnic tables await. Lobster, served hot and fresh, is the specialty, of course, but they also serve steamed mussels (in wine and garlic) and clams. This place is a la carte —buy a crock of baked beans and sodas and a bag of ice while waiting for your lobsters to cook. It's also BYOB, and you can bring in other food, provided they don't sell it here.

IN THE YORKS

⭐ **Cape Neddick Inn Restaurant.** 1233 Rte. 1, Cape Neddick. ☎ **207/363-2899.** Reservations recommended. Main courses $16–$28. DISC, MC, V. Late June–Labor Day daily 5:30–9:30pm; open year-round Wed–Sat; call ahead for days. CONTEMPORARY AMERICAN.

This fine inn has consistently offered some of the best dining in southern Maine since 1979, and continues to do so under its current ownership. Located in an elegant structure on a relatively quiet stretch of Route 1, the Cape Neddick Inn has an open, handsome dining area that mixes traditional and modern. The old comes in the cozy golden glow of the room. The modern is the artwork, which changes frequently and showcases some of the region's better painters and sculptors. The creative menu changes seasonally to make the most of local products. There's an extensive selection of appetizers, including goat cheese with a roasted beet terrine, and applewood-smoked seafood (smoked on premises) tossed in an apple cider vinaigrette and served on Rhode Island johnnycakes. Depending on the season, main courses could include chargrilled steak with Vidalia onions and cob-smoked bacon, or salmon glazed with a Sichuan barbecue sauce. The wine list offers more than 100 choices and was recognized in 2000 with an award from *Wine Spectator.*

Goldenrod Restaurant. Railroad Rd. and Ocean Ave., York Beach. ☎ **207/363-2621.** www.thegoldenrod.com. Breakfast $2.65–$5.25; lunch and dinner entrees $2.75–$7.50. MC, V. Memorial Day–Labor Day daily 8am–10pm (until 9pm in June); Labor Day–Columbus Day Wed–Sun 8am–3pm. Closed Columbus Day–Memorial Day. FAMILY-STYLE.

This beach-town classic is *the* place for local color—it has been a summer institution in York Beach since it first opened in 1896. It's easy to find: look for visitors gawking through plate glass windows at the ancient taffy machines hypnotically churning out taffy in volumes enough (nine million candies a year) to make busloads of dentists very wealthy. The restaurant is behind the taffy and fudge operation, and is low on frills and long on atmosphere. Diners sit on stout oak furniture around a stone fireplace, or at the antique soda fountain. There are dark beams overhead and the sort of linoleum floor you don't see much anymore. Breakfast offerings are the standards (omelets, waffles, griddle cakes, and bakery items).

Lunch features traditional, yet well presented, American fare (soups, club sandwiches, hamburgers, hot dogs). As for dinner, you'd probably be better served heading to some place more creative.

2 Ogunquit

Ogunquit is a bustling beachside town that's attracted vacationers and artists for well over a century. While notable for its elegant summer resort architecture, Ogunquit is most famous for its 3½-mile white-sand beach, which is backed by grassy dunes. The beach serves as the town's front porch, and everyone drifts over there at least once a day when the sun is shining.

Ogunquit's fame as an art colony dates to around 1890, when Charles H. Woodbury arrived and declared the place an "artist's paradise." He was followed by artists such as Walt Kuhn, Elihu Vedder, Yasuo Kuniyoshi, and Rudolph Dirks.

In the past few decades of the last century, the town found quiet fame as a destination for gay travelers, at a time when one's sexual orientation was rarely publicly acknowledged. Ogunquit has retained its appeal for gays through the years, and many local enterprises are run by gay entrepreneurs. The scene is very low-key compared to Provincetown, Massachusetts—it's more like a understated family resort, where a good many family members just happen to be gay.

Despite the architectural gentility and the overall civility of the place, the town is overrun with tourists during the peak summer season, especially on weekends. The teeming crowds are part of the allure for some Ogunquit regulars. If you're not a crowd person, you would do well to visit here in the off-season.

Those hoping to avoid the close company of others might consider other destinations along the coast, or at the least come early or late in the season. If you arrive early in the morning, you can hike a bit and stake out one of the more remote sections of the town's famous beach, which is long enough to allow most of the teeming masses to disperse.

ESSENTIALS
GETTING THERE

Ogunquit is located on Route 1 between York and Wells. It's accessible from either Exit 1 or Exit 2 of the Maine Turnpike.

VISITOR INFORMATION

The **Ogunquit Welcome Center,** P.O. Box 2289, Ogunquit, ME 03907 (☎ **207/646-5533** or 207/646-2939; www. ogunquit.org), is on Route 1 south of the village center. It's open daily 9am to 5pm Memorial Day to Columbus Day (until 8pm weekends during the peak summer season) and Monday to Saturday during the off-season.

GETTING AROUND

The village of Ogunquit is centered around an awkward three-way intersection that seems fiendishly designed to cause massive traffic foul-ups during the summer. Parking in and around the village is also tight and relatively expensive (expect to pay $6 per day or more). As a result, Ogunquit is best explored on foot or by bike.

A number of trackless trolleys (with names like Dolly and Ollie—you get the idea) run all day long from mid-May to Columbus Day between Perkins Cove and the Wells town line to the north, with detours to the sea down Beach and Ocean streets. The cost is $1 per adult and 50¢ per child every time you board; the driver can't make change. It's well worth the small expense to avoid the problems of driving and parking.

EXPLORING THE TOWN

The village center is good for an hour or two of browsing among the boutiques, or sipping a cappuccino at one of the several coffee emporia.

From the village you can walk a mile to scenic Perkins Cove along **Marginal Way,** a mile-long oceanside pathway once used for herding cattle to pasture. Earlier in this century, the land was bought by a local developer who deeded the right-of-way to the town. The pathway, which is wide and well-maintained, departs across from the Seacastles Resort on Shore Road. It passes tidepools, pocket beaches, and rocky, fissured bluffs, all of which are worth exploring. The seascape can be spectacular (especially after a storm), but Marginal Way can also be spectacularly crowded during fair-weather weekends. To elude the crowds, we recommend heading out in the very early morning.

Perkins Cove, accessible either from Marginal Way or by driving south on Shore Road and veering left at the Y intersection, is a small, well-protected harbor that seems custom-designed for photos. As such, it attracts visitors by the busload, carload, and boatload, and is often heavily congested. A handful of galleries, restaurants, and T-shirt shops catering to the tourist trade occupy a cluster of quaint buildings between the harbor and the sea. An intriguing pedestrian drawbridge is operated by whomever happens to be handy, allowing sailboats to come and go. (If crowds of tourists make you unpleasantly edgy, steer well clear of Perkins Cove.)

Not far from the cove is The **Ogunquit Museum of American Art,** 183 Shore Rd. (☎ **207/646-4909**), one of the best small art museums in the nation. Set back from the road in a grassy glen overlooking the rocky shore, the museum's spectacular view initially overwhelms the artwork as visitors walk through the door. But stick around a few minutes—the changing exhibits in this architecturally engaging modern building of cement block, slate, and glass will get your attention soon enough, since the curators have a track record of staging superb shows and attracting national attention. (Be sure to note the bold, underappreciated work of Henry Strater, the Ogunquit artist who founded the museum in 1953.) A 1,400-square-foot wing opened in 1996, adding welcome new exhibition space. The museum is open July 1 to September 30 from 10:30am to 5pm Monday to Saturday, and 2 to 5pm on Sunday. Admission is $4 for adults, $3 for seniors and students, and children under 12 are free.

For evening entertainment, head to the **Ogunquit Playhouse,** Route 1 (☎ 207/646-5511), a 750-seat summer stock theater that has garnered a solid reputation for its careful, serious attention to stagecraft. The theater has entertained Ogunquit since 1933, attracting noted actors such as Bette Davis, Tallulah Bankhead, and Gary Merrill. Reserved seats are $25.

BEACHES

Ogunquit's main beach is more than 3 miles long, and width varies with the tides. There are three paid parking lots (around $2 per hour) along its length. The most popular access point is at the foot of Beach Street, which connects to Ogunquit Village. The beach ends at a sandy spit, where the Ogunquit River flows into the sea; facilities here include changing rooms, bathrooms, and a handful of informal restaurants. It's also the most crowded part of the beach. Less congested options are at Footbridge Beach (turn on Ocean Avenue off Route 1 north of the village center) and Moody Beach (turn on Eldridge Avenue in Wells). Restrooms are maintained at all three beaches.

ON THE WATER

Perkins Cove is home to a handful of deep-sea fishing and tour boat operators, who offer trips of various durations. The **Deborah Ann** (☎ 207/361-9501) chugs some 25 miles off shore twice daily in search of whales (usually humpback, minke, and finback). There are two four-and-a-half-hour tours daily from mid-April to mid-October ($35 for adults, $25 for children, and $30 for seniors) For deep-sea fishing, the **Ugly Anne** (☎ 207/646-7202) runs half- and full-day trips for up to 35 passengers between May and Columbus Day. The fare is $35 for a half-day trip, $50 for a full day. Reservations are encouraged.

Excursions Coastal Maine Outfitting Co., Route 1, Cape Neddick (☎ 207/363-0181; www.excursionsinmaine.com), offers two-hour ($40) and half-day ($65) sea-kayaking tours along area rivers near the coast. For more dramatic paddling, ask about sunrise, sunset, and full-moon kayaking trips. Excursions is located on Route 1 approximately four miles north of Exit 1 on I-95.

A ROAD TRIP TO LAUDHOLM FARM

A short drive north of Ogunquit, just above the beach town of Wells, is **Laudholm Farm** (☎ 207/646-1555), a historic saltwater farm owned by the nonprofit Laudholm Trust since 1986. The 1,600-acre property was originally the summer home of 19th-century railroad baron George Lord, but is now used for estuarine research. The farm has 7 miles of trails through diverse ecosystems, which range from salt marsh to forest to dunes. A visitor center in the regal Victorian farmhouse will get you oriented. Tours are available, or you can explore the grounds on your own. Parking costs $2 per adult ($10 per car maximum) daily in summer and on spring weekends; it's by donation the rest of the year. There's no admission charge to the grounds or visitor center. The trails are open daily from 8am to 8pm (5pm in fall and winter); the visitor center is open 10am to 4pm Monday to Saturday, and noon to 4pm on Sunday (closed weekends in the off-season).

The farm is reached by turning east from Route 1 on Laudholm Farm Road at the blinking light just north of

Harding Books. Bear left at the fork, then turn right into the farm's entrance.

WHERE TO STAY

Just a few steps from Ogunquit's main downtown intersection is the meticulously maintained **Studio East Motel,** 267 Main St. (☎ **207/646-7297**). It's open April to mid-November, with peak season rates running $95 to $119. The rooms are basic, but all have refrigerators; Microwaves are available for free to those staying three nights or more. A restaurant serving traditional New England fare is on the premises.

Beachmere Inn. Beachmere Rd., Ogunquit, ME 03907. ☎ **800/336-3983** or 207/646-2021. Fax 207/646-2231. www.beachmereinn.com. 53 units. A/C TV TEL. Peak season $85–$210, mid-season $75–$160, off-season $55–$110. Rates include continental breakfast. 3-night minimum in summer. AE, CB, DC, DISC, MC, V. Closed mid-Dec–Apr 1.

Run by the same family since 1937, the Beachmere Inn sprawls across a grassy hillside (the inn occupies about 4 acres) and nearly every room has a view northward up Ogunquit's famous beach. Guests choose from two buildings on the main grounds. The Beachmere Victorian dates to the 1890s and is all turrets and porches; two rooms have fireplaces. Next door is the mid-century modern Beachmere South, a two-story motel-like structure designed in 1960s style, featuring concrete slathered with a stucco finish. The rooms at Beachmere South are spacious (some are mini-suites), interestingly angled, and all have private balconies or patios and great views. The inn is located on Marginal Way, which is great for walks, and offers foot access to the beach. When rooms in the two main buildings are filled, guests are offered rooms in the Bullfrog Cottage nearby. The five units are darker, lack views, and are less impressively furnished, but are spacious and appropriate for families. Larger families or groups of friends traveling together should ask about Hearthstone, an elegant cottage with fireplace and barbecue shelter a short walk from the inn.

Grand Hotel. 108 Shore Rd. (P.O. Box 1526), Ogunquit, ME 03907. ☎ **207/646-1231**. www.thegrandhotel.com. E-mail: info@thegrandhotel. com. 28 suites. A/C TV TEL. Peak season $170–$220 double; mid-season $95–$200; off-season $70–$160. Rates include continental breakfast. 2- or 3-night minimum on weekends and peak season. AE, DISC, MC, V. Closed early Nov–early Apr.

The modern Grand Hotel, built in 1990, seems a bit ill at ease in Victorian Ogunquit. Constructed in a vaguely Frank Lloyd Wright–inspired Prairie style, the hotel centers around a three-story atrium and consists of 28 two-room suites. All rooms have refrigerators and VCRs (tapes available for rent). The modern, tidy guest rooms have a generic, chain-hotel character, and each has a private deck from which to enjoy the Maine air (no ocean views). The five top-floor penthouses are airy and bright, with cathedral ceilings and Duraflame-log fireplaces. The hotel is located on busy Shore Road, and is about ten minutes' walk to the beach. Other nice touches: parking (one car per party) is underground and connected to the rooms by elevator, and there's a small indoor pool.

Marginal Way House. Wharf Lane (P.O. Box 697), Ogunquit, ME 03907. ☎ **207/646-8801** or 207/363-6566 in winter. www.marginalwayhouse. com. 30 units (1 with private bathroom down hall). A/C TV. Peak season $93–$185 double; shoulder seasons $45–$155 double. Minimum stay requirements on some weekends. MC, V. Closed late Oct–mid-Apr. Pets allowed off-season; advance notice required.

This old-fashioned, nothing-fancy compound centers around a four-story, mid-19th-century guest house, with summery, basic rooms that feature white painted furniture. Room 7 is among the best, with a private porch and canopy and an ocean view. The guest house is surrounded by four outbuildings of more recent vintage, which lack charm and feature motel-style rooms yet are generally comfortable and bright. The whole affair is situated on a large, grassy lot on a quiet cul-de-sac. It's hard to believe that you're smack in the middle of Ogunquit, with both the beach and the village just a few minutes' walk away. All rooms have refrigerators; one- and two-bedroom efficiencies are available for longer stays.

Nellie Littlefield House. 9 Shore Rd., Ogunquit, ME 03907. ☎ **207/646-1692.** www.visit-maine.com/nellielittlefieldhouse/. 8 units. A/C TV TEL. Peak season $150–$210; mid-season $95–$150; off-season $80–$125. Rates include full breakfast. 2-night minimum weekends, 3 nights on holidays. DISC, MC, V. Closed late Oct–late Apr. Children over 12 are welcome.

This 1889 home stands impressively at the edge of Ogunquit's compact commercial district. This prime location and the handsome Queen Anne architecture are the main draws here. All of the rooms are carpeted and feature a mix of modern and antique reproduction furnishings; several have refrigerators. Four rooms to the rear have private decks, but views are limited—mostly to the unlovely motel next door. The most spacious room is the third floor J.H. Littlefield suite, with two TVs and a jacuzzi. The most unique? The circular Grace Littlefield room, located in the upper turret and overlooking the street. The basement features a compact fitness room with modern equipment.

WHERE TO DINE

Just north of Ogunquit in the town of Wells is **Congdon's Doughnuts,** 1090 Post Rd. (☎ **207/646-4219**), a local institution since 1955. The old-fashioned, irregularly shaped donuts are of the antique sort that explode wonderfully in soft bursts of powdered sugar when you bite into them, leaving a tracery of white on your shirt. It's the way donuts used to be. Open from 6am to 2pm.

✪ **Arrows.** Berwick Rd. ☎ **207/361-1100.** www.arrowsrestaurant.com. Reservations strongly recommended. Main courses $36.95–$39.95; tasting menu $75. MC, V. Mid-Apr to Memorial Day weekend Fri–Sun 6–9:30pm; June–Columbus Day Tues–Sun 6–9:30pm; Columbus Day–mid-Dec Fri–Sun 6–9:30pm. Open Thanksgiving Day. Closed mid-Dec–mid-Apr. Turn uphill at the Key Bank in the village; the restaurant is 1.9 miles on your right. NEW AMERICAN.

When owner/chefs Mark Gaier and Clark Frasier opened Arrows in 1988 they quickly put Ogunquit on the national culinary map. They've done so not only by creating an elegant and intimate atmosphere but by serving up some of the freshest, most innovative cooking in New England. The emphasis is on local products—often very local. The salad greens are grown in gardens on the grounds, and much of the rest is produced or raised locally. The food transcends traditional New England, and is deftly prepared with exotic twists and turns. The menu changes nightly, but among the more popular recurring appetizers is the homemade prosciutto (hams are hung in the restaurant to cure in the off-season) served with baby artichoke hearts, toasted pine nut butter, and balsamic vinegar. Entrees might include a lobster tail and sautéed cod with caramelized Belgian endive, leek cream, caviar, and an asparagus and Parmesan custard; or tenderloin of beef with a celery root pancake, fiddleheads, and black truffle potato chips. The wine list is top-rate. The prices are not for the faint-hearted, but committed foodies will find an evening here memorable.

Aunt Marie's. Rte. 1 (north of town). ☎ **207/646-9144.** Breakfast $2.85–$5.75, lunch $3.95–$7.95. AE, DISC, MC, V. Daily 7am–2pm. Closed late Oct to Apr. BREAKFAST JOINT.

Located on a cluttered stretch of Route 1 with its view of the ocean blocked by graceless condos, Aunt Marie's is still the best spot for breakfast any time of the day. Don't expect your taste buds to be titillated, but do expect to leave very full. Fearless of fat? Try the Bucks Port Pie—a sausage and cheese omelet served atop french fries and beans and slathered with hollandaise sauce.

✪ **Hurricane.** Oarweed Rd., Perkins Cove. ☎ **800/649-6348** (ME and NH only) or 207/646-6348. www.perkinscove.com. Reservations recommended for either lunch or dinner. Lunch items $7–$15; main dinner courses $16–$28; lobster dishes priced daily (to $39). AE, DC, DISC, MC, V. May–Oct daily 11:30am–3:30pm, 5:30–10:30pm; Nov–Apr daily 5:30–9:30pm. Closed briefly in January (call ahead). NEW AMERICAN.

Tucked away amid the T-shirt kitsch of Perkins Cove is one of southern Maine's classiest and most enjoyable dining experiences. The plain-shingled exterior of the building, set along a curving, narrow lane, doesn't hint at what you'll find inside. The narrow dining room is divided into two smallish halves, but soaring windows overlooking the Gulf of Maine create a sense that this place is larger than it actually is. The menu changes daily, and owner Brooks MacDonald is known for his consistently creative concoctions, like an appetizer of deviled Maine lobster cakes served with a tangy fresh salsa (so popular it's always available). At lunch look for salmon burgers with a dill aioli, or walnut-and-brie stuffed swordfish served over an apple-pear slaw. At dinner, there's a delectable lobster stew and a wonderful lobster cioppino (the signature dish), herb-encrusted venison, or pan-seared snapper over a spicy cucumber and daikon slaw. Among the more intriguing desserts: warm pumpkin bread pudding served with a pecan-bourbon sauce. Added bonus: Hurricane makes the best martini in town.

98 Provence. 104 Shore Rd. (P.O. Box 628), Ogunquit, ME 03907. ☎ **207/646-9898** or 207/646-7350. Fax 207/641-8786. www.98provence.com. Reservations recommended. Main courses $18–$30, Table d'hote (appetizer, main course, and dessert) $32. Summer Wed–Mon 5:30–9:30pm; off season Thurs–Mon 5:30–9pm. BISTRO.

Candlelight reflects off the warm wood interior and infuses the surroundings with a romantic glow; tables are covered with two layers of Provençal-style linens, lace curtains drape the windows, and diners eat off colorful china. 98 Provence is charming if a bit on the precious side. The décor almost, but not quite, distracts one from the delicious food. Chef Pierre Gignac relies on fresh, local ingredients to create such dishes as terrine of lobster delicately flavored with mandarin orange. The menu changes thrice yearly to reflect the seasons. You might start with the lobster in a puff pastry with ginger cream sauce or seared duck foie gras with fig sauce. Entrees wander the barnyard, from rabbit to cassoulet to lamb in puff pastry. The venison is quite popular; in fall it's prepared with stuffed pumpkin and dried fruits.

3 The Kennebunks

"The Kennebunks" consist of the villages of Kennebunk and Kennebunkport, both situated along the shores of small rivers. The region was first settled in the mid-1600s and flourished after the American Revolution, when ship captains, shipbuilders, and prosperous merchants constructed the imposing, solid homes. The Kennebunks are famed for their striking historic architecture and expansive beaches. Leave time to explore both.

While summer is the busy season along the coast, winter has its charms: The grand architecture is better seen through leafless trees. When the snow flies, guests find solace in front of a fire at one of the inviting inns.

ESSENTIALS
GETTING THERE
Kennebunk is located off Exit 3 of the Maine Turnpike. Kennebunkport is 3.5 miles southeast of Kennebunk on Port Road (Route 35).

VISITOR INFORMATION
The **Kennebunk-Kennebunkport Chamber of Commerce**, P.O. Box 740, Kennebunk, ME 04043 (☎ **800/982-4421** or 207/967-0857), can answer your questions year-round by phone or at their offices on Route 9 next to Meserve's Market. The **Kennebunkport Information Center** (☎ **207/967-8600**), operated by an association of local businesses, is off Dock Square (next to Ben & Jerry's) and is open daily throughout the summer and fall.

The local trolley (a bus, really), ☎ **207/967-3686,** makes several stops in and around Kennebunkport and also serves the beaches. The fare, $7 per person per day, includes unlimited trips.

EXPLORING KENNEBUNK

Kennebunk's downtown, located inland, is just off the turnpike, and is a dignified, small commercial center of white clapboard and brick. The **Brick Store Museum,** 117 Main St. (☎ **207/985-4802**), hosts shows of historical art and artifacts throughout the summer, switching to contemporary art in the off-season. The museum is housed in a historic former brick store—yes, a store that once sold bricks!—and three adjacent buildings. The buildings have been renovated and all have the polished gloss of a well-cared-for gallery. Admission is $5 for adults, $2 for students, and free for under 6. Open Tuesdays to Saturdays 10am to 4:30pm from June to December. Call for winter hours.

Tom's of Maine (☎ 207/985-3874), a natural toothpaste maker, is headquartered here. Tom and Kate Chappell sell their all-natural toothpaste and other personal care products worldwide, but are almost as well-known for their green, socially-conscious business philosophy. (Tom wrote a 1993 book on the subject.) Tom's factory outlet sells firsts and seconds of its own products (some at a tremendous markdown), as well as a selection of other natural products. The shop is at Lafayette Center (corner of Main and Water streets) an historic industrial building converted to shops and offices. It's open Monday to Saturday 10am to 5pm.

When en route to or from the coast, be sure to note the extraordinary homes that line Port Road (Route 35). This includes the famously elaborate "Wedding Cake House," which you should be able to identify all on your own. (It looks like . . . well, you know.) Local lore claims that the house was built by a guilt-ridden ship captain, who left for sea before his bride could enjoy a proper wedding cake. It's made of brick, with a surfeit of ornamental trim. It's sometimes mistakenly regarded as a fine example of Gothic architecture, but it's nothing of the sort. Underneath all the trimmings is a plain house with a classic Federal form. The house is privately owned but can be enjoyed from the outside.

EXPLORING KENNEBUNKPORT

Kennebunkport is the summer home of former President George Bush, whose family has summered here for decades. Given that, it has the tweedy, upper-crust feel that one might expect of the place. This historic village, whose streets were laid out during days of travel by boat and horse, is subject to monumental traffic jams around the town center. If the municipal lot off the square is full, head north on North Street. a few minutes to the free long-term lot and catch the trolley back into town. Or walk—it's a pleasant walk of about 10 or 15 minutes from the satellite lot to Dock Square.

Dock Square has a pleasantly wharf-like feel to it, with low buildings of mixed vintages and styles, but the flavor is mostly clapboard and shingles. The boutiques in the area are attractive, and many feature creative artworks and crafts. But Kennebunkport's real attraction is found in the surrounding blocks, where the side streets are lined with one of the nation's richest assortments of early-American homes. The neighborhoods are especially ripe with examples of Federal-style homes; many have been converted to B&B's (see "Where to Stay," below).

A bit further afield, in an affluent neighborhood near the Colony Hotel (about one mile east on Ocean Avenue), is a superb collection of homes of the uniquely American shingle style. It's worth a detour on foot or bike to ogle these icons of the 19th- and early 20th-century leisure class.

Aimless wandering is a good tactic for exploring Kennebunkport, but at the least make an effort to stop by the **Richard A. Nott House,** 8 Maine St. (☎ **207/967-2751**), in your travels. Situated on Maine Street at the head of Spring Street, this imposing Greek Revival house was built in 1853 and is a Victorian-era aficionado's dream. It remained untouched by the Nott family through the years, and was donated to the local historical society with the stipulation that it remain forever unchanged. It still has the original wallpaper, carpeting, and furnishings. Tours run about 40 minutes; open mid-June to mid-October 1 to 4pm Tuesday to Friday, and Saturday 10am to 1pm. Admission is $5 for adults, $2 for children under 18.

Ocean Drive from Dock Square to **Walkers Point** and beyond is lined with opulent summer homes overlooking surf and rocky shore. You'll likely recognize the former president's home at Walkers Point when you arrive. If it's not familiar from the several years it spent in the national spotlight, look for crowds with telephoto lenses. If they're not out, look for the shingle-style secret service booth at the head of a drive. That's it.

⊘ **The Seashore Trolley Museum.** 195 Log Cabin Rd., Kennebunkport. ☎ **207/967-2800.** www.trolleymuseum.org. $7 adults, $4.50 children 6–16, $5 seniors, $23 family. Open daily May 29–Oct 21 (10am–5pm) weekends only May 6–May 27 and Oct 21–Nov 5. Closed early Nov–early May. Head north from Kennebunkport on North Street for 1.7 miles; look for signs.

A short drive north of Kennebunkport is a local marvel: a scrap yard masquerading as a museum ("world's oldest and largest museum of its type"). Quirky and engaging, this museum was founded in 1939 to preserve a disappearing way of life, and today the collection boasts more than 200 trolleys, including specimens from Glasgow, Moscow, San Francisco, and Rome. (Naturally, there's also a streetcar named "Desire" from New Orleans.)

About 40 of the cars still operate, and the admission charge includes rides on a 2-mile track. Other cars, some of which still contain early 20th-century advertising, are on display outdoors and in vast storage sheds. A good museum inspires awe and educates its visitors on the sly. This one does so deftly. It's not until you drive away that you're likely to realize how much you've learned about transportation before there were cars in every garage.

REACHING THE BEACH

A word about beach parking: Finding a spot is often difficult, and all beaches require a parking permit, which may be obtained at the town offices or from your hotel. You can avoid parking hassles by renting a bike and leaving your car behind at your inn or hotel. A good spot for rentals is **Cape Able Bike Shop** (☎ **800/220-0907** or 207/967-4382; www.capeable. com), which rents three-speeds (all you'll need here) for $10 a day or $40 per week. There are also mountain bikes, along with kid trailers and baby seats. (Helmets and locks are free with rental.) The bike shop is on North Street north of Kennebunkport at Arundel Road. Some inns (such as The Colony) will rent bikes to guests; others have free bikes for guests to use. Ask when you reserve a room.

The local trolley also offer beach access (see above); the fare is $7 per person per day for unlimited trips.

BEACHES

The coastal area around Kennebunkport is home to several of the state's finest beaches.

Southward across the river (technically this is Kennebunk, although it's much closer to Kennebunkport) are **Gooch's Beach** and **Kennebunk Beach.** Head eastward on Beach Street (from the intersection of routes 9 and 35) and you'll soon wind into a handsome colony of eclectic shingled summer homes (some improbably grand, some modest). The narrow road twists past sandy beaches and rocky headlands. The area can be frightfully congested when traveling by car in the summer; avoid the local version of gridlock by exploring on foot or bike.

Goose Rocks Beach, north of Kennebunkport off Route 9 (watch for signs), is a good choice for those who like their crowds light, and prefer beaches to beach scenes. You'll find an enclave of beach homes set amid rustling oaks just off a fine sand beach. Just offshore is a narrow barrier reef that has historically attracted flocks of geese—the geese in turn lent their name to the beach.

WHERE TO STAY

A unique choice for budget accommodations is the **Franciscan Guest House,** Beach Street (☎ 207/967-2011), a former dormitory on the 200-acre grounds of the St. Anthony's Monastery. The 60 rooms are institutional, basic, and clean and have private bathrooms; guests can stroll the attractive riverside grounds or walk over to Dock Square, about 10 minutes away. Rooms are $64 to $69. No credit cards; open mid-June to mid-September.

EXPENSIVE

Beach House Inn. 211 Beach Ave., Kennebunk Beach, ME 04043. ☎ **207/ 967-3850.** Fax 207/967-4719. www.beachhseinn.com. E-mail: innkeeper@ beachhseinn.com. 35 units. Peak season $190–$350; off-season $95–$350. Rates include continental breakfast. 2-night minimum on weekends. AE, MC, V.

This is good choice if you'd like to be amid the action of Kennebunk Beach. The inn was built in 1891 but has been extensively modernized and expanded—in 1999 it was purchased by the same folks who own the legendary White Barn Inn, and upgraded with down comforters and pillows. The rooms aren't necessarily historic, but they are carpeted and most have Victorian furnishings and accenting. The main draw is the lovely porch, where you can stare out at the pebble beach across the road and idly watch the bikers and in-line skaters. The inn has bikes and canoes for guests to use, and provides beach chairs and towels.

Captain Jefferds Inn. 5 Pearl St. (P.O. Box 691), Kennebunkport, ME 04046. ☎ **800/839-6844** or 207/967-2311. www.captainjefferdsinn.com. E-mail: capjeff@captainjefferdsinn.com. 15 units. A/C. $135–$285 double. Rates include full breakfast. AE, MC, V. 2-night minimum weekends. Dogs $20 additional by advance reservation.

This 1804 Federal home was fully done over in 1997, and the innkeepers have done a superb job in coaxing out the historic feel of the place while giving each room its own personality. Fine antiques abound throughout, and guests will need some persuading to come out of their wonderful rooms once they've settled in. Among the best are "Manhattan," with a four-poster bed, fireplace, and beautiful afternoon light; and "Assisi," with a restful indoor fountain and rock garden (sounds weird, but it works). "Winterthur" is the only room with a television (though there is a TV in the common room), and "Winterthur" and "Santa Fe" both have whirlpools. The price range reflects the varying room sizes, but even the smallest rooms—like "Katahdin"—are comfortable and far exceed the merely adequate. Bright common rooms on the first floor offer alluring lounging space; an elaborate breakfast is served before a fire on cool days and on the terrace when summer weather permits.

⭐ **Captain Lord.** Pleasant St. and Green St. (P.O. Box 800), Kennebunkport, ME 04046. ☎ **207/967-3141.** Fax 207/967-3172. www.captainlord.com. E-mail: innkeeper@captainlord.com. 16 units. A/C TEL. Summer and fall $199–$399 double; winter and spring from $99 midweek, from $175 weekends. Rates include full breakfast. 2-night minimum weekends and holidays year-round (some holidays 3-night minimum). DISC, MC, V. Children 12 and older welcome.

Captain Lord is one of the most architecturally distinguished inns anywhere, housed in a pale-yellow Federal-style home that peers down a shady lawn toward the river. The adjective "stately" is laughably inadequate. When you enter the downstairs reception area, you'll know immediately that this is the genuine article, with grandfather clocks and Chippendale highboys—and that's just the front hallway. Off the hall is a comfortable common area with piped-in classical music and a broad brick fireplace. There's also a conference room with a sofa and TV for those who need their fix.

Head up the elliptical staircase to the guest rooms, which are furnished with splendid antiques; all feature gas fireplaces. The Captain Lord does not have a single unappealing room (although "Union" is a little dark). Among my favorites: "Excelsior," a large corner room with a massive four-poster, a love seat in front of the gas fire, a two-person jacuzzi in the bathroom with heated tile floor; "Hesper," which is the nicest of the less expensive rooms, featuring a burnished historic gloss and a bathroom with a large stained-glass window; and "Merchant," a spacious first-floor suite that pampers you with two large rooms, marble-floored bathroom with large jacuzzi, and a mini-spa with NordicRider bike and foot massager. Four rooms are at Phebe's, an historic gray clapboard home behind the main inn, where guests are served breakfast at a long table in a colonial-style kitchen. The rooms here are less opulent but still very well-appointed.

The Colony Hotel. 140 Ocean Ave. (P.O. Box 511), Kennebunkport, ME 04046. ☎ **800/552-2363** or 207/967-3331. Fax 207/967-8738. www. thecolonyhotel.com/maine. E-mail: reservations@thecolonyhotel.com. 123 units. TEL. $180–$430 double in July and Aug; off-season rates available. Rates include breakfast. 3-night minimum on summer weekends and holidays in main hotel. Closed mid-Oct–mid-May. AE, MC, V. Pets allowed.

The Colony is one of the handful of oceanside resorts that has preserved, intact, the classic New England vacation experience. This mammoth white Georgian Revival (built in 1914) lords over the ocean and the mouth of the Kennebunk River. The three-story main inn has 91 rooms, all of which have been renovated over the last three years. The rooms are bright and cheery, simply furnished with summer cottage antiques. Rooms in two of the three outbuildings carry over the rustic elegance of the main hotel; the exception is the East House, a 1950s-era motor hotel at the back edge of the property with 20 uninteresting motel-style rooms.

Guest rooms lack TVs in the main inn, and that's by design. The Boughton family, which has owned the hotel since 1948, encourages guests to socialize in the evening downstairs in the lobby, on the porch, or at the shuffleboard court, which is lighted for night-time play. A staff naturalist leads guided coastal ecology tours Saturday mornings in July and August.

Dining: The Porch Dining Room seats 100 (open to the public). Dinners begin with a classic relish tray, then progress to creative regional entrees ($15 to $32). On Fridays there's a lobster buffet, and lunch is served daily (poolside in July and August).

Amenities: Bike rental, putting green, library, heated saltwater pool, small beach, conference rooms, poolside sundeck, cocktail lounge, gift shop, afternoon tea in lobby, room service, social director, free newspaper, safe deposit boxes. Health club nearby.

Maine Stay Inn and Cottages. 34 Maine St. (P.O. Box 500-A), Kennebunkport, ME 04046. ☎ **800/950-2117** or 207/967-2117. Fax 207/967-8757. www.mainestayinn.com. E-mail: innkeeper@mainestayinn.com. 17 units. A/C TV. Summer-foliage season $160–$235 double, late fall–spring $95–$200 double. Rates include full breakfast. 2-night minimum stay on weekends; 3 nights on major holiday weekends. AE, MC, V.

Innkeepers Carol and Lindsay Copeland have maintained a strong sense of history in this 1860 home. Guest room decor might best be described as traditional-without-going-overboard-to-be-authentic. The common room is comfortably furnished; be sure to note the exceptional staircase in the main hall. The cottages, arrayed along the property's perimeter, are equally appealing. Constructed in the 1950s, they've been updated with small kitchens, and many have gas or wood fireplaces. The inn is happy to accommodate children in cottage rooms (minimum age is 6 in the main building), and there's a small playground on the edge of the lawn. Feeling stressed? Six rooms have jacuzzis.

The Tides Inn. Goose Rocks Beach, Kennebunkport, ME 04046. ☎ **207/967-3757.** www.tidesinnbythesea.com. E-mail: tidesinn@cybertours. com. 22 units (4 share 2 bathrooms). Peak season $195–$285 double with private bathroom (from $135 off-season); $135 with shared bathroom (from $115 off-season). Closed mid-Oct–mid-May. 3-night minimum stay in peak season (mid-June–Labor Day and all weekends). AE, MC, V.

This is the best bet in the region for a peaceful getaway. Located just across the street from Goose Rocks Beach, the Tides Inn is a yellow clapboard and shingle affair dating from 1899 that retains a seaside boarding house feel while providing up-to-date comfort. (Past guests have included Teddy Roosevelt and Sir Arthur Conan Doyle.) The rooms tend toward the small side, but are comfortable and you can hear the lapping of surf from all of them. Among the brightest and most popular rooms are #11, #15, #24, and #29, some of which have bay windows and all of which have ocean views.

The parlor has old wicker, TV, and chess for those rainy days. The pub is cozy and features a woodstove and dartboard.

Dining/Diversions: The Belvedere Room offers upscale traditional dining in a Victorian setting with options such as rack of lamb, shellfish ragout, filet mignon, and boiled lobster. Entrees are $18.95 to $27.95. Less elaborate meals, including salads, burritos, and burgers ($4.50 to $10.25), are served in the pub. Breakfast is also offered, but not included in room rates.

Old Fort Inn. Old Fort Rd. (P.O. Box M), Kennebunkport, ME 04046. ☎ **207/967-5353.** Fax 207/967-4547. www.oldfortinn.com. E-mail: oldfort@cybertours.com. 16 units (includes 2 suites). A/C TV TEL MINIBAR. $155–$250 double, suites to $350. Rates include full breakfast. AE, DC, DISC, MC ,V.

The sophisticated Old Fort Inn is located in a quiet and picturesque neighborhood of magnificent late-19th-century summer homes about two blocks from the ocean and not far from The Colony Hotel. Guests check in at the tidiest antiques shop I've ever seen, and most park around back at the large carriage house, an interesting amalgam of stone, brick, shingle, and stucco. The 14 rooms here are modern (once inside you could be in a building constructed last year), but are solidly wrought and delightfully decorated with antiques and reproductions. About half of the rooms have in-floor heated tiles in the bathrooms; all have welcome amenities like robes, refrigerators, irons, coffeemakers, hair-dryers, Neutrogena products, and a reasonably priced self-serve snack bar. Two 500-square-foot suites are located in the main house; #216 faces east and the pool, and is flooded with morning light. A full buffet breakfast is served in the main house; in nice weather guests often take waffles, pancakes, croissants, or fresh fruit on wicker trays outside to enjoy the morning sun.

Amenities: The inn is located on 15 acres that include a heated outdoor pool and tennis court (1 hour free daily). A beach is within walking distance; two golf courses are within five minutes. Also: Laundromat or laundry service, dry cleaning.

✪ **White Barn Inn.** Beach Ave. (1/4-mile east of junction of Routes 9 and 35; P.O. Box 560-C), Kennebunkport, ME 04046. ☎ **207/967-2321.** Fax 207/967-1100. www.whitebarninn.com. E-mail: innkeeper@whitebarninn.com. 25 units. A/C TEL. $230–$250 double, suites $365–$550. Rates include continental breakfast and afternoon tea. 2-night minimum weekends; 3 nights holiday weekends. AE, MC, V.

The White Barn Inn pampers its guests like no other in Maine. Upon checking in, guests are shown to one of the inn's parlors and offered port or brandy while valets in crisp uniforms gather luggage and park the cars. After a tour of the inn, guests are left to their own devices. They can avail themselves of the inn's free bikes (including a small fleet of tandems) to head to the beach, or walk cross the street and wander the quiet, shady pathways of St. Anthony's Franciscan Monastery. The rooms are individually decorated in a refined country style that's elegant without being obtrusive. The inn has an atmosphere that's distinctly European, and the emphasis is on service. I'm not aware of any other inn of this size that offers as many unexpected niceties, like robes, fresh flowers in the rooms, bottled water, and turn-down service at night. Nearly half the rooms have wood-burning fireplaces.

Dining: See "Where to Dine," below.

Amenities: Concierge, room service (breakfast only), free newspaper, in-room massage, twice-daily maid service, valet parking, guest safe, afternoon tea, outdoor heated pool, bicycles, nearby ocean beach, conference rooms, sundeck.

MODERATE

Lodge at Turbat's Creek. Turbat's Creek Rd., Kennebunkport, ME 04046. ☎ **207/967-8700.** 26 units. A/C TV TEL. June–Aug $119–$129 double, off-season $109–$119 double. Rates include continental breakfast. AE, MC, V. Closed late-Oct–Apr (open two weeks in Dec). Directions: From Dock Square, drive to top of hill, turn right on Maine St., left at first fork, right at second. Pets allowed; inquire before arriving.

A classy, unusually clean motel in a quiet residential neighborhood about a five minutes' drive from Dock Square. The grounds are attractive and amply endowed with Adirondack chairs. The inn has eight mountain bikes for guests to borrow (no charge), and there's also a heated pool. The rooms, located on two floors, are standard motel size and decorated with rustic pine furniture and painted a cheerful lemony-yellow color. The complimentary continental breakfast may be enjoyed on the lawn in pleasant weather.

WHERE TO DINE

Those in mind of a quick lobster have a couple of options in the Kennebunkport area, although the prices tend to be a bit more expensive than at other casual lobster spots further north along the coast. **Nunan's Lobster Hut,** (☎ **207/967-4362)**

Route 9 north of Kennebunkport at Cape Porpoise, is a classic lobster shack. No reservations or credit cards; open daily for dinner, starting at 5pm in summer. There's also **Cape Porpoise Lobster Co.,** 15 Pier Rd. (☎ **800/967-4268** or 207/967-4268), a compact spot overlooking the sparkling water. There's limited outdoor dining, but most everything is served on Styrofoam plates, so beware of rogue winds that strive to dump your meal on your lap. No reservations; credit cards are accepted. It's usually open daily from 8am to 8pm for breakfast, lunch, and dinner in season; closed from late fall to around Memorial Day.

Federal Jack's Restaurant and Brew Pub. 8 Western Ave., Lower Village (south bank of Kennebunk River), Kennebunkport. ☎ **207/967-4322.** www.federaljacks.com. Main courses (lunch or dinner) $5.95–$14.95; lobster dinners priced to market. AE, DISC, MC, V. Daily 11:30am–10pm. PUB FARE.

This light, airy, and modern restaurant, named after a schooner built at Cape Porpoise a century ago, is in a retail complex of recent vintage that sits a bit uneasily amid the boatyards lining the south bank of the Kennebunk River. From the second floor perch (look for a seat on the spacious three-season deck in warmer weather), you can gaze across the river toward the shops of Dock Square. The upscale pub menu features regional fare with a creative twist, and also offers standard fare like hamburgers, steamed mussels, and pizza. This is good bet for a basic meal without any pretensions; locals keep a sharp eye on the specials board, which features treats like a grilled crab and havarti sandwich. The restaurant is best known for its Shipyard ales, lagers, and porters, which they've been brewing since 1992 and are among the best in New England. Non-tipplers can enjoy a zesty homemade root beer, or fresh-roasted coffees at the coffee bar.

Grissini. 27 Western Ave., Kennebunkport. ☎ **207/967-2211.** www. restaurantgrissini.com. Reservations encouraged. Entrees $7.95–$18.95. AE, MC, V. Sun–Fri 5:30–9:30pm; Sat 5–9pm (closed Wed Jan–Mar). TUSCAN.

Opened by the same folks who run the White Barn Inn, Grissini is a handsome trattoria that offers great value for the money. The mood is a sort of elegant but writ large rustic Italian: oversized Italian advertising posters line the walls of the soaring, barn-like space, and burning logs in the handsome stone fireplace take the chill out of a cool evening. In fact, everything seems larger than life, including the plates, flatware, and water goblets. The menu changes weekly; meals are likewise luxuriously sized and nicely presented, and include a wide range of pastas and pizza, served with considerable flair. More far-ranging entrees include osso buco with vegetables, lemon zest and rosemary served over garlic mashed potatoes, and wood-grilled salmon served with a roasted pepper ragu. Desserts include crème caramel and tiramisu.

Seascapes. 77 Pier Rd., Cape Porpoise, Kennebunkport. ☎ **207/967-8500.** www.seascapesrestaurant.com. Reservations recommended. Entrees $19–$25. AE, MC, V. Daily 12:30–2:30pm and 5–9pm (open until 10pm Fri and Sat in peak season). Closed late Oct–Apr. UPSCALE NEW ENGLAND.

A tony restaurant with a wonderful ocean view, Seascapes is decorated in what might be termed traditional country-club bamboo, with a few creative touches like rustic handpainted table settings. It's fancy but not overly fussy, a popular spot with regular visitors to the coast yet with food several notches above the tried and true. All the fish is fresh (excepting shrimp), and all the breads and desserts are made on premises. The menu offers traditional favorites like onion-crusted Black Angus sirloin steak with potato Swiss au gratin, along with more adventurous dishes like cashew-crusted Chilean sea bass served with a citrus-tamari sauce. Christina's shrimp (served with feta cheese and Kalamata olives) is a favorite here. The restaurant has garnered *Wine Spectator's* award of excellence annually since 1993.

✪ **White Barn Inn.** Beach Ave., Kennebunkport. ☎ **207/967-2321.** Reservations recommended. Fixed-price dinner $73. AE, MC, V. Daily 6–9pm. Closed two weeks in Jan. REGIONAL/NEW AMERICAN.

The setting is magical. The restaurant (attached to an equally magical inn, see above) is housed in an ancient, rustic barn with a soaring interior. There's a copper-topped bar off to one side, rich leather seating in the waiting area, a pianist, and an eclectic collection of country antiques displayed in the hay loft. The service is impeccable, although those accustomed to more informal settings might find it overly attentive.

The excellent menu changes frequently, but depending on the season you might start with a lobster spring roll with daikon, carrots, snow peas, and cilantro, then graduate to a crab-glazed poached fillet of halibut on sweet-pea puree, or pan-seared veal and venison on bacon-roasted butternut squash. Among the more popular dishes is the Maine lobster served on homemade fettuccini with cognac-coral butter sauce. Anticipate a meal to remember. The White Barn won't let you down.

3

Portland

*P*ortland is Maine's largest city, and easily one of the more attractive and livable small cities on the East Coast. Actually, Portland feels more like a large town than a small city. Strike up a conversation with a resident, and you're likely to get an earful about how easy it is to live here. You can buy superb coffee, see great movies, and get good Thai food to go (Portland has several Thai restaurants). Yet it's still small enough to walk from one end of town to the other, and postal workers and bank clerks know your name soon after you move here. Despite its outward appearance of being an actual metropolis, Portland has a population of just 65,000.

Like most successful downtowns, Portland has been forced to reinvent itself every couple of generations as economic and cultural trends overturn old paradigms. The city was a center for maritime trade in the 19th century, when a forest of ship masts obscured the view of the harbor. It's been a manufacturing hub, with locomotive factories, steel foundries, and fish-packing plants. It's been a mercantile center with impressive downtown department stores and a slew of wholesale dealers.

Today, as the sprawling, could-be-anywhere mall area of South Portland siphons off much of the local commercial energy, the city is bent on reshaping downtown as a tourist destination and regional center for the arts. The newest attraction, a public market featuring Maine-grown fresh foods and flowers, opened in the summer of 1998; plans for a $50 million modern aquarium are underway; and talk of a new convention center periodically erupts. The verdict is still out on whether this current reincarnation will ultimately succeed. But unlike other deteriorating downtowns nationwide, today Portland has few vacant storefronts. Office space is in short supply, and there's a sort of brisk urban vitality that's eluded other cities many times its size.

1 Orientation

GETTING THERE

Portland is off the Maine Turnpike (I-95). Coming from the south, downtown is most easily reached by taking Exit 6A, then following I-295 to downtown. Exit at Franklin Street and follow this eastward until you arrive at the waterfront at the Casco Bay Lines terminal. Turn right on Commercial Street and you'll be at the lower edge of the Old Port. Continue on a few blocks to the visitors center (see below).

Concord Trailways (☎ **800/639-3317** or 207/828-1151) and **Vermont Transit** (☎ **800/537-3330** or 207/772-6587) offer bus service to Portland from Boston and Bangor. The Vermont Transit bus terminal is located at 950 Congress St. Concord Trailways, which is a few dollars more expensive, offers movies and headsets on its trips. The Concord terminal is inconveniently located on Sewall Street (a 35-minute walk from downtown), but it has plenty of free parking and is served by local buses from nearby Congress Street ($1 fare).

The **Portland International Jetport** is served by regularly scheduled flights on **Air Nova** (☎ 902/873-5000; www.airnova.ca), **American Airlines** (☎ 800/433-7300; www.aa.com), **Delta/Business Express** (☎ 800/638-7333; www.delta-air.com), **Continental** (☎ 800/525-0280; www.flycontinental.com), **US Airways** (☎ 800/428-4322; www.usairways.com), **United** (☎ 800/241-6522; www.ual.com), and **Northwest Airlines** (☎ 800/225-2525; www.nwa.com). The airport has grown in fits and starts in recent years (ongoing construction and tight parking can be frustrating at times) but is still quite easily navigated. It's located just across the Fore River from downtown. Metro buses ($1) connect the airport to downtown; cab fare runs about $12.

VISITOR INFORMATION

The **Convention and Visitor's Bureau of Greater Portland,** 305 Commercial St., Portland, ME 04101 (☎ **207/772-5800** or 207/772-4994), stocks a large supply of brochures and is happy to dispense information about local attractions, lodging, and dining. The center is open in summer weekdays 8am to 6pm and weekends 10am to 5pm; hours are shorter during the off-season. Ask for the free "Greater Portland Visitor Guide" with map.

Portland has two free weekly alternative newspapers—*Casco Bay Weekly* and the *Portland Phoenix* —and both offer close-to-comprehensive listings of local events, films, nightclub performances and the like. Copies are widely available at restaurants, bars, and convenience stores.

CITY LAYOUT

The city of Portland is divided into two areas: on-peninsula and off-peninsula. (There are also the islands, but more on that below.) Most travelers are destined for the compact peninsula, which is home to the downtown and where most of the city's cultural life and much of its retail activity takes place.

Viewed from the water, Portland's peninsula is shaped like a sway-backed horse, with the Old Port in the belly near the waterfront, and the peninsula's two main residential neighborhoods (Munjoy Hill and the West End) on the gentle rises overlooking downtown. Congress Street, Portland's main artery of commerce, connects these two neighborhoods. The western stretch of Congress Street (roughly between Monument Square and State Street) is home to Portland's emerging Arts District, where you can find a handsome art museum, several theaters, the campus of the Maine College of Art (located in an old department store), an L.L. Bean outlet, and a growing number of restaurants and boutiques.

PARKING

Parking is notoriously tight in the Old Port area, and the city's parking enforcement notoriously efficient. Several parking garages are convenient to the Old Port, with parking fees less than $1 per hour.

SPECIAL EVENTS

New Year's/Portland (☎ 207/772-9012) rings in January with a smorgasbord of events and entertainment throughout downtown Portland. Events for families are scheduled in the afternoon; entertainment more oriented for adults—including loads of live music—kicks off later in the evening at numerous locales, including auditoriums, shops, and churches. The emphasis is on enjoying New Year's without alcohol. One admission fee buys entrance to all events.

The **Old Port Festival** (☎ 207/772-6828) takes place in early June when tens of thousands of revelers descend upon

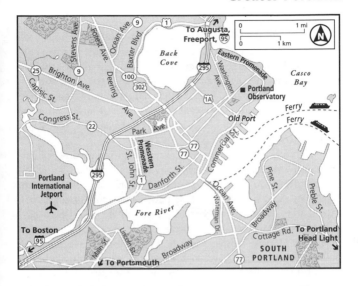

the historic Old Port section to herald the arrival of summer. Several blocks of the Old Port are blocked to traffic, and the throngs order food and buy goods from street vendors. Several stages provide entertainment, ranging from kids' sing-alongs to raucous blues. Admission is free.

2 Exploring the City

Any visit to Portland should start with a stroll around the historic **Old Port.** Bounded by Commercial, Congress, Union, and Pearl streets, this several-square-block area near the waterfront contains the city's best commercial architecture, a plethora of fine restaurants, a mess of boutiques, and one of the thickest concentrations of bars you'll find anywhere. (The Old Port tends to transform as night lengthens, with the crowds growing younger and rowdier.) The narrow streets and intricate brick facades reflect the mid-Victorian era during which most of the area was rebuilt following a devastating fire in 1866. Leafy, quaint **Exchange Street** is the heart of the Old Port, with other attractive streets running off and around it.

Just outside the Old Port, don't miss the **First Parish Church** at 425 Congress St., an uncommonly beautiful granite meeting house with an impressively austere interior that's changed little since it first opened its doors in 1826. A few doors down the block is Portland's **City Hall,** at the head of Exchange Street. Modeled after New York's City Hall, Portland's seat of government was built of granite in 1909. It houses the Merrill Auditorium, the city's premier venue for concerts and Broadway road shows. In a similarly regal vein is the **U.S. Custom House** at 312 Fore St. During business hours feel free to wander inside to view the elegant woodwork and marble floors dating back to 1868.

Flanking the Old Port on the two low hills are downtown's main residential areas. Drive eastward on Congress Street up and over Munjoy Hill and you'll come to the **Eastern Promenade,** a 68-acre hillside park with broad, grassy slopes extending down to the water and superb views of Casco Bay and its islands. Along the base of the park you'll find the Eastern Prom Pathway, which wraps along the waterfront between the Casco Bay Lines ferry terminal near the Old Port and the East End Beach. The pathway is suitable for walking or biking, and offers wonderful views of the harbor and its constant boat traffic. The easiest place to park is at the bottom of the hill near the beach and boat ramp.

Atop Munjoy Hill, above the Eastern Promenade, is the distinctive **Portland Observatory,** a quirky shingled tower dating from 1807, used to signal the arrival of ships into port. After four years of extensive structural repairs, the tower reopened in the summer of 2000. Exhibits inside provide a quick glimpse of Portland's past, but the real draw is the expansive view from the top of the city and the harbor. It is open daily (when flags are flying from the cupola); admission is $3 for adults, $2 for children. For more information, call ☎ 207/774-5561.

On the other end of the peninsula is the **Western Promenade.** (Follow Spring Street westward to Vaughan; turn right and then take your first left on Bowdoin Street to the prom.) This narrow strip of lawn atop a forested bluff has views across the Fore River, which is lined with less-than-scenic light industry, to the White Mountains in the distance. It's a great spot to watch the sunset. Around the Western Prom are some of the grandest and most imposing houses in the city that include a wide array of architectural styles, from Italianate to shingle to stick.

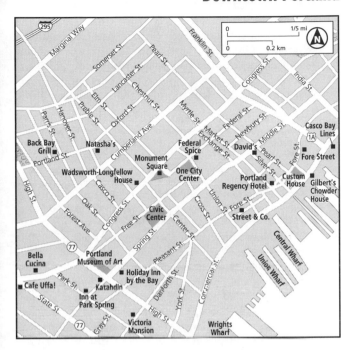

THE TOP ATTRACTIONS: FROM LIGHTHOUSES TO LONGFELLOW

Children's Museum of Maine. 142 Free St. (next to the Portland Museum of Art). ☎ **207/828-1234.** Admission $5 per child or adult (free for children under 1). AE, MC, V. Mon–Sat 10am–5pm, Sun noon–5pm; closed Mon–Tues fall–spring. Discounted parking at Spring St. Parking Garage.

The centerpiece exhibit here is the camera obscura, a room-sized "camera" located on the top floor of this stout, columned downtown building next to the art museum. Children gather around a white table in a dark room, where they see magically projected images that include cars driving on city streets, boats plying the harbor, and seagulls flapping by. The camera obscura never fails to enthrall, and it provides a memorable lesson in the workings of a lens—whether in a camera or an eye.

That's just one attraction. There's plenty more to do here: from running a supermarket checkout counter to sliding down the firehouse pole to piloting a mock space shuttle from a high cockpit. The Explore Floor offers a series of interactive science exhibits focusing on Maine's natural resources; through fall 2001: Ship Ahoy!, which features a newly built 40-foot schooner on main gallery floor. Make a deal with your kids: they behave during a trip to the art museum (just next door), and they'll be rewarded with a couple of hours in their own museum.

❂ **Portland Head Light & Museum.** Fort Williams Park, 1000 Shore Rd., Cape Elizabeth. ☎ **207/799-2661.** www.portlandheadlight.com. Free admission for grounds; museum admission $2 adults, $1 children 6–18. Park grounds open daily year-round sunrise–sunset (until 8:30pm in summer); museum open daily June–Oct 10am–4pm; open weekends only in spring and late fall. From Portland, follow State St. across the Fore River; continue straight on Broadway. At third light turn right on Cottage Rd., which becomes Shore Rd.; follow until you arrive at the park, on your left.

Just a 10-minute drive from downtown Portland, this 1794 lighthouse is one of the most picturesque in the nation. (You'll probably recognize it from its cameo role in numerous advertisements and posters.) The light marks the entrance to Portland Harbor and was occupied continuously from its construction until 1989, when it was automated and the graceful keeper's house (1891) converted to a small, town-owned museum focusing on the history of navigation. The lighthouse itself is still active and thus closed to the public, but visitors can stop by the museum, browse for lighthouse-themed gifts at the gift shop, wander the park grounds, and watch the sailboats and cargo ships come and go. The park has a pebble beach, grassy lawns with ocean vistas, and picnic areas well suited for informal barbecues.

Portland Museum of Art. 7 Congress Sq. (corner of Congress and High streets). ☎ **207/775-6148.** www.portlandmuseum.org. E-mail: pma@maine. rr.com. $6 adults, $5 students and seniors, $1 children 6–12. (Free admission Fri 5–9pm.) Tues–Wed and Sat–Sun 10am–5pm (June–mid-Oct also open Mon 10am–5pm), Thurs–Fri 10am–9pm.

This bold, modern museum was designed by I.M. Pei & Partners in 1983, and features selections from its own fine collections along with a parade of touring exhibits. (Summer exhibits are usually targeted at a broad audience.) The museum is particularly strong in American artists with Maine connections, including Winslow Homer, Andrew Wyeth, and Edward Hopper, and has fine displays of early American furniture and crafts. The museum shares the Joan Whitney

Payson Collection with Colby College (the college gets it one semester every other year), which includes wonderful European works by Renoir, Degas, and Picasso. Guided tours are daily at 2pm.

Portland Public Market. 25 Preble St. (½ block west of Monument Square). ☎ **207/228-2000.** www.portlandmarket.com. Open year-round. Mon–Sat 9am–7pm, Sun 10am–5pm.

The Portland Public Market features some of the best food that Maine is producing, and it's the perfect place to lay in supplies for a picnic or snacks. There are more than two-dozen vendors selling fresh foods and flowers, much of which is Maine grown. The architecturally distinctive building is at once classic and modern, and houses fishmongers, butchers, fresh fruit dealers, a seafood cafe, a wine shop, and a new restaurant called Commissary (see below). There's free parking (with validated ticket) at the connected parking garage on the west side of Cumberland Avenue.

Victoria Mansion. 109 Danforth St. ☎ **207/772-4841.** $7 adults, $3 children 6–17, free for children under 6. May–Oct Tues–Sat 10am–4pm, Sun 1–5pm; tours offered at quarter past and quarter of each hour. Closed Nov–Apr, except for holiday tours from end-Nov to mid-Dec. From the Old Port, head west on Fore St., veer right on Danforth St. at light near Stonecoast Brewing; proceed three blocks to the mansion, at the corner of Park St.

Widely regarded as one of the most elaborate Victorian brownstone homes ever built in the United States, this mansion (also known as the Morse-Libby House) is a remarkable display of high Victorian style. Built between 1858 and 1863 for a Maine businessman who made a fortune in the New Orleans hotel trade, the towering, slightly foreboding home is a prime example of the Italianate style once in vogue. Inside, it appears that not a square inch of wall space was left unmolested by craftsmen or artisans (11 painters were hired to create the murals). The décor is ponderous and somber, but it offers an engaging look at a bygone era. This home is a must for architecture buffs and is often mentioned in books on the history of American architecture. A gift shop sells Victorian-themed gifts and books.

Wadsworth-Longfellow House & Center for Maine History. 489 Congress St. ☎ **207/879-0427.** www.mainehistory.com. Gallery and Longfellow house tour $6 adults, $2 children (6–18). Gallery only $4 adults, $2 children. Longfellow House open June–Oct daily 10am–4pm, gallery 10am–5:30pm; Nov–May gallery only Wed–Sat noon–4pm.

Maine Historical Society's "history campus" includes three widely varied buildings on busy Congress Street in downtown Portland. The austere brick Wadsworth-Longfellow House dates to 1785 and was built by Gen. Peleg Wadsworth, father of noted poet Henry Wadsworth Longfellow. It's furnished in an early 19th century style, with many samples of Longfellow family furniture on display. Adjacent to the home is the Maine History Gallery, located in a garish post-modern building, formerly a bank. Changing exhibits here explore the rich texture of Maine history. Just behind the Longfellow house is the library of the Maine Historical Society, a popular destination among genealogists.

ON THE WATER

The 3.5-mile **Back Cove Pathway** loops around Portland's Back Cove, offering attractive views of the city skyline across the water, glimpses of Casco Bay, and a bit of exercise. The pathway is the city's most popular recreational facility; after work in summer Portlanders flock here to walk, bike, jog, and windsurf (there's enough water two-and-a-half hours before and after high tide). Part of the pathway shares a noisy bridge with I-295 and it can be fulsome at a dead low tide, but when tides and weather cooperate it's a pleasant spot for a walk. The main parking lot is located across from Shop 'n Save Plaza at the water's edge. Take Exit 6 (Forest Avenue north) off I-295; turn right at the first light on Baxter Boulevard; at the next light turn right again and park in the lot ahead on the left.

Another fine place to take in a water view is the **Eastern Prom Pathway,** which wraps for about a mile along the waterfront between the Casco Bay Lines ferry terminal and the East End Beach (the path continues onward to connect with the Back Cove Pathway). The paved pathway is suitable for walking or biking and offers wonderful views out toward the islands and the boat traffic on the harbor. The easiest place to park is near the beach and boat ramp. From downtown head east on Congress Street until you can't go any farther; turn right, then take your first left on the road down the hill to the water's edge.

Casco Bay Lines. Commercial and Franklin Sts. ☎ **207/774-7871.** www.cascobaylines.com. Fares vary depending on the run and season, but summer rates typically $5.25–$13.75 round-trip. Frequent departures 6am–10pm.

Six of the Casco Bay islands have year-round populations and are served by scheduled ferries from downtown Portland. Except for Long Island, the islands are part of the city of Portland. The ferries offer an inexpensive way to view the bustling harbor and get a taste of island life. Trips range from a 20-minute (one-way) excursion to Peaks Island (the closest thing to an island suburb with 1,200 year-round residents), to the 5½-hour cruise to Bailey Island (connected by bridge to the mainland south of Brunswick) and back. All of the islands are well suited for walking; Peaks Island has a rocky back shore that's easily accessible via the island's paved perimeter road (bring a picnic lunch). Cliff Island is the most remote of the bunch, and has a sedate turn-of-the-century island retreat character.

Eagle Island Tours. Long Wharf (Commercial St.). ☎ **207/774-6498.** $17.50 adults, $13.50 seniors, $10.50 children under 12 (includes state park fee of $1.50 adult, 50¢ child). One departure daily at 10am.

Eagle Island was the summer home of famed Arctic explorer and Portland native Robert E. Peary, who claimed in 1909 to be the first person to reach the North Pole. (His accomplishments have been the subject of exhaustive debates among Arctic scholars, some of whom insist he inflated his claims.) In 1904, Peary built a simple home on a remote, 17-acre island at the edge of Casco Bay; in 1912 he added flourishes in the form of two low stone towers. After his death in 1920 his family kept up the home, then later donated it to the state, which has since managed it as a state park. The home is open to the public, maintained much the way it was when Peary lived here. Island footpaths through the scant forest allow exploration to the open, seagull-clotted cliffs at the southern tip. Eagle Tours offers one trip daily from Portland. The four-hour excursion includes a 1½-hour stopover on the island.

Old Port Mariner Fleet. Commercial St. (Long Wharf and Custom House Wharf). ☎ **207/775-0727.** www.marinerfleet.com. Excursions $10–$75. Several departures daily.

This fleet of three boats tied up off Commercial Street offers a number of ways to enjoy the bay. The *Indian II* runs deep-sea fishing trips far beyond Portland Harbor in search of cod, cusk, hake, pollack, and more. Most are daylong trips (8am to 5pm), but several times each summer they offer marathons (5am to 5pm) for real die-hards. On the *Odyssey* you search for

Ferries to Nova Scotia

A trip to northern New England can serve as a springboard for an excursion to Atlantic Canada. The most hassle-free way to link the two is by ferry. Two ferries connect Yarmouth, Nova Scotia with Maine, saving hours of driving time and providing a relaxing mini-cruise along the way.

The **Scotia Prince** departs each evening from Portland for an 11-hour crossing to Nova Scotia. The ship is bustling with activity, from its cafe and restaurant to casino and glitzy floor show in the lounge. When the party winds down, you can retire to a cabin for a good night's sleep and awake for breakfast before disembarking in Nova Scotia. Day cabins are available on the return trip, but you'll save some money sitting in the lounge or relaxing on a deck chair and watching for whales.

The Portland to Yarmouth crossing aboard the *Scotia Prince* is approximately 11 hours and costs $80 for adult passengers,

whales by day (10am to 4pm), and in the evening enjoy music and food, including a four-hour Downeast lobster bake with entertainment for $34.50.

SHOPPING

Aficionados of antique and secondhand furniture stores love Portland. Good browsing may be had on Congress Street. Check out the stretches between State and High streets in the arts district, and from India Street to Washington Avenue on Munjoy Hill. About a dozen shops of varying quality (mostly low-end) can be found in these two areas.

For new items, the Old Port, with its dozens of boutiques and storefronts, is well worth browsing. It's especially strong in contemporary one-of-a-kind clothing that's a world apart from generic stuff you'll find at a mall. Artisan and crafts shops are also well represented.

Abacus American Crafts. 44 Exchange St. ☎ **207/772-4880.**

A wide range of bold, inventive crafts of all varieties—from furniture to jewelry—is displayed on two floors of this centrally located shop. Even if you're not in a buying frame of mind, this is a great place for browsing.

$40 for children, and $98 for each vehicle. Cabins are available for an additional fare, ranging from $32 for a day cabin to $165 for an overnight suite. Advance reservations are essential. Call **Prince of Fundy Cruises** at ☎ **800/341-7540** or 207/775-5616; www.princeoffundy.com.

Bay Ferries (☎ **888/249-7245**) operates the Bar Harbor–Yarmouth ferry aboard *The Cat* (short for catamaran), which claims to be the fastest ferry in North America. Since going into service in 1998, the new ship has cut the crossing time from 6 hours to 3 hours, zipping along at up to 50 miles per hour. There's an open deck on the rear, but passengers trying to enjoy the fresh air sometimes find it mingled with exhaust fumes. Summer season rates are U.S.$55 adult, U.S.$50 senior, U.S.$25 child (5 to 12), and U.S.$70 for automobile. Off-season rates are available. As with the Prince of Fundy line, advance reservations are vital during the peak summer season.

Amaryllis Clothing Co. 41 Exchange St. ☎ 207/772-4439.

Portland's original creative clothing store, Amaryllis offers unique clothing for women that's as comfortable as it is casually elegant. The colors are rich, the patterns unique, and some items are designed by local artisans. It's open until 9pm daily in summer.

D. Cole Jewelers. 10 Exchange St. ☎ 207/772-5119.

Dean and Denise Cole are longtime Old Port artisans and entrepreneurs, producing wonderfully handcrafted gold and silver jewelry. Browse through elegant traditional designs as well as more eccentric work at their brightly lit, low-pressure shop.

Fibula. 50 Exchange St. ☎ 207/761-4432.

Original, handcrafted jewelry by Maine's top designers is beautifully displayed at this tasteful shop in the heart of the Old Port. There's also a collection of loose gemstones on display.

Green Design Furniture. 267 Commercial St. ☎ 207/775-4234.

This inventive shop sells a line of beautiful, mission-inspired furniture that disassembles for easy storage and travel. These beautiful works are creatively crafted of cherry.

Harbor Fish Market. 9 Custom House Wharf (across from end of Pearl St.).
☎ **800/370-1790** or 207/775-0251.

This classic waterfront fish market is worth a trip just to see
the mounds of fresh fish. It's a great spot for lobsters-to-go
(they're packed for travel and will easily last 24 hours), or to
buy smoked fish for a local picnic.

L.L. Bean Factory Store. 542 Congress St. ☎ **207/772-5100.**

Sporting goods retailer L.L. Bean opened its first downtown
factory outlet here in 1996. Look for last year's fashions,
returns, and slightly damaged goods, along with a small selection of first-run, full-price items.

Maine Potters Market. 376 Fore St. ☎ **207/774-1633.**

Maine's largest pottery collective has been in operation for
nearly 2 decades. You can select from a variety of styles;
shipping is easily arranged.

Resourceful Home. 111 Commercial St. ☎ **207/780-1314.**

Environmentally sound products for the home and garden,
linens, and cleaning products are the specialties here.

Stonewall Kitchen. 182 Middle St. ☎ **207/879-2409.**

Stonewall is a frequent winner in food trade shows for its
innovative and delicious mustards, jams, and sauces. Among
them: ginger peach tea jam, sun-dried tomato and olive relish,
and maple chipotle grill sauce. You can browse and sample at
their Old Port store (also stores in Camden and in York).

The Whip and Spoon. 161 Commercial St. ☎ **800/937-9447** or
207/774-4020.

Look for great kitchen gadgets, Maine-made food products,
and the city's best selection of wine (including a Maine blueberry variety).

3 Where to Stay

The **Holiday Inn by the Bay,** 88 Spring St. (☎ **207/
775-2311**), offers great views of the harbor from about half
the rooms, along with the usual chain-hotel creature comforts.
Peak-season rates are approximately $140 for a double.
Budget travelers seeking chain hotels typically head toward the
area around the Maine Mall in South Portland, about a
10-minute drive away from the attractions of downtown. Try

Days Inn (☎ 207/772-3450) or **Coastline Inn** (☎ 207/772-3838).

✪ **Black Point Inn.** 510 Black Point Rd., Prouts Neck, ME 04074. ☎ **800/258-0003** or 207/883-2500. Fax 207/883-9976. www.blackpointinn.com. 80 units (includes 12 two-room suites). A/C TV TEL. July–Labor Day $345–$470 double, cottages $420–$520 double. Spring and fall from $290; winter from $210. Rates include breakfast and dinner. AE, CB, DC, DISC, MC, V.

Located about 15 minutes from downtown Portland, the Black Point Inn is a Maine classic. Situated on 9 acres with views along the coast both north and south, the Black Point was built as a summer resort in 1873 in an area enshrined in some of the work of noted American painter Winslow Homer. It's been under new ownership since 1998 (by the same people who own the Portland Regency), and the new owners have retained its famous old-world graciousness and charm. Sixty guest rooms are located in the main shingled lodge. Even the smaller rooms are generously sized, with enough room for two wing chairs and a writing desk. All are carpeted and have a quaint, summery feel, with Martha Washington bedspreads, original glass door knobs, and reproduction furnishings. There are also four tidy cottages on the property, and the guest rooms here have more of a rustic L.L. Bean look to them; my pick would be the Sprague Cottage, with its flagstone floors in the common area and five rooms with private balconies, some with ocean views. Since 1999, the inn has been open year-round. Note that it's popular for weddings on summer weekends, when you'll encounter accompanying bustle and noise.

Dining/Diversions: The main dining rooms have heavy beams, Windsor chairs, toile wallpaper, views of the garden or ocean, and a menu that favors creative resort fare, such as seafood fettuccine, cedar-planked salmon, crusted rack of lamb and, of course, boiled lobster with butter and lemon. On staff are a social director and, in summer, a children's program director.

Amenities: Olympic sized outdoor pool, indoor pool, ocean swimming at two adjacent beaches, shuttle to 5 area golf courses, hot tub, sauna, fitness room, nearby tennis courts, trails through bird sanctuary, massage, children's program (summers), free valet parking, limited rooms service, laundry and dry cleaning, baby-sitting, safe deposit boxes, afternoon refreshments, robes, irons, hair dryers, and coffee delivery to room.

The Danforth. 163 Danforth St., Portland, ME 04102. ☎ **800/991-6557** or 207/879-8755. Fax 207/879-8754. www.danforthmaine.com. E-mail: danforth@maine.rr.com. 10 units. A/C TV TEL. Summer $139–$329 double; off-season $119–$229. Rates include continental breakfast; discounts available in off-season. AE, MC, V. Pets sometimes allowed ($10 fee), call ahead.

Located in an exceptionally handsome brick home constructed in 1821, The Danforth opened in 1994 and is now one of Portland's most desirable small inns. The guest rooms are handsomely decorated, many in rich and vibrant tones. The inn's extra touches are exceptional throughout, from working fireplaces in all guest rooms (but one) to the richly paneled basement billiards room to the direct-line phones. Especially appealing is Room 1, with a sitting room and private second-floor deck, and Room 2, with high ceilings and superb morning light; rooms 5 and 6, housed in the old servant's wing, are smaller. The inn is located at the edge of the Spring Street Historic District, and is within a ten-minute walk from downtown attractions. It's very popular for weddings and other events, so if you're in search of a quiet weekend retreat, ask first if anything is planned.

Amenities: Newspaper delivery, in-room massage, billiards room, bicycle rental, sundeck, access to in-town health club.

Inn at Park Spring. 135 Spring St., Portland, ME 04101. ☎ **800/437-8511** or 207/774-1059. www.innatparkspring.com. E-mail: psinn@javanet.com. 6 units. A/C. May–Oct $130–$145 double; Nov–April $95–$105. Rates include full breakfast and off-street parking. 2-night minimum weekends. AE, MC, V. Children over 10 are welcome.

This small, tasteful B&B is located on a busy downtown street in a historic brick home that dates back to 1835. It's well-located for exploring the city on foot. The Portland Museum of Art is just two blocks away, the Old Port about 10 minutes, and great restaurants are all within easy walking distance. Guests can linger or watch TV in the front parlor, or chat at the table in the kitchen. The rooms are all corner rooms, and most are bright and sunny. Especially nice is "Spring," with its great morning light and wonderful views of the historic row houses on Park Street, and "Gables," on the third floor, which gets abundant afternoon sun.

The Percy Inn. 15 Pine St., Portland ME 04104. ☎ **207/871-7638.** Fax 207/775-2599. www.percyinn.com. E-mail: innkeeper@percyinn.com. 4 units. A/C TV TEL. June–Oct $129–$179 double; Nov–May $89–$159. Rates include continental breakfast. MC, V. Children over 8 welcome.

The handsome Percy Inn was opened in 1998 by innkeeper Dale Northrup at the edge of Portland's west end. Housed in a brick 1830 town house in an up-and-coming but not-quite-there area, the inn is close to good restaurants and the Center for Cultural Exchange (see below), as well as about a 15-minute walk to the Old Port. The four guest rooms are located atop a narrow and twisting staircase. The third-floor "Dorothy Parker Room" has a Dickensian view of the brick skyline, along with a decent-sized bathroom and dressing area. The second-floor "Henry W. Longfellow Room" has wonderful random-width floorboards, a small snack room with mini-fridge, and a corner sitting area. Nice touches abound: All rooms have weather radios, CD players, VCRs, complimentary soft drinks, and coolers with beach blankets for day trips. There's limited common space; self-serve breakfasts are offered in a second-floor breakfast room.

✪ **Pomegranate Inn.** 49 Neal St., Portland, ME 04102. ☎ **800/356-0408** or 207/772-1006. Fax 207/773-4426. www.pomegranateinn.com. 8 units. A/C TV TEL. Summer and fall $165–$205 double; winter and spring $95–$145. Rates include full breakfast. 2-night minimum summer weekends; four nights at Christmas and Thanksgiving. AE, DISC, MC, V. On-street parking. Directions: From the Old Port, take Middle Street (which turns into Spring Street) to Neal Street in the West End (about 1 mile); turn right and proceed to inn. Children 16 and older are welcome.

This is Portland's most appealing B&B, and one of the better choices in all of northern New England. Housed in an imposing, dove-gray 1884 Italianate home in the architecturally distinctive Western Prom neighborhood, the interiors are wondrously decorated with whimsy and elegance—a fatally cloying combination when attempted by someone without impeccably good taste. Look for the bold and exuberant wall paintings by a local artist, and the eclectic antique furniture collected and tastefully arranged by owner Isabel Smiles. If you have the chance, peek in some of the unoccupied rooms—they're all different with painted floors and boisterous faux-marble woodwork. Most rooms have gas fireplaces; the best of the lot is in the carriage house, which has its own private terrace, kitchenette, and fireplace. Tea and wine is served upon arrival, and the sit-down breakfasts in the cheery dining room are invariably creative and tasty. The inn is well situated for exploring the West End, and downtown is about a 20-minute walk away.

Portland Regency Hotel. 20 Milk St., Portland, ME 04101. ☎ **800/ 727-3436** or 207/774-4200. Fax 207/775-2150. www.theregency.com. public@theregency.com. 95 units. A/C MINIBAR TV TEL. Summer $199–$249 double; off-season $159–$239. AE, CB, DISC, MC, V.

Centrally located on a cobblestone courtyard in the middle of the trendy Old Port, the Regency boasts the city's premier hotel location. But it's got more than location going for it— it's also one of the more architecturally striking and better-managed hotels in the state. Housed in an 1895 brick armory, the hotel inside is thoroughly modern and offers attractive guest rooms nicely appointed and furnished with all the expected amenities. The architects have had to work within the quirky layout of the building; as a result, the top-floor rooms lack windows but have skylights, and the windows are knee-high in some other rooms. The hotel has three different style suites; for a splurge, ask for Room 332 or Room 336, both corner rooms with handsome (nonworking) brick fireplaces and sitting areas. The one complaint is the noise: the interior guest room walls are a bit thin so noise travels from room to room, and on weekends the revelry in the Old Port streets sometimes penetrates even the dense brick walls.

Dining: The hotel is home to The Armory Restaurant, which serves breakfast, lunch, and dinner. Dinners include traditional favorites like steak au poive and surf-and-turf, with entree prices ranging from $14.95 to $26.95.

Amenities: Limited room service, valet parking, dry cleaning (Monday to Friday), baby-sitting (with prior notice), valet parking ($8 per day), courtesy car to airport, safety deposit boxes, jacuzzi, VCR rental, sauna, fitness club, conference rooms, aerobics classes.

4 Where to Dine

More than anything else, Portland is a city of creative cheap eats. In addition to the places listed under the "Inexpensive" category below, you'll find filling fare at the cafeteria-style **Fresh Market Pasta,** 43 Exchange St. (☎ **207/773-7146**), and classic breakfasts served all day to hungry fishermen and well-scrubbed college kids alike at **Becky's,** 390 Commercial St. (☎ **207/773-7070**).

EXPENSIVE

✪ **Back Bay Grill.** 65 Portland St. ☎ **207/772-8833.** www. backbaygrill.com. Reservations recommended. Main courses $18–$33. AE, DC, DISC, MC, V. Mon–Thurs 5–9pm, Fri and Sat 5–9:30pm. NEW AMERICAN.

Back Bay Grill is one of Portland's consistently best restaurants, offering an upscale, contemporary ambiance amidst a rather downscale neighborhood near the main post office. There's light jazz in the background, and bold artwork on the walls that goes several notches above mere atmosphere. The menu is revamped seasonally, although dishes change more frequently to emphasize the local produce and meats that are available. Diners begin an evening with the popular terrine of house-cured gravlax and smoked salmon with marinated red onions, or sautéed foie gras on brioche with a poached pear and dried cherries. For main courses, look for heavenly dishes like rack of lamb with porcini-infused potato gratin and lavender demi-glacé; halibut with a chorizo-saffron sauce; or seared salmon on vanilla-scented Vidalia onions with fresh fava beans and a baby arugula-lobster salad. The fresh pastas are memorable and might include fettuccini with smoked tomatoes and oyster mushrooms, or ravioli filled with maple butternut squash and served with a tangy cranberry, orange, and ginger sauce. The restaurant offers a good selection of moderately priced wines by the glass.

Commissary. 25 Preble St. (in Portland Public Market). ☎ **207/228-2057.** Reservations recommended. Main courses $17–$23. AE, DC, DISC, MC, V. Daily 5–10pm (closed 9pm Sun & Mon). NEW AMERICAN.

This new spot (it opened in late 2000) brings an unaccustomed gloss to the Portland restaurant scene. It was created by Maine native, Matthew Kenney, who is the author of the cookbook *Matthew Kenney's Mediterranean Cooking*. Kenney developed a following with his three Manhattan restaurants, Matthew's, Mezze and Monzu. The soaring, spare space is urbane (if noisy), and the menu employs fresh fare from the market and beyond, with a seasonal emphasis. Among typical offerings: wood-roasted char, chicken stuffed with foie gras and pears, and a risotto of wild mushrooms. Side dishes are extra and ambitiously priced ($5 for wilted greens), but the main dishes offer good value. The wine list is honorable, with whites priced mostly in the $20s, reds in the $30s and up.

Fore Street. 288 Fore St. ☎ **207/775-2717.** Reservations recommended. Main courses, $14.95–$25.95. AE, MC, V. Mon–Sat 5:30–10pm; Sun 5:30–9:30pm. CONTEMPORARY GRILL.

During the long summer evenings, light floods in through the huge windows at this loft-like space; later at night, it takes on a more intimate glow with soft lighting against the brick walls, buttery narrow-plank maple floors, and copper-topped tables. But the place always feels bustling—the sprawling open kitchen is located in the middle of it all and filled with a team of chefs busy stoking the wood-fired brick oven and grilling fish and meats. Grilled foods are the specialty here. The menu changes nightly, but you might start with the local quail roasted in the wood oven or mussels served with a garlic almond butter, then move on to the turnspit-roasted Maine rabbit or choose among the applewood grilled dishes, including steak, chicken, duckling, venison, or fresh fish. Meals are consistently well prepared here, and the service is attentive on all but the busiest nights.

Street & Co. 33 Wharf St. ☎ **207/775-0887.** Reservations recommended. Main courses $15.95–$34.95. AE, MC, V. Sun–Thurs 5:30–9:30pm, Fri–Sat until 10pm. MEDITERRANEAN/SEAFOOD.

A pioneer establishment on now-bustling Wharf Street, Street & Co. specializes in seafood cooked just right. There's no smoke and mirrors—you pass the open kitchen as you're seated, and you can watch the talented chefs perform their magic in their tiny space. This intimate spot is a bit like something you might imagine stumbling onto while touring Provence: low beams, dim lighting, and drying herbs hanging overhead. Diners are seated at copper-topped tables, designed such that the waiters can deliver steaming skillets right from the stove. In the mood for lobster? Try it grilled and served over linguini in a butter-garlic sauce. If you're partial to calamari, this is the place. They know how to cook it so it's perfectly tender, a knack that's been lost elsewhere. Street & Co. fills up early, so reservations are strongly recommended. One-third of the tables are reserved for walk-ins each night, so it can't hurt to ask if you're in the neighborhood. In summer, there's outdoor seating along the cobblestone street.

MODERATE

Bella Cucina. 653 Congress St. ☎ **207/828-4033.** Reservations recommended. Main courses, $9–$17. AE, CB, DISC, MC, V. Open daily 5–10pm. RUSTIC ITALIAN.

Situated in one of Portland's less elegant commercial neighborhoods, Bella Cucina sets an inviting mood with rich colors, stylized fish sculptures, soft lighting, and pinpoint spotlights over the tables that carve out alluring islands of light. The eclectic menu changes frequently but dances deftly between rustic Italian and regional, with options like a robust cioppino with haddock and lobster, and a mélange of veal, pork, and chicken served with a prosciutto and mushroom ragout. Three or four vegan entrees are always offered. About half the seats are kept open for walk-ins, so take a chance and stop by even if you don't have a reservation. There's a fitting selection of wines, and free parking at night behind Joe's Smoke Shop.

Café Uffa!. 190 State St. ☎ **207/775-3380.** Breakfast $4–$7, dinner $10–$18. MC, V. Wed 5:30–10pm; Thurs–Fri 7–11am and 5:30–10pm, Sat 8am–noon and 5:30–10pm, Sun 9am–2pm. CONTEMPORARY AMERICAN.

Café Uffa! offers a little bit of everything, from vegetarian entrees to grilled steak, but try the fish, which is grilled to a wonderful tenderness over a wood-stoked fire (the salmon is especially good). Dishes might include grilled mahi-mahi on a shiitake mushroom risotto cake, and pan-seared scallops with a pesto broth. With its mismatched chairs, last-week's–flea-market decor, aggressively informal styling, and high ceilings, Uffa appeals to a young (and young-minded) crowd. Sunday brunches are superb, but be prepared to wait. There's often a line to get in.

Katahdin. 106 High St. ☎ **207/774-1740.** Reservations not accepted. Main courses $13–$22. DISC, MC, V. Tues–Thurs 5–9:30pm, Fri–Sat until 10:30pm. CREATIVE NEW ENGLAND.

Katahdin is a lively, often noisy spot that prides itself on its eclectic cuisine. Artists on slim budgets dine on the nightly blue plate special, which typically features something basic like meatloaf or pan-fried catfish. Wealthy business folks dine on more delicate fare, like the restaurant's crab cakes. Other recommended specialties include main courses of grilled sea scallops with an apricot-lobster reduction, and London broil marinated in a ginger, scallion, and garlic mix. Sometimes the kitchen nods, but for the most part, food is good, made more palatable by the reasonable prices. There's a small but decent selection of wines. No reservations are accepted, but you can enjoy one of the restaurant's fine martinis while waiting for a table at the bar.

Natasha's. 40 Portland St. ☎ **207/774-4004.** Reservations recommended. Main courses, brunch $4.50–$8.50, lunch $4.50–$9.95 (mostly $5–$6), dinner $13–$20. AE, DISC, MC, V. Mon–Fri 9am–2:30pm, Sat–Sun 8am–2:30pm, Tues–Sat 5–9:30pm. NEW AMERICAN.

Natasha's, located between the main post office and the Portland Public Market, has a setting that borders on industrial chic—battered concrete floors and drop ceilings, combined with tomato-red walls, a handsome black pew-like bench that lines the wall, and white tablecloths topped with butcher's paper. The menu is delightfully creative in its simplicity—a smoked salmon chowder, and Maine crab and goat cheese rangoon for starters. Dinner entrees (served Tuesday to Saturday) include lobster and crab ravioli served with leeks and lemon, pork loin grilled and served with a spicy pepper jam, and a crispy peanut tofu with pad Thai seasoning. Brunch is served until 2:30, featuring great omelets, corned beef hash, and granola. (Try the tortillas with scrambled eggs and other fixin's.) Lunch is equally inviting, with options including creative sandwiches (like a grilled vegetarian napoleon with artichoke hearts) and salads, along with wraps and noodles. Owner Natasha Carleton believes in giving back to the community: on Mondays lunch is free—you pay what you can afford, with the more affluent covering the cost for the less so.

INEXPENSIVE

✪ **Becky's.** 390 Commercial St. ☎ **207/773-7070.** Breakfast items $3–$6.25, sandwiches $1.75–$4.75. AE, DISC, MC, V. Daily 4am–9pm. BREAKFAST/LUNCH JOINT.

Becky's got a glowing write-up by noted food writers Jane and Michael Stern in *Gourmet* magazine in 1999, but it obviously hasn't gone to the proprietor's head (she's a mother of six and doesn't have time for a swelled head). This waterfront institution is located in a squat maroon building of concrete block on the non-quaint end of the waterfront, and has drop ceilings, fluorescent lights, and scruffy counters, booths, and tables. It's populated early (it opens 4am) and often by local fishermen grabbing a cup of joe and a plate o' eggs before setting out; later in the day it attracts high school kids and businessmen and just about everyone else. The menu is extensive, offering about what you'd expect, including lots of inexpensive sandwiches (fried haddock and cheese, corn dogs, tuna melt). But it's most noted for its breakfasts, including 13 different omelets, eggs anyway you'd like them, fruit bowls (made with fresh fruit in season), pancakes, and French toast. And where else can you choose among five different types of home fries?

Federal Spice. 225 Federal St. ☎ **207/774-6404.** Main courses $2.50–$6. No credit cards. Mon–Sat 11am–9pm. WRAPS/GLOBAL.

Portland's best bet for a quick, cheap, and filling nosh. Located beneath a parking garage (just off Temple Street), Federal Spice is a breezy, informal spot with limited dining inside and a few tables outside. There's quesadillas, salads, and soft tacos, along with great wraps full of inventive fillings (the curried coconut chicken is our favorite). The yam fries are excellent and nicely accompany just about everything on the menu.

Gilbert's Chowder House. 92 Commercial St. ☎ **207/871-5636.** Reservations not accepted. Chowders $2.50–$9.75, sandwiches $2.25–$9.95, main courses $6.95–$22.95. Mon–Thurs 11am–10pm, Fri–Sat 11am–11pm, Sun 11am–9pm (closed earlier in winter). CHOWDER/SEAFOOD.

Gilbert's is an unprepossessing waterfront spot that's nautical without being too cute. Angle for the outdoor tables overlooking a parking lot and the working waterfront; sometimes it smells pleasantly nautical, sometimes unpleasantly so. The chowders are flavorful if pasty. If you're looking to bulk up, consider getting your chowder in a bread bowl. Other meals include fried clams and haddock sandwiches, and a mess of other seafood available broiled or fried. There's also a basic lobster dinner, which includes corn on the cob and a cup of clam chowder. Limited microbrews are on tap; the homemade cheesecake makes a fitting dessert.

✪ **Silly's.** 40 Washington Ave. ☎ **207/772-0360.** Lunch and dinner $2.25–$6.50; pizza $7.50–$20. MC, V. Mon–Sat 10am–10pm; closed Sun. ECLECTIC/TAKE-OUT.

Silly's is the favored cheap-eats joint among even jaded Portlanders. Situated on an aggressively charmless urban street, the interior is informal, bright and spunky, with an excellent selection of mismatched 1950s-era dinettes and funky-retro accessories. The menu is creative, the selections tasty, and everything made fresh and from scratch. The place is locally noted for its "fast abdullahs," which consist of tasty fillings rolled up in fresh tortillas. (Among the favorites: the shish kebab with feta cheese, and the big and sloppy "Diesel," made with pulled pork barbecue and coleslaw.) The pizza is also excellent, and there's beer on tap. Don't overlook the great mound of hand-cut french fries, or the huge old-fashioned milkshakes and malts.

5 Portland After Dark

BARS & MUSIC

Portland is usually lively in the evenings, especially on summer weekends when the testosterone level in the Old Port seems to rocket into the stratosphere with young men and women prowling the dozens of bars and spilling out onto the streets.

Among the Old Port bars favored by locals are **Three-Dollar Dewey's,** at the corner of Commercial and Union streets (try the great french fries); **Gritty McDuff's Brew Pub,** on Fore Street near the foot of Exchange Street; and **Brian Ború,** on Center St. All three bars are casual and pubby, with guests sharing long tables with new companions.

Beyond the active Old Port bar scene, a number of clubs offer a mix of live and recorded entertainment throughout the year. As is common in other small cities where there's more venues than attendees, the clubs have come and gone, sometimes quite rapidly. Check one of the two free weekly newspapers, *Casco Bay Weekly* or the *Portland Phoenix,* for current venues, performers, and show times.

FILM

Downtown Portland is blessed with three movie houses, allowing travelers in the mood for a flick to avoid the disheartening slog out to the boxy, could-be-anywhere mall octoplexes. The **Keystone Theatre Cafe,** 504 Congress St. (☎ 207/871-5500), offers surprisingly good pub fare and beer while you enjoy second-run films that are often more arty than you'll find at the mall. **Nickelodeon Cinemas,** 1 Temple St. (☎ 207/772-9751), has six screens showing second-run films at discount prices. **The Movies,** 10 Exchange St. (☎ 207/772-9600), is a compact art-film showcase in the heart of the Old Port featuring a line-up of foreign and independent films of recent and historic vintage.

PERFORMING ARTS

Portland has a growing creative corps of performing artists. Theater companies typically take the summer off, but it doesn't hurt to call or check the local papers for special performances.

Center for Cultural Exchange. 1 Longfellow Square (corner of Congress and State Sts.). ☎ **207/761-1545.** www.artsandculture.org. Tickets $8–$27.

The center is devoted to bringing acts from around the globe to Portland. Venues range from area theaters and churches to the center's small but handsome performance space located in a former dry cleaning establishment! Acts range from pan-Caribbean dance music to klezmer bands to Quebecois step-dancing. It's worth stopping by the center (it hosts a tiny cafe) to see what coming up. You just never know.

Portland Stage Company. Portland Performing Arts Center, 25A Forest Ave. ☎ **207/774-0465.** www.portlandstage.com. Tickets $20–$32.

The best-polished and most consistent of the Portland theater companies, Portland Stage offers crisply produced shows staring local and imported equity actors in a handsome, second-story theater just off Congress Street. About a half-dozen shows are staged throughout the season, which runs from October to May. Recent (spring 2000) shows included Graham Greene's "Travels With My Aunt" and Pearl Cleage's "Blues for an Alabama Sky."

Portland Symphony Orchestra. 477 Congress St.. ☎ **207/842-0800** for tickets or 207/773-6128 for more information. www.portlandsymphony.com. Tickets $23–$51.

The well-regarded Portland Symphony, headed by Toshiyuki Shimada, offers a variety of performances throughout the season (typically September to May), ranging from pops concerts to Mozart. Summer travelers should consider a Portland detour on the week of July Fourth, when the "Independence Pops" is held (weather permitting) at various sites around southern Maine, including the grounds of the Portland Head Lighthouse in Cape Elizabeth. The latter is a memorable outdoor picnic concert that features the 1812 Overture and concludes with fireworks.

6 Side Trips

OLD ORCHARD BEACH

About 12 miles south of Portland is the unrepentantly honky-tonkish beach town of Old Orchard Beach, which offers considerable stimulus for most of the senses. This venerable Victorian-era resort is famed for its amusement park, pier, and long, sandy beach, which attracts sun worshippers from all over (especially Canada). Be sure to spend time and money on the stomach-churning rides at the beachside amusement park of **Palace Playland** (☎ 207/934-2001), then walk on the 7-mile-long beach past the mid-rise condos that sprouted in the 1980s like a scale-model Miami Beach.

The beach is broad and open at low tide; at high tide, space to plunk your towel down is at a premium. In the evenings, teens and young adults dominate the town's culture, spilling out of the video arcades and cruising the main strip. For dinner, do as the locals do and buy hot dogs and pizza and cotton candy; save your change for the arcades.

Old Orchard is just off Route 1 south of Portland. The quickest route is to leave the turnpike at Exit 5, then follow I-195 and the signs to the beach. Don't expect to be alone here: Parking is tight, and the traffic can be horrendous during the peak summer months.

SEBAGO LAKE & DOUGLAS HILL

Maine's second-largest lake is also its most popular. Ringed with summer homes of varying vintages, many dating from the early part of this century, Sebago Lake attracts thousands of vacationers to its cool, deep waters.

You can take a tour of the outlying lakes and the ancient canal system between Sebago and Long lakes on the *Songo Queen,* a faux-steamship berthed in the town of Naples (☎ 207/693-6861). Or just lie in the sun along the sandy beach at bustling **Sebago Lake State Park** (☎ 207/693-6613) on the lake's north shore (the park is off Route 302; look for signs between Raymond and South Casco). The park has shady picnic areas, a campground, a snack bar, and lifeguards on the beach (entrance fee charged). It can be uncomfortably crowded on sunny summer weekends; it's best on weekdays. Bring food and charcoal for barbecuing at the shady picnic areas off the beach. The park's campground has a separate beach, is at a distance from the day-use area, and is less congested during good weather. It books up early in the season, but you might luck into a cancellation if you need a spot to pitch your tent.

To the west of the lake, the rolling wooded uplands hold some surprises. For a low-key excursion, head to the **Jones Museum of Glass and Ceramics** (☎ 207/787-3370), a place that captivates even visitors who have little interest in either. Housed in a beautiful old farm building near a compound of summer homes, the museum has hundreds of pieces of old and contemporary glass displayed in highly professional exhibits. The museum is just off Route 107 south of Sebago (the town, not the lake), on the lake's west side, and is conscientious about posting signs directing you there; watch for them. It's open 10am to 5pm Monday to Saturday May to mid-November (1 to 5pm only on Sunday). Admission is $5 for adults, $3 for students, free for children under 12.

A short hop up the hill from the museum is **Douglas Mountain,** whose summit is capped with a medieval-looking 16-foot stone tower. The property is open to the public; the summit is reached via an easy one-quarter mile trail from the parking area. Look for wild blueberries in late summer.

✪ SABBATHDAY LAKE SHAKER COMMUNITY

Route 26 from Portland to Norway is a speedy highway past new housing developments and through hilly farmland. At one point the road pinches through a cluster of stately historic buildings that stand proudly beneath towering shade trees. That's the **Sabbathday Lake Shaker Community** (☎ 207/926-4597), the last active Shaker community in the nation. The half-dozen or so Shakers living here today still embrace their traditional beliefs and maintain a communal, pastoral way of life. The bulk of the community's income comes from the sale of herbs, which have been grown here since 1799.

Tours are offered daily in summer and early fall except on Sundays (when visitors are invited to attend Sunday services). Docents provide tours of the grounds and several buildings, including the graceful 1794 meeting house. Exhibits in the buildings showcase the famed furniture handcrafted by the Shakers, and include antiques made by Shakers at other U.S. communes. You'll learn plenty about the Shaker ideology with its emphasis on simplicity, industry, and celibacy. After your tour, browse the gift shop for Shaker herbs and teas. The introductory tour lasts one hour and 15 minutes ($6 adult, $2 children 6 to 12, free for children under 6). In July and August the community also offers an extended tour, which lasts two hours ($7.50 adult, $2.75 children). It is open daily (except Sunday) 10am to 4:30pm, Memorial Day to Columbus Day. The last tour is at 3:15pm.

The Shaker village is about 45 minutes from Portland. Head north on Route 26 (Washington Avenue in Portland). The village is 8 miles from Exit 11 (Gray) of the Maine Turnpike.

4

Freeport to Port Clyde

*V*eteran Maine travelers contend this part of the coast is fast losing its native charm—it's too commercial, too developed, too much like the rest of the United States. The grousers do have a point, especially regarding Route 1's roadside, but get off the main roads and you'll find pockets where you can catch glimpses of another Maine. Among the sights back road travelers will stumble upon are quiet inland villages, dramatic coastal scenery, and a rich sense of history, especially maritime history.

The best source of information for the region in general is found at the **Maine State Information Center** (☎ 207/ 846-0833) just off Exit 17 of I-95 in Yarmouth. This state-run center is stocked with hundreds of brochures and free newspapers, and is staffed with a helpful crew that can provide information on the entire state, but is particularly well-informed about the mid-coast region.

Just across the road from the information center is the ○ **DeLorme Map Store** (☎ 888/227-1656). Here you'll find a wide selection of maps, including the firm's trademark state atlases and a line of CD-ROM map products. The store's fun to browse even if you're not a map buff, but what makes the place worth a detour off the interstate is Eartha, "the world's largest rotating and revolving globe." The 42-foot diameter globe, which occupies the whole of the atrium lobby, is constructed on a scale of 1:1,000,000, and is the largest satellite image of the earth ever produced.

1 Freeport

If Freeport were a mall (and that's not a far-fetched analogy), L.L. Bean would be the anchor store. It's the business that launched Freeport, elevating its status from just another town off the interstate to one of the two outlet capitals of Maine (the other is Kittery). Freeport still has the form of a classic coastal village, but it's a village that's been largely taken over by the national fashion industry. Most of the old homes and stores have been converted to upscale shops, and now sell name-brand clothing and housewares. Banana Republic occupies an exceedingly handsome brick Federal-style home; even the McDonald's is in a tasteful, understated Victorian farmhouse—you really have to look for the golden arches.

While a number of more modern structures have been built to accommodate the outlet boom, strict planning guidelines have managed to preserve much of the local charm, at least in the village section. Huge parking lots off Main Street are hidden from view, making this one of the more aesthetically pleasing places to shop. But even with these large lots, parking can be scarce during the peak season, especially on rainy summer days when every cottage-bound tourist between York and Camden decides that a trip to Freeport is a winning idea. Bring a lot of patience, and expect teeming crowds if you come at a busy time.

ESSENTIALS
GETTING THERE
Freeport is on Route 1, but is most commonly reached via I-95 from either Exit 19 or 20.

VISITOR INFORMATION
The **Freeport Merchants Association,** P.O. Box 452, Freeport, ME 04032 (☎ **800/865-1994** or 207/865-1212; www.freeportusa.com), publishes a map and directory of businesses, restaurants, and overnight accommodations. The free map is widely available around town, or you can contact the association to have them send you one.

SHOPPING
Freeport has more than 100 retail shops between Exit 19 of I-95 at the far lower end of Main Street and Mallett Road, which connects to Exit 20. Shops have recently begun to spread south of Exit 19 toward Yarmouth. If you don't want to miss a single shopping opportunity, get off at Exit 17 and head north on Route 1. The bargains can vary from extraordinary to "eh?", so plan on racking up some mileage if you're intent on finding outrageous deals. National chains with a presence in Freeport are, among many others, The Gap, Banana Republic, Burberry's, Levi's, Calvin Klein, Patagonia, North Face, Abercrombie & Fitch, J. Crew, Coach, Chaudier

Cookware ("the cookware of choice aboard Air Force One"), Timberland, and Maidenform.

Stores in Freeport are typically open daily 9am to 9pm during the busy summer season.

Cuddledown of Maine. 231 U.S. Rte. 1 (between exits 17 and 19). ☎ **207/ 865-1713.** www.cuddledown.com.

Cuddledown started producing down comforters in 1973, and now makes a whole line of products much appreciated in northern climes and beyond. Down pillows are made right in the outlet shop, which carries a variety of European goose-down comforters in all sizes and weights. Look also for linens and home furnishings. This is the company's only outlet store.

Freeport Knife Co. 148 Main St. ☎ **207/865-0779.**

The largest selection of knives for kitchen and camp is found in this shop. Look for the custom knives, and bring your dull camp blade for sharpening.

J.L. Coombs, Fine Casuals and Footwear. 15 Bow St., and 278 Rte. 1 (between exits 17 and 19). ☎ **800/683-5739** or 207/865-4333.

A Maine shoemaker since 1830, J.L. Coombs today carries a wide assortment of imported and domestic footwear at its two Freeport shops, including Finn Comfort, Dr. Martens, Ecco, and Mephisto. There's also outerwear by Pendleton and Jackaroos.

☉ L.L. Bean. Main and Bow Sts. ☎ **800/341-4341.** www.llbean.com.

Monster outdoor retailer L.L. Bean traces its roots to the day Leon Leonwood Bean decided that what the world really needed was a good weatherproof hunting shoe. He joined a watertight gum shoe with a laced leather upper. Hunters liked it. The store grew. An empire was born.

Today L.L. Bean sells millions of dollars worth of clothing and outdoor goods to customers nationwide through its well-respected catalogs, and it continues to draw hundreds of thousands through its door. This modern, multilevel store is the size of a regional mall, but tastefully done with its own indoor trout pond and lots of natural wood. L.L. Bean is open 365 days a year, 24 hours a day (note the lack of locks or latches on the front doors), and it's a popular spot even in the dead of night, especially in summer and around holidays. Selections include Bean's own trademark clothing, along with home furnishings, books, shoes, and plenty of outdoor gear for camping, fishing, and hunting. A 2-minute walk away is the L.L. Kids store, with goods for the younger set.

In addition to the main store, L.L. Bean stocks an outlet shop with a relatively small but rapidly changing inventory at discount prices. It's in a back lot between Main Street and Depot Street—ask at the front desk of the main store for walking directions. L.L. Bean also has outlets in Portland, Ellsworth, and North Conway, N.H.

Mangy Moose. 112 Main St. ☎ **207/865-6414.**

A cute souvenir shop with a twist: virtually everything in the place is moose-related. There are moose hackey sacks, moose wine glasses, moose trivets, moose cookie cutters, and, of course, moose T-shirts. And much more. The merchandise is a notch above that you'll find in other tourist-oriented shops.

Thos. Moser Cabinetmakers. 149 Main St. ☎ **207/865-4519.**

Classic furniture reinterpreted in lustrous wood and leather is the focus at this shop, which thanks to a steady parade of ads in *The New Yorker* and elsewhere has become almost as much an icon of Maine as L.L. Bean. Shaker, mission, and modern styles have been wonderfully reinvented by the shop's designers and woodworkers—who produce heirloom-quality signed pieces. Nationwide delivery is easily arranged.

EXPLORING FREEPORT

While Freeport is nationally known for its outlet shopping, that's not all it offers. Just outside of town you'll find a lovely pastoral landscape, picturesque country walks, and scenic drives that make for a handy retreat from all that spending.

Head by car east on Bow Street (down the hill from L.L. Bean's main entrance), and wind around for 1 mile to the sign for **Mast Landing Sanctuary** (☎ **207/781-2330**). Turn left, then turn right in .10 miles into the sanctuary parking lot. A network of trails totaling about 3 miles crisscrosses through a landscape of long-ago eroded hills and mixed woodlands; streams trickle down to the marshland estuary. The 140-acre property is owned by the Maine Audubon Society and is open to the public until dusk.

Back at the main road, turn left and continue eastward for 1.4 miles, then turn right on Wolf Neck Road. Continue 1.7 miles, then turn left for one-half mile on a dirt farm road. **Wolfe's Neck Farm,** owned and operated by a non-profit trust, has been experimenting with ways to produce beef without chemicals, and it sells its own line of chemical-free meat. All this happens to take place at one of the most scenic coastal farms in Maine (it's especially beautiful near sunset). Stop at the gray farmhouse and pick up some tasty frozen steaks or flavorful hamburger. Open Monday to Friday 1 to 6pm, Saturday 9am to 3pm (☎ **207/865-4469**).

Continue south on Wolf Neck Road and you'll soon come to 233-acre **Wolfe's Neck Woods State Park** (☎ **207/ 865-4465**). This compact, attractive park has quiet woodland trails that run through forests of white pine and hemlock, past estuaries, and along the rocky shoreline of the bay. Googins Island, just offshore, has an osprey nest on it. This is a good destination for enjoying a picnic brought from town.

WHERE TO STAY

Freeport is blessed with more than 600 guest rooms, ranging from quiet B&Bs with three rooms to chain motels with several dozen. Reservations are strongly recommended during the peak summer season.

Harraseeket Inn. 162 Main St., Freeport, ME 04032. ☎ **800/342-6423** or 207/865-9377. www.harraseeketinn.com. E-mail: harraseeke@aol.com. 84 units. A/C TV TEL. Summer and fall $180–$265 double; spring and early summer $140–$235; winter $110–$215. All rates include breakfast buffet. AE, DC, DISC, MC, V. Take Exit 20 off I-95 to Main St.

The Harraseeket Inn is a large, thoroughly modern hotel two blocks north of L.L. Bean. It's to the inn's credit that, despite its size, a traveler could drive down Main Street and not immediately notice it. A late-19th century home is the soul of the hotel, but most of the rooms are in later additions built in 1989 and 1997. Guests can relax in the well-regarded dining room, read the paper in the common room with the baby grand player piano, or sip a cocktail in the homey Broad Arrow Tavern with its wood-fired oven and grill. The guest rooms are on the large side and tastefully done, with quarter-canopy beds and a nice mix of contemporary and antique furniture. All have hair dryers and coffee makers; about a quarter have gas or wood-burning fireplaces, and more than half feature single or double whirlpools.

Dining: There are two restaurants on the premises. The Maine Dining Room offers New American dining with an emphasis on local ingredients; entree prices are $21 to $28.

The Broad Arrow Tavern has a more informal setting with a less ambitious menu, which includes an array of burgers, steaks, pizzas, and pastas; entrees range from $7.50 to $21.95.

Amenities: Concierge, room service (7am to 10pm), afternoon tea, dry cleaning, laundry service, safe deposit boxes, indoor heated lap pool, business center, conference rooms.

Isaac Randall House. 5 Independence Dr., Freeport, ME 04032. ☎ **800/ 865-9295** or 207/865-9295. Fax 207/865-9003. www.isaacrandall.com. 12 units (1 private hall bathroom). A/C TEL. Summer and holidays $100–$175 double; off-season weekends $75–$145; off-season midweek $65–$100. 2-night minimum on holiday and midsummer weekends. AE, DISC, MC, V. Located ½ mile south of the L.L. Bean store on Rte. 1. Pets accepted.

Freeport's first bed-and-breakfast, the Isaac Randall House is located in an 1823 farmhouse that's been refurbished with a dozen handsome guest rooms, all with private bathroom, about half with televisions. The most charming of the bunch is the "Pine" room, built in an adjoining shed with rustic barnboards and decorated in a Southwestern motif. (It also features a unique antique copper tub.) The least charming are the two smaller, modern rooms in an addition in back, and a dark "Loft" room upstairs. Breakfast is served in a homey country kitchen. The inn is well situated for exploring Freeport; its main disadvantage is its location sandwiched between busy Route 1 and I-95. The sound of traffic is never far away.

Kendall Tavern. 213 Main St., Freeport, ME 04032. ☎ **800/341-9572** or 207/865-1338. 7 units. Peak season $100–$125 double; off-season $75–$95. Rates include full breakfast. AE, DISC, MC, V.

If you want to be out of the bustle of town but not too far from the shopping, this is a good choice. This handsome B&B is in a cheerful yellow farmhouse on 3.5 acres at a bend in the road a half-mile north of the center of Freeport. The rooms are all plushly carpeted and appointed with comfort in mind. Everything is decorated in a bright and airy style, with framed posters on the walls and a mix of antique and new furniture. The rooms facing Route 1 (Main Street) may be a bit noisier than the others, but the traffic is still not likely to be too disruptive. There's a piano in one of the two downstairs parlors, and a sizable hot-tub in a spacious private room in the back (no extra charge). An all-you-can-eat breakfast is served in the pine-floored dining room.

Maine Idyll Motor Court. 1411 U.S. Route 1, Freeport, ME 04032. ☎ **207/865-4201.** www.freeportusa.com/maineidyll. 20 cottages. TV. $48–$72 double; $68–$90 2- and 3-bedroom cottages. Includes continental breakfast. No credit cards (checks OK). Closed early Nov–late Apr. Pets allowed.

The 1932 Maine Idyll Motor Court is a Maine classic—a cluster of 20 cottages scattered about a grove of beech and oak trees. Each has a tiny porch, wood-burning fireplace (birch logs provided), TV, modest kitchen facilities (no ovens), and time-worn furniture. The cabins are not lavishly sized but are comfortable and spotlessly clean. If you need a phone, you're out of luck—the cabins lack them, and there's no pay phone on the premises (the owners are good about letting guests use the office phone if they're in a pinch). The only interruption to an idyll here is the omnipresent sound of traffic: I-95 is just through the trees on one side, Route 1 on the other side. Get past the drone, and you'll find very good value for your money here.

Nicholson Inn. 25 Main St., Freeport, ME 04032. ☎ **800/344-6404** or 207/865-6404. 3 units (showers only). A/C. Double peak season $100 ; off-season $75. Rates include full breakfast. No credit cards.

If your goal in Freeport is to visit as many outlets as humanly possible, then as far as proximity to the shopping there's no better place. Located right on Main Street just a minute's walk from the heart of the shopping district, this comfortable home built in the mid-1920s has just three guest rooms, all with private bathrooms. The common rooms and guest rooms have a pleasant floral motif. Furnishings are country contemporary and oak Victorian; a huge three-course breakfast is served daily. A front porch with wicker furniture is a good spot to rest up between forays, and there's plenty of parking for guests, who are allowed to leave their cars in the inn lot even after they check out.

WHERE TO DINE

Despite all the outlet glitz of Freeport, a couple of small-town restaurants have persisted. For a quick and simple meal, you might head down Mechanic Street (near the Mangy Moose at 112 Main St.) to the **Corsican Restaurant,** 9 Mechanic St. (☎ **207/865-9421**), for a 10-inch pizza, calzone, or king-sized sandwich. A favored spot for a quick, reasonably priced lunch close to L.L. Bean is the **Falcon Restaurant,** 8 Bow St.

(☎ **207/865-4031**). Also nearby is the **Chowder Express &
Sandwich Shop,** 2 Mechanic St. (☎ **207/865-3404**), a hole-
in-the-wall with counter seating for about a dozen. They serve
fish, lobster, and clam chowder in paper bowls with plastic
spoons. It's not a destination restaurant, but good for a quick
bite between shops.

For fine dining, see also the Harraseeket Inn, above.

Gritty McDuff's. Lower Main St., Freeport. ☎ **207/865-4321.** Reservations
not accepted. Main courses $6.50–$13.95. AE, DISC, MC, V. Daily 11:30am–
11pm. BREW PUB.

Spacious, informal, and air-conditioned in summer, Gritty's is
an offshoot of Portland's first and most successful brew pub.
It's located a short drive south of the village center and is best
known for its fine and varied selection of craft beers. The pub
offers a wide ranging bar menu for both lunch and dinner,
with few standout offerings but decent, consistent fare. The
burgers and stone-oven pizzas are reliable; pub classics
like shepherd's pie and barley-coated fish also tend to be popular. During the busy summer season the kitchen and wait-
staff can get a bit overwhelmed; bring your patience and a
newspaper.

Harraseeket Lunch & Lobster. Main St., South Freeport. ☎ **207/
865-4888.** Lobsters market price (typically $8–$12). No credit cards. Open
daily 11:30am–8:30pm. Closed mid-Oct–May 1. Directions: From I-95 take Exit
17 and head north on Route 1; turn right on S. Freeport Rd. at the huge Indian
statue; continue to stop sign in South Freeport; turn right to waterfront. From
Freeport take South St. (off Bow St.) to Main St. in South Freeport; turn left to
waterfront. LOBSTER POUND.

Located at a boatyard on the Harraseeket River about 10 minutes drive from Freeport's main shopping district, this lobster
pound is an especially popular destination on sunny days—
although with its heated dining room, it's a worthy destination
any time. Order a crustacean according to how hungry you are
(from 1 pound on up), then take in the river view from the
dock while waiting for your number to be called. Be prepared
for big crowds; a good alternative is to come in late afternoon
between the crushing lunch and dinner hordes.

Jameson Tavern. 115 Main St. ☎ **207/865-4196.** Reservations encouraged.
Main courses, tap room $6.95–$16.95; dining room lunch $5.25–$10.95,
dinner $11.95–$22.95. AE, DC, DISC, MC, V. Tap room daily 11am–11pm;
dining room daily in summer 11am–10pm, winter 11:30am–9pm. AMERICAN.

Located in a handsome, historic farmhouse literally in the shadow of L.L. Bean (it's just north of the store), the Jameson Tavern touts itself as the birthplace of Maine. In 1820 the papers were signed here legally separating Maine from Massachusetts. Today, it's a dual restaurant under the same ownership. As you enter the door you can head left to the historic Tap Room, a compact, often crowded spot filled with the smell of fresh-popped popcorn. (Ask to sit outside on the brick patio if the weather's good.) Meals here include fare like crab-cake burgers, lobster croissants, and a variety of build-your-own burgers. The other part of the house is the Dining Room, which is rather more formal in a country-colonial sort of way. Meals here are more sedate and gussied up, with an emphasis on steak and hearty fare. Entrees include filet mignon oscar (with asparagus, crabmeat, and hollandaise), seafood fettuccini, and pan-blackened haddock. (Look also for heart-healthy selections.) While not overly creative, the meals in both the dining room and tap room will hit the spot.

2 Brunswick & Bath

Brunswick and Bath are two handsome, historic towns that share a strong commercial past. Many travelers heading up Route 1 pass through both towns eager to reach areas with higher billing on the marquee. That's a shame, for both are well worth the detour to sample the sort of slower pace that's being lost elsewhere.

Brunswick was once home to several mills along the Androscoggin River; these have since been converted to offices and the like, but Brunswick's broad Maine Street still bustles with activity. (Idiosyncratic traffic patterns can lead to snarls of traffic in the late afternoon.) Brunswick is also home to Bowdoin College, one of the nation's most respected small colleges. The school was founded in 1794, offered its first classes 8 years later, and has since amassed an illustrious roster of prominent alumni, including Nathaniel Hawthorne, Henry Wadsworth Longfellow, President Franklin Pierce, and Arctic explorer Robert E. Peary. Civil War hero Joshua Chamberlain served as president of the college after the war.

Eight miles to the east, Bath is pleasantly situated on the broad Kennebec River, and is a noted center of shipbuilding. The first U.S.-built ship was constructed downstream at the

Popham Bay colony in the early 17th century; in the years since, shipbuilders have constructed more than 5,000 ships hereabouts. Bath shipbuilding reached its heyday in the late 19th century, but the business of shipbuilding continues to this day. Bath Iron Works is one of the nation's preeminent boatyards, constructing and repairing ships for the U.S. Navy. The scaled-down military has left Bath shipbuilders in a somewhat tenuous state, but it's still common to see the steely gray ships in the dry dock (the best view is from the bridge over the Kennebec), and the towering red-and-white crane (topped by a lighted Christmas tree in December) moving supplies and parts around the yard.

ESSENTIALS
GETTING THERE

Brunswick and Bath are both on Route 1. Brunswick is accessible via Exits 22 and 23 off I-95. If you're bypassing Brunswick and heading north up Route 1 to Bath or beyond, continue up I-95 and exit at the "coastal connector" exit in Topsham, which avoids some of the slower traffic going through Brunswick.

For bus service from Portland or Boston, contact **Vermont Transit** (☎ **800/451-3292**) or **Concord Trailways** (☎ **800/ 639-3317**).

VISITOR INFORMATION

The **Bath-Brunswick Region Chamber of Commerce,** 59 Pleasant Street, Brunswick, ME 04011 (☎ **207/725-8797** or 207/443-9751), offers information and lodging assistance Monday to Friday 8:30am to 5pm from its offices near downtown Brunswick. The chamber also staffs an information center 10am to 7pm daily in summer on Route 1 between Brunswick and Bath.

FESTIVALS

In early August look for posters for the ever-popular ✪ **Maine Festival** (☎ **207/772-9012**), which takes place at Thomas Point Beach between Brunswick and Bath. What started as a sort of counterculture celebration of Maine people and crafts has evolved and grown to a hugely popular mainstream event. Performers from throughout Maine gather at this pretty coveside park (it's a private campground the rest of the summer), and put on shows from noon past dark throughout the first weekend in August. Displays of crafts, artwork, and the products of small Maine businesses are also on display. An admission fee is charged.

WHAT TO SEE AND DO

Collectibles buffs and aficionados of antiques malls should schedule in an hour or so at **Cabot Mill Antiques,** 14 Maine St., Brunswick (☎ 207/725-2855; www.cabotiques.com), located on the ground floor of a restored textile mill in downtown Brunswick.

IN BRUNSWICK

Bowdoin Museum of Art. Walker Art Building, Bowdoin College. ☎ 207/725-3275. Free admission. Tues–Sat 10am–5pm, Sun 2–5pm.

This stern, neo-classical building on the Bowdoin campus was designed by the prominent architectural firm of McKim, Mead, and White. While the collections are small, they include a number of exceptionally fine paintings from Europe and America, along with early furniture and artifacts from classical antiquity. The artists include Andrew and N.C. Wyeth, Marsden Hartley, Winslow Homer, and John Singer Sargent. The older upstairs galleries have soft, diffused lighting from skylights high above; it feels a bit as if you're underwater. The basement galleries, which feature rotating exhibits, are modern and spacious. *Note:* Construction and expansion may close or disrupt visits to the gallery over the next two years.

Peary-MacMillan Arctic Museum. Hubbard Hall, Bowdoin College. ☎ 207/725-3416. Free admission. Tues–Sat 10am–5pm, Sun 2–5pm.

While Admiral Robert E. Peary (class of 1887) is better known for his accomplishments (he "discovered" the North Pole at age 53 in 1909), Donald MacMillan (class of 1898) also racked up an impressive string of achievements in Arctic research and exploration. You can learn about both men and the wherefores of Arctic exploration in this altogether manageable museum on the Bowdoin campus. The front room features mounted animals from the Arctic, including some impressive polar bears. A second room outlines Peary's historic 1909 expedition, complete with excerpts from Peary's journal. The last room includes varied displays of Inuit arts and crafts, some historic, some modern. You can visit this compact museum in about 20 minutes or so; the art museum (see above) is just next door.

IN BATH

Maine Maritime Museum & Shipyard. 243 Washington St. ☎ **207/ 443-1316.** www.bathmaine.com. Admission $8.75 adult, $6 child 6–17, $26 family. Open daily 9:30am–5pm.

On the shores of the Kennebec River, this museum (just south of the very obvious Bath Iron Works shipyard) features a wide array of displays and exhibits related to the boat-builder's art. The museum is housed at the former shipyard of Percy and Small, which built some 42 schooners in the late 19th and early 20th century. The centerpiece of the museum is the handsomely modern Maritime History Building. There's also a gift shop with a nice selection of books about ships. The 10-acre property houses a fleet of additional displays, including an intriguing exhibit on lobstering and a complete boat building shop. Kids enjoy the play area (they can search for pirates from the crow's nest of the play boat). Be sure to wander down to the docks on the river to see what's tied up, or to inquire about the occasional river cruises ($30 per person), which include lighthouse tours, and adventures up the Kennebec River to Merrymeeting Bay.

WHERE TO STAY

Brunswick Bed & Breakfast. 165 Park Row, Brunswick, ME 04011. ☎ **800/299-4914** or 207/729-4914. www.brunswickbnb.com. E-mail: info@ brunswickbnb.com. 8 units. A/C TEL. $90–$130 double, including full breakfast. MC, V. Closed January. Children 6 and over accepted.

This handsome B&B is located in downtown Brunswick facing the green, and is within walking distance to Bowdoin College, area theaters, and restaurants along Maine Street. The rooms in this Federal-style home with wraparound porch are quite spacious and are furnished serviceably in a sort of country-modern style, some with wingback or wicker chairs, and all with attractive quilts; ask for one of the brighter, cheerier corner rooms. There's a TV downstairs in the common room; in-room telephones allow only outgoing calls.

Grey Havens. Seguinland Rd., Georgetown Island, ME 04548. ☎ **207/ 371-2616.** Fax 207/371-2274. www.greyhavens.com. E-mail: greyhavens@ clinic.net. 13 units (2 with private hall bathrooms). $100–$220 double including full breakfast. Closed Nov–May. Directions: From Rte. 1 head south on Rte. 127 then follow signs for Reid State Park; watch for inn on left. MC, V. No children under 12.

This is the inn first-time visitors to Maine fantasize about when planning their vacation. Located on Georgetown Island off the beaten track southeast of Bath, this graceful, 1904 shingled home with prominent turrets sits on a high, rocky bluff overlooking the sea. Inside and out, it feels like the setting of a novel involving several generations. In the spacious common room you can relax in cozy chairs in front of the cobblestone fireplace while listening to classical music. The guest rooms are simple but comfortably furnished. The ocean-front rooms command a premium, but are worth it. (If you're looking to save a few dollars, ask for an oceanfront room where the bathroom is located just across the hall from the room.) Guests can use the inn's canoe or bikes to explore the outlying area. One caveat: The inn itself has been only lightly modernized, which is good but means rather thin walls. If you have loud neighbors, you'll learn more about their lives than you may care to know.

Sebasco Harbor Resort. Rte. 217, Sebasco Estates, ME 04565. ☎ **800/ 225-3819** or 207/389-1161. Fax 207/389-2004. www.sebasco.com. E-mail: info@sebasco.com. 115 units. TEL. July–Labor Day $169–$249 double; May–June $129–$209; Sept–Oct $149–$229. Service charge additional; ask about modified American plan rates. AE, DISC, MC, V. 2-night minimum on weekends. Closed late Oct–early May. Directions: South from Bath 11 miles on Rte. 209; look for Rte. 217 and signs for Sebasco.

Sebasco is a grand old seaside resort that's fighting a generally successful battle against time and irrelevance. It's a self-contained resort of the sort that flourished 50 years ago, and today is being rediscovered by families. Some guests have been coming here for 60 years and love the timelessness of it; newcomers are starting to visit now that much of it has benefited from a facelift.

The 664-acre grounds remain the real attraction here—guests enjoy sweeping ocean views, a lovely seaside pool, and great walks around well-cared-for property. The guest rooms, it should be noted, are adequate rather than elegant, and may seem a bit short of the mark given the high prices charged. Most lack a certain style—especially the 40 rooms in the old inn, which are dated, and I don't mean that in a good way. (The small wooden decks on many rooms are a plus, though.) Better are the quirky rooms in the octagonal Lighthouse Building—rooms #12 and #20 have among the best views in the state. Most (not all) rooms have TVs; ask first if it's important to you. If you're coming for more than two days, it's probably best to book one of the cottages, which come in all sorts and sizes.

Dining/Diversions: The Pilot House Dining Room is airy, contemporary, and the best place to enjoy the sunsets. You'll find white linens and a jackets-recommended-on-men policy; the menu is contemporary resort style, with dishes like grilled swordfish with a pesto butter, and prime rib with a Parmesan Yorkshire pudding. Another restaurant, Ledges, is a more informal spot downstairs that serves a lighter menu.

Amenities: Swimming in outdoor saltwater pool and ocean, 9-hole golf course, tennis courts, hot tub, sauna, health club, bay cruises, canoe and kayak rentals, shuffleboard, snack bar, children's center and programs, video games, candlepin bowling, movies, nature trails, sailing lessons, bike rentals. Popham Beach is five miles away.

WHERE TO DINE

Both downtown Brunswick and downtown Bath offer plenty of casual places to dine, ranging from burgers to barbecue and better. For informal fare, it's hard to go wrong at these cafes and restaurants. The two places I've listed below are 20 minutes or so southeast of Bath, but are featured because they're both so distinctive they're well worth the detour.

Five Islands Lobster Co. Route 127, Georgetown. ☎ **207/371-2990.** Typically $6–$9 per lobster; 75¢ for corn on the cob. MC, V. Daily 11am–8pm in July and Aug; shorter hours during the off-season. Closed Columbus Day–Mother's Day. LOBSTER POUND.

The drive alone makes this lobster pound a worthy destination. It's located about 12 miles south of Route 1 down winding Route 127, past bogs and spruce forests with glimpses of azure ocean inlets. (Head south from Woolwich, which is just across the bridge from Bath.) Drive until you pass a cluster of clapboard homes, then keep going until you can't go any farther.

Wander out to the wharf with its unbeatable island views, and place your order. This is a down-home affair, owned jointly by local lobstermen and the proprietors of Grey Havens, a local inn (see above). While you're awaiting your lobster, you can wander next door to the Love Nest Snack Bar for extras like soda or the sinful onion rings. Gather up your grub and settle in at one of the wharf picnic tables, or head over to the grassy spots at the edge of the dirt parking lot. And bring some patience: despite its edge-of-the-world feel, the lobster pound draws steady traffic and it can be crowded on weekends.

✪ **Robinhood Free Meetinghouse.** Robinhood Rd., Robinhood. ☎ **207/ 371-2188.** www.robinhood-meetinghouse.com. Reservations encouraged. Main courses $18–$25. AE, DISC, MC, V. Open daily May–Oct 5:30–9pm. Limited days late fall–spring; call first. FUSION.

Chef Michael Gagne seems to follow architect Daniel Burnham's dictum: "Make no little plans." His menu features between 30 and 40 entrees, and they're wildly eclectic—from saltimboca to Szechuan swordfish to Wiener schnitzel Viennese. Ordering from the menu is like playing stump the chef: Let's see you make *this!* And you know what? Gagne almost always hits his notes and rarely serves a mediocre meal. You just can't go wrong here. The Meetinghouse has attracted legions of dedicated local followers, who appreciate the extraordinary attention paid to detail, like the foam baffles glued discreetly to the underside of the seats to dampen the echoes in the sparsely decorated, immaculately restored 1855 Greek Revival Meetinghouse. Even the sorbet served between courses is homemade. While no means a budget restaurant, the Meetinghouse offers good value for the price.

3 Harpswell Peninsula

Extending southwest from Brunswick and Bath is the picturesque Harpswell region. It's actually three peninsulas, like the tines of a pitchfork, if you include the islands of Orrs and Bailey, which are linked to the mainland by bridges. While close to some of Maine's larger towns (Portland is only 45 minutes away), the Harpswell Peninsula has a remote, historic feel with sudden vistas across meadows to the blue waters of northern Casco Bay. No hiking trails, no garish attractions— just winding roads good for country drives. (Narrow shoulders and fast cars make for poor biking, however.)

The region is an amalgam—old houses with picturesque peeling paint next to manufactured homes, summer houses next to the homes of Brunswick commuters. Toward the southern tips of the peninsulas, the character changes as clusters of colorful Victorian-era summer cottages displace the farmhouses found farther inland. Some of these cottages rent by the week, but savvy families book up many of them years in advance. Ask local real estate agents if you're interested.

There's no set itinerary for exploring the area. Just drive south from Brunswick on Route 24 or 123 until you can't go any farther, then backtrack for a bit and strike south again. Among the "attractions" worth looking for are the wonderful ocean and island views from **South Harpswell** at the tip of the westernmost peninsula (park and wander around for a bit), and the clever **Cobwork Bridge** connecting Bailey and Orrs islands. The hump-backed bridge was built in 1928 of granite blocks stacked in such a way that the strong tides could come and go and not drag the bridge out with it. No cement was used in its construction.

WHERE TO STAY

Driftwood Inn & Cottages. Washington Ave., Bailey Island, ME 04003. ☎ **207/833-5461,** off-season 508/947-1066. 17 double units, 7 single units, 6 cottages (most units share hallway bathrooms). $70–$110 double; weekly $375 per person including breakfast and dinner (July and Aug only); cottages $550–$600 per week. Open late May–mid-Oct; dining room open late June–Labor Day. No credit cards.

The oceanside Driftwood Inn dates back to 1910. This family-run rustic summer retreat on three acres at the end of a dead-end road, is a compound of four weathered, shingled buildings and a handful of housekeeping cottages on a rocky, oceanside property. The rooms of time-aged pine have a simple turn-of the last-century flavor that hasn't been gentrified in the least. Most rooms share bathrooms down the hall, but some have private sinks and toilets. (The inn has seven rooms for solo travelers, which are a rare find these days; single prices start at $55.) Cottages are set along a small and private cove, and they are furnished in a budget modern style. It's nothing fancy: expect industrial carpeting and plastic shower stalls. Some beds could stand replacing, yet where else can you sleep at the water's edge for under $100 per night? The inn has an old saltwater pool and porches with wicker furniture to while away the afternoons; bring plenty of books and board games.

Dining: The dining room serves basic fare (roasts, fish, etc.) in a wonderfully austere setting overlooking the sea; meals are extra, although a weekly American plan is available. Dining is open to outside guests if you make reservations by 4:30pm.

WHERE TO DINE

If a steamed lobster is on your mind, several sprawling establishments specialize in delivering crustaceans fresh from the sea. On the Bailey Island side there's **Cook's Lobster House**

(☎ **207/833-2818**), which has been serving up a choice of shore dinners since 1955. The restaurant has two decks for outdoor dining. Near Harpswell is the **Estes Lobster House** (☎ **207/833-6340**), which serves lobster (including an artery-clogging triple lobster plate) amid relaxed, festive surroundings.

✪ **Dolphin Marina.** Basin Point, South Harpswell. ☎ **207/833-6000.** Breakfast items $1.25–$3; sandwiches $3.50–$7.95; complete dinners $13.95–$16.95. Open for breakfast Fri–Sun only 8am–10:30am; daily 11am–8pm. MC, V. Closed early Nov–Apr. Directions: Drive 12.2 miles south of Brunswick on Route 123, turn right at Ash Point Rd. near the West Harpswell School, then take the next right on Basin Point Rd. and continue to the end. TRADITIONAL NEW ENGLAND.

One of the premier places for chowder in the state is the down-home Dolphin Marina at Basin Point. At road's end you'll find yourself at a boatyard; wander inside the shingled building with small-paned windows, where you'll discover a tiny counter, simple wooden tables, and great views of lobster boats bobbing on Casco Bay. If it's crowded, you can get a meal to go…except the chowder. It's against Dolphin tradition that you walk out with chowder; you have to sit down and enjoy it here. It's worth the wait—the chowders and lobster stew are exceptionally creamy and flavorful, and are served with the blueberry muffins that are often warm and capped with a crispy crown. The servers can be flummoxed at busy times, so bring some patience.

4 Wiscasset & the Boothbays

Wiscasset is a lovely riverside town and it's not shy about letting you know: "The Prettiest Village in Maine," is the boast on the sign at the edge of town and on many brochures. Whether or not you agree with this self-assessment, the town is attractive (although the sluggish and persistent line of traffic snaking through on Route 1 diminishes the charm), and makes a good stop for stretching legs, taking in an attraction or two, or grabbing a bite to eat en route to coastal destinations further along. Take the time to walk through the elegant neighborhoods both north and south of Route 1, which have kept much of their historic integrity in tact.

The Boothbays, 11 miles south of Route 1 on Route 27, consist of several small and scenic villages—East Boothbay, Boothbay Harbor, and Boothbay, among them—which are closer than Wiscasset to the open ocean. The former fishing port of Boothbay Harbor was discovered in the last century by wealthy rusticators who built imposing seaside homes and retreated here in summer to avoid the swelter of the cities along the Eastern Seaboard.

Having embraced the tourist dollar, the harborfront village never really looked back, and in more recent years it has emerged as one of the premier destinations of travelers in search of classic coastal Maine. This embrace has had an obvious impact. The village is often regarded as a mandatory stop on bus tours, which has in turn attracted kitschy shops and a slew of mediocre restaurants that seem to specialize in baked stuffed haddock.

If Boothbay Harbor is stuck in a time warp, it's Tourist Trap circa 1974—bland and boxy motels hem in the harbor, and side-by-side boutiques hawk the same mass-market trinkets (Beanie Babies, T-shirts emblazoned with puffins). Despite it all, there's still an affable charm that manages to rise above the clutter and cheese, especially on foggy days when the horns bleat mournfully at the harbor's mouth. If you avoid the tourist clutter of the downtown harbor area itself, some of the outlying areas are uncommonly beautiful.

ESSENTIALS
GETTING THERE

Wiscasset is on Route 1 midway between Bath and Damariscotta. Boothbay Harbor is south of Route 1 on Route 27. Coming from the west, look for signs shortly after crossing the Sheepscot River at Wiscasset.

VISITOR INFORMATION

Wiscasset lacks a tourist information booth, but a phone call to the **Wiscasset Regional Business Association** (☎ **207/882-9617**) should answer any questions you may have.

As befits a place where tourism is a major industry, the Boothbay region has three visitor information centers in and around town, reflecting the importance of the travel dollars to the region. At the intersection of Route 1 and Route 27 is a center that's open May to October and is a good place to stock up on brochures. A mile before you reach the village is the seasonal **Boothbay Information Center** on your right (open June to October). If you zoom past it or it's closed, don't fret. The year-round **Boothbay Harbor Region Chamber of**

Commerce, P.O. Box 356, Boothbay Harbor, ME 04538 (☎ 207/633-2353), is at the intersection of routes 27 and 96.

WHAT TO SEE & DO
IN WISCASSET

Aside from enjoying the town's handsome architecture and vaunted prettiness, there are several quirky, low-key attractions that will nicely break up a trip along the coast. You'll also find a handful of worthwhile antiques shops. Next to Red's Eats is the Wiscasset Hardware Co., a sublimely old-fashioned hardware store that has retained its roots while also stocking wares of interest to souvenir hunters.

Castle Tucker. Lee and High Sts. ☎ 207/882-7364. $4 adults, $2 children. Tours leave on the hour noon–4pm Wed–Sun; open July–Aug only.

This fascinating mansion at the edge of town overlooking the river was first built in 1807, then radically added to and altered in a more ostentatious style in 1860. The home remains more or less in the same state it was in when reconfigured by cotton trader Capt. Richard Tucker; his descendent Jane Tucker still lives on the top floor. Tours of the lower floor are offered by the Society of New England Antiquities, which was given the house by Ms. Tucker in 1997. The detailing is exceptional and offers insight into the life of an affluent sea captain in the late 19th century. Be sure to note the extraordinary elliptical staircase and the painted plaster trim (it's not oak).

Maine Coast Railroad. Rte. 1 (just before the bridge). ☎ 800/795-5404 or 207/882-8000. $10 adults, $5 children 6–12, free for children under 5. Daily late June–mid-Sept 10am and 1pm; weekends only mid-Sept–mid-Oct 10am and 1pm.

Weary of Route 1 traffic? Hop on the Maine Coast Railroad and let somebody else do the driving while you put your feet up and enjoy the scenery. The 90-minute excursions are offered to either Bath or Newcastle, and both routes follow along forest and field, offering fleeting glimpses of the Maine of an earlier era. The railcars date from the 1930s.

✪ Musical Wonder House. 18 High St. ☎ 207/882-7163. $15 for full downstairs tour; $8 for half downstairs; $30 full house tour. Late May–mid-Oct daily 10am–5pm. Closed late Oct–late May.

Talk about your obsession! Danilo Konvalinka has been collecting music boxes both grand and tiny for decades, and nothing seems to delight him more than to play them for awestruck visitors. The collection includes massive and ancient music boxes that sound as resounding as an orchestra (an 1870 Girard music box from Austria), to the tinnier, more ethereal sounds of the smaller contraptions. Music boxes are displayed (and played) in four rooms in a stately 1852 home; admission is charged by the room. It is quite pricey; if you're undecided whether it's worth the fee, try this: Visit the free gift shop and sample some of the coin-operated 19th-century music boxes in the adjoining hallway. Intrigued? Sign up for the next tour.

IN THE BOOTHBAYS

Coastal Maine Botanical Garden. Barters Island Rd., Boothbay (near Hogdon Island). ☎ **207/633-4333.** Open daylight hours. Free admission. Directions: From Route 27 in Boothbay Center bear right at the monument at the stop sign, then make the first right on Barters Island Rd.; drive one mile; look for the stone gate on your left.

This 128-acre waterside garden is relatively new and a work in progress, but already worth exploring. It's not a fancy, formal garden like you'll find elsewhere in Maine, but rather a natural habitat that's being gently coaxed into a more mannered state. Those overseeing this nonprofit organization have blazed several short trails through the mossy forest, good for a half-hour's worth of exploring, cutting through terrain that's delightfully quiet and lush. One trail follows along much of the 3,600 feet of tidal shoreline that's part of the property. Plans call for ornamental gardens featuring Maine's indigenous plants to be completed by 2005.

Marine Resources Aquarium. McKown Point Rd., West Boothbay Harbor. ☎ **207/633-9542.** $3 adult, $2.50 children 5–18. Daily 10am–5pm. Closed after Columbus Day to just before Memorial Day.

Operated by the state's Department of Marine Resources, this compact aquarium offers context for life in the sea around Boothbay and beyond. You can view rare albino and blue lobsters, and get your hands wet at a 20-foot touch tank—a sort of petting zoo of the slippery and slimy. Parking is tight at the aquarium, which is located on a point across the water from Boothbay Harbor, so visitors are urged to use the free shuttle bus (look for the Rocktide trolley) that connects downtown with the aquarium and runs frequently throughout the summer.

BOAT TOURS

The best way to see the timeless Maine coast around Boothbay is on a boat tour. Nearly two dozen tour boats berth at the harbor or nearby, offering trips ranging from an hour's outing to a full-day excursion to Monhegan Island. You can even observe puffins at their rocky colonies far offshore.

Balmy Day Cruises (☎ **800/298-2284** or 207/633-2284) runs several trips from the harbor, including an all-day excursion to Monhegan Island on the 65-foot *Balmy Days II* (this allows passengers about four hours to explore the island before returning—see "Monhegan Island" section below). The Monhegan trip is $30 (children $18). The company also offers one-harbor tours for $9 (children $4.50). If you'd rather be sailing, ask about the 90-minute cruises on the *Bay Lady,* a 15-passenger Friendship sloop ($18). It's a good idea to call ahead for reservations.

The most personal way to see the harbor is via sea kayak. **Tidal Transit Kayak Co.** (☎ **207/633-7140**) offers morning, afternoon, and sunset tours of the harbor for $30 (sunset's the best bet). Kayaks may also be rented for $12 an hour, or $50 per day. Tidal Transit is open daily in summer (except when it rains) on the waterfront at 47 Townshend Ave. (walk down the alley).

WHERE TO STAY

One of the coast's most memorable private campgrounds is located between Bath and Wiscasset. **Chewonki Campgrounds,** off Route 144 (☎ **207/882-7426**), occupies 50 acres overlooking a salt marsh and the confluence of lazy tidal streams. The sites are sizeable and private; there's a nicely maintained pool with a sweeping view; kayaks and canoes are available for rent. Campsites start at $23 per night, which is at the high end of the price scale but decidedly worth it. Directions: Drive 7 miles east of Bath on Route 1; turn right on Route 144, then take the next right past the airport and follow signs for campground.

Five Gables Inn. Murray Hill Rd. (P.O. Box 335), East Boothbay, ME 04544. ☎ **800/451-5048** or 207/633-4551. www.fivegablesinn.com. E-mail: info@fivegablesinn.com. 16 units. TEL. $110–$175 double. Rates include breakfast buffet. MC, V. Closed Nov–mid-May. Drive through East Boothbay on Route 96; turn right after crest of hill on Murray Hill Rd. Children 12 and older are welcome.

The handsome Five Gables Inn was painstakingly restored in the late 1980s, and now sits proudly amid a small colony of summer homes on a quiet road above a peaceful cove. It's nicely isolated from the confusion and hubbub of Boothbay Harbor; the activity of choice here is to sit on the deck and enjoy the glimpses of the water through the trees. The rooms are pleasantly appointed, and five have fireplaces that burn manufactured logs. Room 8 is a corner room with brilliant morning light; Room 14 is the most requested, with a great view and a fireplace with a marble mantle. (Some of the first floor rooms open onto a common deck and lack privacy.) The breakfast buffet is sumptuous, with offerings like tomato-basil frittata, cornbread with bacon and green onions, and blueberry-stuffed French toast.

The Inn at Lobsterman's Wharf. Route 96, East Boothbay. ☎ **207/ 633-5481.** www.lobstermanswharf.com. 9 units. TV. $56–$85 double, including continental breakfast. MC, V. Pets allowed in 2 rooms.

This is our budget pick for the region. A clean, comfortable no-frills place located adjacent to a working boatyard, this nine-room inn was originally a coal depot and later a boarding house. It still has some of the boarding house informality to it (although all rooms now have small private bathrooms), but you get a lot for your money. Seven rooms face the water, and the innkeeper invited local people to decorate each of the rooms to reflect local history, giving them a unique, home-spun flair. "Hodgon Suites" is the largest, located under the eaves with a view of the Hodgon Yacht boatyard. The Lobsterman's Wharf restaurant (see below) is just next door.

Lawnmeer Inn & Restaurant. Rte. 27, Southport, ME 04576. ☎ **800/ 633-7645** or 207/633-2544. www.lawnmeerinn.com. E-mail: cooncat@ lawnmeerinn.com. 32 units. TV TEL. Summer rates $85–$195 double; spring and fall from $75–$180. 2-night minimum on holiday weekends. MC, V. Closed mid-Oct–mid-May. Pets accepted on limited basis; $10 extra per pet.

The Lawnmeer, situated a short hop from Boothbay on the northern shore of Southport Island, offers easy access to town and a restful environment. This was originally built as a guest home in the late 19th century, and the main inn has been updated with some loss of charm. More than half of the guest rooms are located in a motel-like annex, which makes up for a lack of character with private balconies offering views of the placid waterway that separates Southport Island from the mainland.

Dining: Regional and global cuisine is served in a comfort-able, homey dining room with windows overlooking the waterway. The inn serves some of the most consistently reliable food in a town that's come to expect high restaurant turnover. Look for contemporary fare, with entrees like grilled venison with a cranberry chutney, chicken satay, and rainbow trout with chanterelles. Entrees are priced $16 to $22; reservations are recommended.

Newagen Seaside Inn. Route 27 (P.O. Box 68), Cape Newagen, ME 04552. E-mail: seaside@wiscasset.net. ☎ **800/654-5242** or 207/633-5242. www.newagenseasideinn.com. 26 units. $130–$225 double, including full breakfast. Ask about off-season discounts. MC, V. Closed mid-Oct—mid-May. Located on south tip of Southport Island; take Route 27 from Boothbay Harbor and continue on until the inn sign.

This 1940s-era resort has seen more glamorous days, but it's still a superb small, low-key resort offering stunning ocean views and walks through a fragrant spruce forest. The inn is housed in a low, wide, white-shingled building that's furnished simply with country pine furniture. There's a classically austere dining room, narrow cruise-ship–like hallways with pine wainscotting, and a lobby with a fireplace. The rooms are plain and the inn can be a bit threadbare in spots, but never mind that. Guests flock here for the 85-acre oceanside grounds filled with decks, gazebos, and walkways that border on the magical. It's hard to convey the magnificence of the ocean views, which may be the best of any inn in Maine.

Dining: The handsome, simple dining room with ocean views offers a menu with creative New England fare like grilled salmon with a cucumber dill relish, and pork roast with apple fennel compote (entrees $13.95 to $28.95). Closed Tuesday for dinner.

Amenities: Freshwater and saltwater pools, badminton, horseshoes, tennis, sundeck, free rowboats.

Spruce Point Inn. Atlantic Ave. (P.O. Box 237), Boothbay Harbor, ME 04538. ☎ **800/553-0289** or 207/633-4152. www.sprucepointinn.com. E-mail: thepoint@sprucepointinn.com. 93 units. TV TEL. Mid-July–Aug $155–$325 double; fall $105–$250; spring $110–$250; early summer $115–$225. 2-night minimum weekends; 3 nights holidays. AE, DC, DISC, MC, V. Closed mid-Oct–Memorial Day. Turn seaward on Union St. in Boothbay Harbor; proceed 2 miles to the inn. Pets accepted; $50 deposit, $100 cleaning fee.

The Spruce Point Inn was originally built as a hunting and fishing lodge in the 1890s, and evolved into a summer resort in 1912. After some years of quiet neglect, it has benefited greatly from an overall spiffing up that's been ongoing since the late 1980s. A number of new units were built in the late 1990s; they match the older buildings architecturally, and blend in nicely. Those looking for historic authenticity may be disappointed. Those seeking modern resort facilities (Jacuzzis, carpeting, updated furniture) along with accenting to provide a bit of historic flavor, will be delighted. (Those who prefer their gentility a bit less polished should consider the Newagen Seaside Inn, see above.) Anyway, it's hard to imagine anyone being let down by the 15-acre grounds, situated on a rocky point facing west across the harbor. Guests typically fill their time idling in the Adirondack chairs, or partaking of more strenuous activities that include croquet, shuffleboard, tennis on clay courts, or swimming. Children's programs accommodate the growing number of families who vacation here.

Dining: Diners are seated in an elegant formal dining room (men are requested to wear jackets) and enjoy wonderful sunset views across the mouth of Boothbay Harbor as they peruse the evening menu. The menu features creative adaptations of traditional New England meals. Appetizers include grilled barbecue shrimp with a tomato and white bean ragout, and crab cakes with wasabi cream, black sesame seeds, and pickled ginger. Main courses are along the lines of rack of lamb with herb crust and pomegranate sauce, and pan-seared swordfish with a tropical salsa. Entrees range from $16 to $29.

Amenities: Two outdoor pools (one heated), Jacuzzi, two outdoor clay tennis courts, fitness center, lawn games (shuffleboard, tetherball, etc.), sundeck, conference rooms, self-service laundromat, concierge, dry cleaning, laundry service, in-room massage, baby-sitting, safe, game room, free shuttle to downtown Boothbay Harbor.

Topside. McKown Hill, Boothbay Harbor, ME 04538. ☎ **877/486-7466** or 207/633-5404. www.gwi.net/topside. E-mail: topside@gwi.net. 25 units. TEL. July 1–Labor Day $67–$155 double (most rooms around $85); Apr–June and Sept–Oct $50–$130 double. Rates include continental breakfast. AE, DISC, MC, V. Closed mid-Oct–late Apr.

The old gray house on the hilltop looming over the dated motel buildings may bring to mind the Bates Motel, especially when a full moon is overhead. But get over that. Because Topside offers spectacular ocean views at a reasonable price from a quiet hilltop compound located right in downtown Boothbay. The inn itself—a former boarding house for shipyard workers—features several comfortable rooms, furnished with a somewhat discomfiting mix of antiques and contemporary furniture. At the edge of the inn's lawn are two outbuildings with basic motel units. These are on the small side, furnished simply with dated paneling and furniture. (You won't find this hotel profiled in *House Beautiful.*) Rooms 9 and 14 have the best views, but most rooms offer a glimpse of the water, and many have decks or patios. All guests have access to the wonderful lawn and the endless views, and the Reed family, which owns and operates the inn, is accommodating and friendly.

WHERE TO DINE
IN WISCASSET

Red's Eats. Water St. (Rte. 1 just before the bridge). ☎ **207/882-6128.** Sandwiches $2–$5.25; lobster rolls vary, but are typically around $11. No credit cards. Mon–Thurs 11am–11pm; Fri–Sat 11am–2am; Sun noon–6pm. Closed Oct–April. TAKE-OUT.

Red's is an innocuous roadside stand smack in downtown Wiscasset that's probably received more than its fair share of media ink about its famous lobster rolls. (They often crop up in "Best of Maine" surveys.) And they *are* good, consisting of moist chunks of chilled lobster placed in a roll served with a little mayo on the side. But be aware they're on the pricey end of the scale—you can find less expensive (although less meaty) versions elsewhere. The few tables behind the stand fill up quickly in summer, but you can walk a minute or two and be on a public riverfront deck, which has a better view anyway. One way to economize: Order one lobster roll and split it with a friend, then fuel up on the budget fare that dominates the rest of the menu.

Sarah's. Water St. and Route 1 (across from Red's). ☎ **207/882-7504.** Sandwiches $4.45–$6.25; pizzas $4.95–16.95. AE, DISC, MC, V. Daily 11am–8pm (until 9pm Fri and Sat). SANDWICHES/TRADITIONAL.

Sarah's is a hometown favorite, which opened quietly in Wiscasset in 1987 then moved down the block to a place with a view of Sheepscot River a decade later. Expect personable service and filling and well-prepared (if unremarkable) food. It's usually crowded for lunch, with offerings including pita pockets (good choice: roasted turkey, tomato, red onion, and sprouts), croissant sandwiches, roll-ups on 12-inch tortillas, burritos, and a local favorite called a whaleboat, which is two-cheese turnovers (like a calzone) served with a broad choice of ingredients. The lobsters are fresh, hauled daily by Sarah's brother and father. This is our choice for an informal lunch break when motoring up Route 1—at least at those times we don't feel like splurging on a lobster roll at Red's.

IN THE BOOTHBAYS

When wandering through Boothbay Harbor, watch for **"King" Brud and his famous hot-dog cart.** Brud started selling hot dogs in town in 1943, and he's still at it. He's usually at the corner of McKown and Commercial streets from 10am until 4pm from June to October.

More innovative dining (in addition to Christopher's Boathouse, see below) may be found in the dining rooms at Spruce Point Inn and Lawnmeer Inn, listed in "Where to Stay," above.

Boothbay Region Lobstermen's Co-op. Atlantic Ave., Boothbay Harbor. ☎ 207/633-4900. No reservations. Fried and grilled foods $1.75–$10.25; dinners $7–$11.95. DISC, MC, V. Open daily May–mid-Oct 11:30am–8:30pm. By foot: cross footbridge and turn right; follow road for ⅓ mile to co-op. SEAFOOD.

"We are not responsible if the seagulls steal your food," reads the sign at the ordering window of this casual, harborside lobster joint. And that sets the tone pretty well. Situated across the harbor from downtown Boothbay, the lobstermen's co-op offers no-frills lobster and seafood. This is the best pick from among the cluster of usually dependable lobster-in-the-rough places that line the waterfront nearby. You order at a pair of windows, then pick up your meal and carry your tray to either the picnic tables on the dock or inside a garage-like two-story prefab building. Lobsters are priced to market (figure $8 to $12), with extras like onion rings ($2.10) or coleslaw ($1). A bank of soda machines provides liquid refreshment. This is a fine place for a lobster on a sunny day, but it's uninteresting at best in rain or fog.

✪ **Christopher's Boathouse.** 25 Union St., Boothbay Harbor. ☎ 207/633-6565. Reservations recommended during peak season. Main courses, lunch $5–$9, dinner $17–$23. MC, V. June 1–Oct 15 daily 5–9pm. July 4–mid-Oct daily 11:30am–3pm. Closed Sun–Mon in winter. CREATIVE AMERICAN/WOOD GRILL.

Christopher's is the exception to the generally unexciting fare found elsewhere around town. Scenically located at the head of the harbor, the restaurant is open, bright, and modern, and a handful of lucky diners get a tremendous view up the boat-clotted harbor. (There's also outside-deck dining when the weather is good.) The chef has a deft touch with spicy flavors, and nicely melds the expected with the unexpected (to wit: lobster and mango bisque with spicy lobster wontons). The meals from the wood grill are excellent, and they include an Asian-spiced tuna with Caribbean salsa, and a barbecue-spiced flank steak. Christopher's is a popular destination in the summer months; make a reservation to avoid disappointment.

Lobsterman's Wharf. Rte. 96, East Boothbay. ☎ **207/633-3443.** Reservations for parties of 6 or more only. Lunch $4.50–$13.95; dinner $13.95–$22.95 (mostly $14–$16). AE, MC, V. Open daily 11:30am–midnight Apr–Oct. Closed Oct–Apr. SEAFOOD.

Located on the water in East Boothbay, the Lobsterman's Wharf has the comfortable, pubby feel of a popular neighborhood bar, complete with pool table. And that's appropriate, since that's what it is. But it's that rarest of pubs—a place that's popular with the locals, but also serves up a decent meal and knows how to make travelers feel at home. If the weather's cooperative, sit at a picnic table on the dock and admire the views of a spruce-topped peninsula across the Damariscotta River; you can also grab a table inside amid the festive nautical decor. Entrees include a mixed-seafood grill, a barbecue shrimp and ribs platter, grilled swordfish with bèarnaise, and succulent fresh lobster offered four different ways. At lunch, there's hamburger, baked haddock, lobster rolls, and steamed lobster.

5 Pemaquid Peninsula

The Pemaquid Peninsula is an irregular, rocky wedge driven deep into the Gulf of Maine. It's much less commercial and trinkety than the Boothbay Peninsula just across the Damariscotta River, and more inviting for off-the-beaten-track exploration. (If you're given to such generalizations, the Boothbay peninsula is for tourists, the Pemaquid peninsula is for travelers.) The inland areas are leafy with hardwood trees, and laced with narrow, twisting back roads that are perfect for bicycling. As you near the southern tip where small harbors and coves predominate, the region takes on a more remote, maritime feel. When the surf pounds Pemaquid Point's rugged, rocky shore at the extreme southern tip of the peninsula, this can be one of the most dramatic destinations in Maine.

ESSENTIALS
GETTING THERE

The Pemaquid Peninsula is accessible from the west by turning southward on Route 129/130 in Damariscotta, just off Route 1. (Stay on Route 130 to Pemaquid Point.) From the east, head south on Route 32 just west of Waldoboro.

VISITOR INFORMATION

The **Damariscotta Region Chamber of Commerce,** P.O. Box 13, Main Street, Damariscotta, ME 04543 (☎ 207/563-8340), is a good source of local information, and maintains a seasonal information booth on Route 1 during the summer months.

EXPLORING THE PEMAQUID PENINSULA

The Pemaquid Peninsula invites slow driving and frequent stops. Start out by heading south on Route 129 toward Walpole from the sleepy head-of-the-harbor village of Damariscotta. Keep an eye on your left for the austerely handsome **Walpole Meeting House,** one of three meeting houses built on the peninsula in 1772. (Only two remain.) It's not regularly open to the public, but Sunday services are held here four times each summer (call for times), or try to sneak a look during the occasional wedding. (Dress well and don't eat too much of the wedding party's food.) History or architecture buffs bound and determined to see the interior when it's closed might also contact Charlene Hunter (☎ 207/563-5318), who has the key.

Just north of the unassuming fishing town of South Bristol on Route 129, watch for the **Thompson Ice Harvesting Museum** (☎ 207/644-8551). During winter's deep freeze (usually in February), volunteers from around town carve out huge blocks of ice and relay them to the well-insulated icehouse (a 1990 replica of the original icehouse) to be packed in sawdust. Summer visitors can peer into the cool, damp depths and see the glistening blocks (the harvest is sold to fishermen throughout the summer to ice down their catch), and learn about the once-common practice of ice harvesting through photos and other exhibits in a tiny museum. The grounds are open during daylight hours year-round; the museum exhibits are open 1 to 4pm Wednesday, Friday, and Saturday in July and August. A $1 donation (50¢ for children) is requested.

About 5 miles north of South Bristol, turn right on Pemaquid Road, which will take you to Route 130. Along the way look for the **Harrington Meeting House** (the other 1772 structure), which is open to the public on occasional afternoons in July and August. It's an architectural gem inside, almost painfully austere, with a small museum of local artifacts on the second floor. Even if it's not open, stop to wander about the lovely cemetery out back, the final resting place of many sea captains.

Head south on Route 130 to the village of New Harbor, and look for signs to **Colonial Pemaquid** (☎ 207/677-2423). Open daily from Memorial Day to Labor Day 9am to 5pm, this state historic site features exhibits on the original 1625 settlement here; archaeological digs take place in the summer. The $1 admission charge (free for children under 12) includes a visit to stout **Fort William Henry,** a 1907 replica of a supposedly impregnable fortress that stood over the river's entrance. (It was not impregnable, as it turned out, with tragic results for the settlement.) Nearby Pemaquid Beach allows for a bracing ocean dip and is a good spot for families.

Pemaquid Point, which is owned by the town, is the place to while away an afternoon (☎ **207/677-2494**). Bring a picnic and a book, and find a spot on the dark, fractured rocks to settle in. The ocean views are superb and the only distractions are the tenacious seagulls, which may take a profound interest in your lunch. While here, be sure to visit the **Fishermen's Museum** (☎ **207/677-2494** or off-season 207/677-2726) in the handsome lighthouse (open daily 10am to 5pm; Sunday from 11am to 5pm). Informative exhibits depict the whys and wherefores of the local fishing trade, and should answer those questions that invariably arise while watching lobstermen at work just offshore. There's a small fee ($1 over 12, 50¢ seniors) to use the park in summer; admission to the museum is by donation.

From New Harbor, you can get a great view of the coast from the outside looking in with **Hardy Boat Cruises** (☎ **800/278-3346** or 207/677-2026; www.hardyboat.com). Tours are aboard the 60-foot *Hardy III,* and excursions include a one-hour sunset and lighthouse cruise ($9 adult, $6 children 12 and under), 90-minute puffin tours out to Eastern Egg Rock ($17 adult, $10 children), and ferry service to

Monhegan Island ($26 adult, $18 children). Extra clothing for warmth is strongly recommended. Closed Columbus Day to mid-May.

Route 32 strikes northwest from New Harbor and it's the most scenic way to leave the peninsula if you plan to continue eastward on Route 1. Along the way look for the sign pointing to the **Rachel Carson Salt Pond Preserve,** a Nature Conservancy property. The noted naturalist Rachel Carson studied these roadside tidepools extensively while researching her 1956 bestseller *The Edge of the Sea,* and today it's still an inviting spot for budding naturalists and experts alike. Pull off your shoes and socks, and wade through the cold waters at low tide looking for starfish, green crabs, periwinkles, and other creatures.

WHERE TO STAY

Bradley Inn. Rte. 130, 3063 Bristol Rd, New Harbor, ME 04554. ☎ **207/677-2105.** Fax 207/677-3367. www.bradleyinn.com. E-mail: bradley@lincoln.midcoast.com. 16 units (including cottage). TEL. Summer and fall $135–$235 double; winter and spring $105–$160. Rates include full breakfast. AE, MC, V.

The Bradley Inn is located within easy walking or biking distance to the point, but there's plenty of reasons to lag behind at the inn. Start by wandering the nicely landscaped grounds, or enjoying a game of croquet in the gardens. If the fog's moved in for a spell, settle in for a game of Scrabble at the pub, which is decorated with a lively nautical theme. The rooms are tastefully appointed; only the carriage house has a television. The third floor rooms are my favorites, despite the hike, thanks to the distant glimpses of John's Bay. The inn is popular with weddings on weekends in summer, so ask in advance if you're seeking solitude and quiet.

Amenities: Free use of bikes, room service (7am to 10pm), access to nearby beach

Dining: The fare served in the inn's handsome first-floor restaurant emphasizes local seafood, but the menu also features duck, steak, and rabbit. Entrees are priced $22 to $28.

Hotel Pemaquid. Rte. 130, Pemaquid Point (mailing address: 3098 Bristol Rd., New Harbor, ME 04554). ☎ **207/677-2312.** www.hotelpemaquid.com. 23 units (4 share 2 bathrooms). Peak season $79–$215 double ($60 for shared bathroom); off season $65–$185 ($52 shared bathroom). 2-night minimum stay on weekends. No credit cards. Closed mid-Oct–mid-May.

This 1889 coastal classic isn't directly on the water—it's only a minute or two walk from Pemaquid Point—but the main inn has the flavor of an old-time seaside boarding house. The outbuildings are a bit more modern and have less character. The inn is aggressively old-fashioned (although most guest rooms now have private bathrooms), with narrow hallways and antiques, including a great collection of old radios and phonographs. The inn has a two- (or three-) bedroom suite, which is ideal for families.

✪ **Newcastle Inn.** River Rd., Newcastle, ME 04553. ☎ **800/832-8669** or 207/563-5685. www.newcastleinn.com. 14 units. Summer $110–$220 double; off-season $95–$185. Rates include full breakfast. 2-night minimum stay some weekends. AE, MC, V. Closed January. Children age 12 and up are welcome.

Located not far from Route 1 and just across the river from Damariscotta, the Newcastle Inn is the most luxurious (and most romantic) option in the Pemaquid region (Pemaquid Point is about 15 miles away). It's especially appealing to gourmands, who rave about the inn's restaurant. The inn has limited views of the tidal Damariscotta River, but the real charm lies within the well-appointed inn, which has an elegant, modern, country feel. Innkeepers Rebecca and Howard Levitan have aggressively expanded guest rooms by combining smaller rooms, and most are now spacious and bright. (Eight have air conditioning, two have televisions, and nine have gas fireplaces.) "Seguin Island" is the smallest room, "West Quoddy" the largest suite (they're named after light-houses). The "Pemaquid Point Suite" is very appealing, with gas fireplace, glimpses of the river, a small sitting room, and a large bathroom with a two-person Jacuzzi.

Dining: The inn's restaurant is top-rate—the Levitans report that Julia Child has dined here on her birthday for three years running. Cocktails are served at 6pm in the inn's common room, followed by dinner at 7pm. The menu focuses on fresh Maine ingredients and changes nightly. Typical entrees might include a seared duck breast with calvados reduction sauce, or beef tenderloin au poive with oven-roasted cherry tomatoes. The four-course meal offers good value at a fixed price of $39.50 (plus tax and gratuity).

WHERE TO DINE

Shaw's Fish and Lobster Wharf. On the water, New Harbor. ☎ **207/677-2200.** Lobster priced to market (typically $7 per pound). MC, V. Open mid-May–mid-October daily 11am–8pm (open until 9pm July and August). Closed mid-Oct–late May. LOBSTER.

Shaw's attracts hordes of tourists, but it's no trick to figure out why: It's one of the best-situated lobster pounds, with postcard-perfect views of the working harbor and the boats coming and going through the inlet that connects to the open sea. Customers stand in line to place their orders, then wait for their name to be called. While waiting, you can stake out a seat on either the open deck or the indoor dining room (go for the deck), or order up some appetizers from the raw bar. This is one of the few lobster joints in Maine with a full liquor license.

6 Monhegan Island

Brawny, wild, and remote, Monhegan Island is Maine's premier island destination. Visited by Europeans as early as 1497 (although some historians insist that earlier Norsemen carved primitive runes on neighboring Manana Island), the island was first settled by fishermen attracted to the sea's bounty in the offshore waters. Starting in the 1870s and continuing to the present day, noted artists discovered the island and came to stay for a spell. Their roster included Rockwell Kent (the artist most closely associated with the island), George Bellows, Edward Hopper, and Robert Henri. The artists gathered in the kitchen of the lighthouse to chat and drink coffee; it's said that the wife of the lighthouse keeper accumulated a tremendously valuable collection of paintings. Today, Jamie Wyeth, scion of the Wyeth clan, claims the island as his part-time home.

It's not hard to figure why artists have been attracted to the place: There's a mystical quality to it, from the thin light to the startling contrasts of the dark cliffs and the foamy white surf. There's also a remarkable sense of tranquility to this place, which can only help focus one's inner vision.

Be aware that this is not Martha's Vineyard—no ATMs, few pay phones, even electricity is in scarce supply. That's what visitors tend to like about it. If you have the time, I'd strongly recommend an overnight on the island at one of the several hostelries. Day trips are easily arranged, but the island's true character doesn't start to emerge until the last day boat sails away and the quiet, rustic appeal of the island starts to percolate back to the surface.

Visiting Port Clyde

Port Clyde's charm lies in the fact that it's still first and foremost a fishing village. While some small-scale tourist enterprises have made their mark on the village, located at the tip of a long finger about 15 miles south of Route 1, it still caters primarily to working fishermen and the ferry workers who keep Monhegan supplied.

Here's a favorite routine for spending a couple of hours in Port Clyde, either while waiting for the ferry or just snooping around. Head to the **Port Clyde General Store** (☎ 207/372-6543) on the waterfront and soak up the cracker-barrel ambiance (there's actually a decent selection of wine here, attesting to encroaching upscalism). Order a sandwich to go, then drive to the **Marshall Point Lighthouse Museum** (☎ 207/372-6450); follow the road along the harbor eastward, and bear right to the point. This small lighthouse received a few moments of fame when Forrest Gump turned around here and headed back west during his cross-country walks in the movie, but it also happens to be one of the more peaceful and scenic lighthouses in the state. Carry your lunch around to the far side of the lightkeeper's house and settle on one of the granite benches to watch the fishing boats come and go through the thoroughfare. Afterwards, tour through the small but engaging museum (free; donations encouraged) and learn a bit about the culture of lighthouses on the Maine Coast.

ESSENTIALS
GETTING THERE

Access to Monhegan Island is via boat from either New Harbor, Boothbay Harbor, or Port Clyde. The hour-and-ten-minute trip from Port Clyde is the favored route among longtime island visitors. The trip from this rugged fishing village is picturesque as it passes the Marshall Point Lighthouse and a series of spruce-clad islands before setting out on the open sea.

Two boats make the run to Monhegan from Port Clyde. The *Laura B.* is a doughty workboat (building supplies and boxes of food are loaded on first; passengers fill in the available niches on the deck and in the small cabin). A newer boat—

the faster (50 minutes), passenger-oriented *Elizabeth Ann*— also makes the run, offering a large heated cabin and more seating. You'll need to leave your car behind, so pack light and wear sturdy shoes. The fare is $25 round-trip for adults; $12 for children 2 to 12 years old; $2 for pets. Reservations are advised: **Monhegan Boat Line,** P.O. Box 238, Port Clyde, ME 04855 (☎ **207/372-8848;** www.monheganboat.com). Parking is available near the dock for an additional $4 per day.

VISITOR INFORMATION

Monhegan Island has no formal visitor center, but it's small and friendly enough that you can make inquiries of just about anyone you meet on the island pathways. The clerks at the ferry dock in Port Clyde are also quite helpful. Be sure to pick up the inexpensive map of the island's hiking trail at the boat ticket office or at the various shops around the island. An informal web site maintained by Clare Durst offers helpful information for first-time visitors: www.briegull.com/monhegan/.

Because wildfire could destroy this breezy island in short order, smoking is prohibited outside the village.

EXPLORING MONHEGAN

Walking is the chief activity on the island, and it's genuinely surprising how much distance you can cover on these 700 acres (about 1½ miles long and a half-mile wide). The village clusters tightly around the harbor; the rest of the island is mostly wild land, laced with some 17 miles of trails. Much of the island is ringed with high, open bluffs atop fissured cliffs. Pack a picnic lunch and hike the perimeter trail, and plan to spend much of the day just sitting and reading, or enjoying the surf rolling in against the cliffs.

The inland trails are appealing in a far different way. Deep, dark **Cathedral Woods** is mossy and fragrant; sunlight only dimly filters through the evergreens to the forest floor.

Bird watching is a popular activity in the spring and fall. Monhegan Island is on the Atlantic flyway, and a wide variety of birds stop at the island along their migration routes. Swapping stories of the day's sightings is a popular activity at island inns and B&Bs.

The sole attraction on the island is the **Monhegan Historical and Cultural Museum,** located next to the 1824 lighthouse on a high point above the village. The museum, open from July to September, has a quirky collection of historic artifacts and provides context for this rugged island's history. Nearby is a small and select art museum that opened in 1998, featuring changing exhibits showcasing the works of illustrious island artists, including Rockwell Kent.

The spectacular view from the grassy slope in front of the lighthouse is the real prize. The vista sweeps across a marsh, past one of the island's most historic hotels, past melancholy Manana Island, and across the sea beyond. Get here early if you want a good seat for the sunset; it seems most visitors to the island congregate here after dinner. (Another popular place is the island's southern tip, where the wreckage of the *D.T. Sheridan,* a coal barge, washed up in 1948.)

If you time it right, you can also visit the studios of Monhegan artists, who still come here in great numbers. Artists often open their workspaces for limited hours, and are happy to have visitors stop by and look at their work, chat, and perhaps buy a canvas or sculpture. Some of the artwork runs along the lines of predictable seascapes and sunsets, but much of it rises above the banal. Look for the bulletin board along the main pathway in the village for a listing of the days and hours the studios are open.

WHERE TO STAY & DINE ON MONHEGAN

Monhegan House. Monhegan Island, ME 04852. ☎ **800/599-7983** or 207/594-7983. Fax 207/596-6472. 33 units (all with shared bathroom). $100 double. AE, DISC, MC, V. Closed Columbus Day–Memorial Day.

The handsome Monhegan House has been accommodating guests since 1870, and it has the comfortable, worn patina of a venerable lodging house. The accommodations at this four-floor walk-up are austere but comfortable; there are no closets, and everyone uses clean dormitory-style bathrooms. The downstairs lobby with fireplace is a welcome spot to sit and take the fog-induced chill out of your bones (even in August it can be cool here). The restaurant offers three meals a day, with a selection of filling but simple meat and (very fresh) fish dishes, along with vegetarian entrees. Main courses range in price from about $10 to $18.

Trailing Yew. Monhegan Island, ME 04852. ☎ **800-592-2520** or 207/596-0440. 37 units in four buildings (all but 1 share bathrooms). $120 double, including breakfast, dinner, taxes, and tips. No credit cards. Closed mid-Oct–mid-May. Pets allowed.

At the end of long summer afternoons, guests congregate near the flagpole in front of the main building of this rustic hillside compound. They sit in Adirondack chairs or chat with new-found friends. But mostly they're waiting for the ringing of the bell, which signals them in for dinner, as if at summer camp. Inside, guests sit around long tables, introduce themselves to their neighbors, then pour an iced tea and wait for the delicious, family-style dinner. (You're given a choice, including vegetarian options, but my advice is to opt for the fresh fish whenever it's available.)

The Trailing Yew, which has been taking in guests since 1929, is a friendly, informal place, popular with hikers and birders. Guest rooms are eclectic and simply furnished in a pleasantly dated summer-home style; only one of the four guest buildings has electricity (most but not all bathrooms have electricity); guests in rooms without electricity are provided a kerosene lamp and instruction in its use (a small flashlight is helpful . . . just in case). Rooms are unheated, so bring an extra layer if the weather's chilly.

5

Penobscot Bay

*T*raveling eastward along the Maine Coast, those who pay attention to such things will notice that they're suddenly heading almost due north around Rockland. The culprit behind this geographic quirk is Penobscot Bay, a sizeable bite out of the Maine Coast that forces a lengthy northerly detour to cross the head of the bay where the Penobscot River flows in at Bucksport.

You'll find some of Maine's more pastoral coastal scenery in this area—spectacular offshore islands and high hills rising above the blue bay. Although the mouth of Penobscot Bay is occupied by two large islands, its waters can still churn with vigor when the tides and winds conspire.

Penobscot Bay's western shore gets a heavy stream of tourist traffic, especially along Route 1 through the scenic village of Camden. Nonetheless, this is a good destination to get a taste of the Maine coast. Services for travelers are abundant, although during the peak season a small miracle will be required to find a weekend guest room without a reservation.

1 Rockland & Environs

Located on the southwest edge of Penobscot Bay, Rockland has long been proud of its brick-and-blue-collar waterfront town reputation. Built around the fishing industry, Rockland historically dabbled in tourism on the side. But with the decline of the fisheries and the rise of the tourist economy in Maine, the balance has shifted—Rockland has recently been colonized by creative restaurateurs and innkeepers and other small-business folks who are painting it with an unaccustomed gloss.

There's a small park on the waterfront from which the fleet of windjammers comes and goes, but more appealing than Rockland's waterfront is its commercial downtown—it's basically one long street lined with sophisticated historic brick architecture. If it's picturesque harbor towns you're seeking, head to Camden, Rockport, Port Clyde, or Stonington. But

Rockland makes a great base for exploring this beautiful coastal region, especially if you have a low tolerance for trinkets and tourist hordes.

ESSENTIALS
GETTING THERE

Route 1 passes directly through Rockland. Rockland's tiny airport is served by **Colgan Air** (☎ **800/272-5488** or 207/596-7604) with daily flights from Boston and Bar Harbor. **Concord Trailways** (☎ **800/639-3317**) offers bus service from Rockland to Bangor and Portland.

VISITOR INFORMATION

The **Rockland/Thomaston Area Chamber of Commerce,** P.O. Box 508, Rockland, ME 04841 (☎ **800/562-2529** or 207/596-0376; e-mail rtacc@midcoast.com), staffs an information desk at Harbor Park. It's open daily 9am to 5pm Memorial Day to Labor Day, and weekdays only the rest of the year.

EVENTS

The **Maine Lobster Festival** (☎ **800/562-2529** or 207/596-0376) takes place at Harbor Park the first weekend in August (plus the preceding Thursday and Friday). Entertainers and vendors of all sorts of Maine products—especially the local crustacean—fill the waterfront parking lot and attract thousands of festival-goers who enjoy this pleasant event with a sort of buttery bonhomie. The event includes the Maine Sea Goddess Coronation Pageant.

TWO FINE MUSEUMS

Farnsworth Museum. 352 Main St., Rockland. ☎ **207/596-6457.** www.farnsworthmuseum.org. E-mail: farnsworth@midcoast.com. $9 adults, $8 seniors, $5 students 18 and older, free for 17 and under (all prices discounted $1 in winter). MC, V. Summer 9am–5pm daily; winter Tues–Sat 10am–5pm, Sun 1–5pm.

Rockland, for all its rough edges, has long and historic ties to the arts. Noted sculptor Louise Nevelson grew up in Rockland, and in 1935 philanthropist Lucy Farnsworth bequeathed a fortune large enough to establish the Farnsworth Museum, which has since become one of the most respected art museums in New England. Located in the middle of downtown, the Farnsworth has a superb collection of paintings and sculptures by renown American artists with a connection to Maine. This

Penobscot Bay

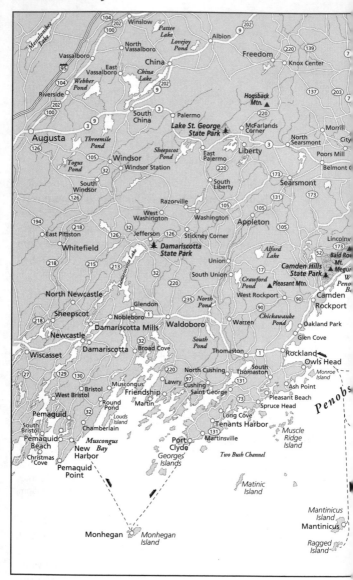

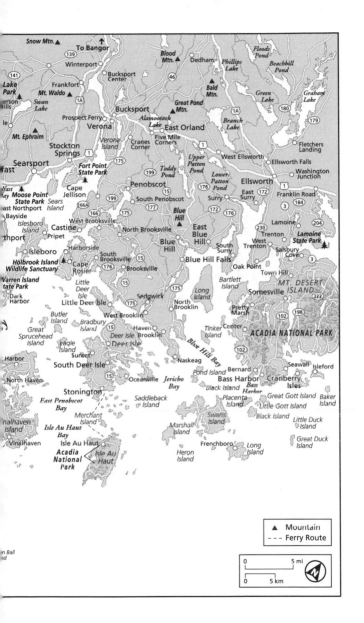

Map Legend

▲ Mountain
- - - Ferry Route

0		5 mi
0		5 km

includes not only Nevelson and three generations of Wyeths (N.C., Andrew, and Jamie), but Rockwell Kent, Childe Hassam, and Maurice Prendergast. The exhibit halls are modern, spacious, and well designed, and the shows professionally prepared. In 1998, the museum expanded with the opening of the **Farnsworth Center for the Wyeth Family,** housed in the former Pratt Memorial Methodist Church and containing Andrew and Betsy Wyeth's personal collection of Maine-related art.

The Farnsworth also owns two other buildings open to the public. The **Farnsworth Homestead,** located behind the museum, offers a glimpse into the life of prosperous coastal Victorians. And a 25-minute drive away in the village of Cushing is the **Olson House,** perhaps Maine's most famous home, immortalized in Andrew Wyeth's noted painting, *Christina's World.* Ask at the museum for directions and information (closed in winter).

Owls Head Transportation Museum. Rte. 73, Owls Head. ☎ **207/ 594-4418.** www.ohtm.org. $6 adults, $5.00 seniors, $4 children 5–12, families $16. Apr–Oct daily 10am–5pm; Nov–Mar daily 10am–4pm.

You don't have to be a car or plane buff to enjoy a day at this museum, located 3 miles south of Rockland on Route 73. Founded in 1974, the museum has an extraordinary collection of cars, motorcycles, bicycles, and planes, nicely displayed in a tidy, hangar-like building at the edge of the Knox County Airport. Look for the beautiful early Harley Davidson, and the sleek Rolls Royce Phantom dating from 1929. The museum is also a popular destination for hobbyists and tinkerers, who drive and fly their classic vehicles here for frequent weekend rallies in the summer. Call ahead or check the museum's web site to ask about special events.

WHERE TO STAY

Capt. Lindsey House Inn. 5 Lindsey St., Rockland, ME 04841. ☎ **800/ 523-2145** or 207/596-7950. Fax 207/596-2758. www.rocklandmaine.com. E-mail lindsey@midcoast.com. 9 units. A/C TV TEL. Peak season $110–$160 double; Columbus Day–Memorial Day $65–$110. Rates include continental breakfast. AE, DISC, MC, V.

The three-story, brick Capt. Lindsey House is located just a couple minutes' walk from the Farnsworth Museum. It was originally erected as a hotel in 1835, but went through several subsequent incarnations, including headquarters of the

Rockland Water Co. (The inn's front desk is where folks once paid their water bills.) Guests enter through a doorway a few steps off Rockland's Main Street, and enter into an opulent first-floor common area done up in rich tones, handsome dark-wood paneling, and a well-selected mix of antique and contemporary furniture. The upstairs rooms are also tastefully decorated in a contemporary country style, generally with bold modern colors and patterns mixed deftly with traditional design. Even the smaller rooms like Room 4 are well done (this in a sort of steamship nouveau style); the rooms on the third floor all feature yellow pine floors and antique oriental carpets. All rooms but two have showers only, but all have pleasing extras, like handmade bedspreads, hair dryers, down comforters, and bathrobes. Reliable pub fare is available at The Waterworks next door (see below), which is owned by the same people who own the inn.

East Wind Inn. P.O. Box 149, Tenants Harbor, ME 04860. ☎ **800/ 241-8439** or 207/372-6366. Fax 207/372-6320. www.eastwindinn.com. E-mail: info@eastwindinn.com. 26 units (7 with shared bathroom). Summer $138 double ($90 with shared bathroom), $165–$275 suites and apartments. Off-season $72–$126 double. Rates include full breakfast. 2-night minimum on suites & apts. AE, DISC, MC, V. Closed Dec–Apr. Drive south on Route 131 from Thomaston to Tenants Harbor; turn left at post office. $10 extra for pets (by reservation). Children 12 and older welcome.

The inn itself, formerly a sail loft, is perfectly situated next to the harbor with water views from all rooms and the long porch. It's a classic seaside hostelry with busy wallpaper, simple colonial reproduction furniture, and tidy rooms. (The 10 guest rooms across the way at a former sea captain's house have most of the private bathrooms.) The atmosphere is relaxed almost to the point of ennui and the service good.

Dining: Traditional New England fare is served in an Edwardian-era dining room (open from April to November). The seafood is usually your best bet; the baked haddock is always popular. Sides include freshly cut french fries, and "country mashed potatoes" ("made with milk, butter, and occasional lumps"). Entrees are priced from $11.95 to $17.95.

LimeRock Inn. 96 Limerock St. Rockland, ME 04841. ☎ **800/546-3762** or 207/594-2257. www.limerockinn.com. 8 units. $100–$185 double. Rates include breakfast. DISC, MC, V.

This beautiful Queen Anne–style inn is located on a quiet side street just 2 blocks from Rockland's Main Street. Originally built for U.S. Rep. Charles Littlefield in 1890, it served as a doctor's residence from 1950 to 1994, after which it was renovated into a gracious inn. The innkeepers have done a commendable job converting what could be a gloomy manse into one of the region's better choices for overnight accommodation. Attention has been paid to detail throughout, from the choice of country Victorian furniture to the Egyptian cotton bed sheets. All the guest rooms are welcoming, but among the best choices is the "Island Cottage Room," a bright and airy chamber wonderfully converted from an old shed and featuring a private deck and jacuzzi. The "Turret Room" has French doors into the bathroom, which features a clawfoot tub. If it's big elegance you're looking for, opt for the "Grand Manan Room," which has a large four-poster bed, a fireplace, and a double jacuzzi.

Samoset Resort. Rockport, ME 04856. ☎ **800/341-1650** (outside Maine) or 207/594-2511. www.samoset.com. E-mail: info@samoset.com. 178 hotel units, plus 72 town house units. A/C TV TEL. Early July–Labor Day $169–$329 double ($339 suite); fall $159–$259 ($289 suite); winter $99–$169 ($189 suite); May–mid-June $129–$219 ($239 suite); mid-June–early July $179–$289 ($299 suite). Meals not included; ask about MAP packages. AE, CB, DC, DISC, MC, V.

The Samoset is a something of a Maine coast rarity—a modern, self-contained resort that offers contemporary styling, ocean views, and lots of golf. Both the hotel and town houses are surrounded by the handsome golf course, which opens up expansive views from almost every window on the property. The lobby is constructed of massive timbers (recovered from an old grain silo in Portland), and the guest rooms all have balconies or terraces. Golfers love the place—it's been called Pebble Beach East—and families will always find plenty of activities for kids (there's a summer camp during high season, and baby-sitting the rest of the year). The resort also has the best sunset stroll in the state—you can ramble across the golf course to a breakwater that leads out to a picturesque lighthouse. The one downside: for the high prices charged, the staff may be less polished than you would expect.

Dining/Diversions: The Samoset offers four dining areas, including the Clubhouse Grill, Breakwater Cafe, and the Poolhouse. The centerpiece restaurant is Marcel's, where specialty dinners are prepared tableside. These include lobster flambé, rack of lamb for two, and steak Diane. Prices for main courses at Marcel's range from $16 to $29.

Amenities: 18-hole golf course ($95 for 18 holes), indoor and outdoor pools, modern health club, hot tub, sauna, indoor video golf driving range, 4 tennis courts (night play), jogging and walking trails, children's program, business center, gift shops, courtesy car, valet parking, massage, free newspaper, concierge, laundry service and dry cleaning, baby-sitting, safe, and safe deposit boxes.

WHERE TO DINE

Cafe Miranda. 15 Oak St., Rockland. ☎ **207/594-2034.** Reservations strongly encouraged. Main courses $9.50–$16.50. DISC, MC, V. Tues–Sat 5:30–9:30pm (until 8:30 in winter). WORLD CUISINE.

Hidden away on a side street, this tiny, contemporary restaurant features a huge menu with big flavors. The fare draws liberally from cuisines from around the globe ("It's comfort food for whatever planet you're from," says owner-chef Kerry Altiero), and given its wide-ranging culinary inclinations it comes as something of a surprise just how well-prepared everything is. The chargrilled pork and shrimp cakes served with a ginger-lime-coconut sauce are superb. Other creative entrees include barbecue pork ribs with a smoked jalapeño sauce, and Indian almond chicken. (The menu changes often, so don't set your heart on these dishes in particular.) Cafe Miranda provides the best value for the buck of any restaurant in Maine. Beer and wine are available.

Cod End Fish House. Next to the Town Dock, Tenants Harbor. ☎ **207/372-6782.** Lunch entrees $2.50–$8; dinner $7.95–$13.95. DISC, MC, V. July–Aug daily 7am–9pm; limited hours June, Sept–Oct; closed Nov–May. LOBSTER POUND.

Part of the allure of Cod End is its hidden and scenic location—it seems as though you've stumbled upon a secret. Situated between the Town Landing and the East Wind Inn, Cod End is a classic lobster joint with fine views of tranquil Tenants Harbor. You walk through the fish market (where you can buy fish or lobster to go, along with various lobster-related souvenirs), then place your order at the outdoor shack. While waiting to be called, you can check out the dock or just sit and relax in the sun. (If it's raining, there's limited seating in the market.) Lobsters are the draw here, naturally, but there's plenty else to choose from, including chowders, stews, linguini with seafood, rolls (like the clam or haddock rolls), and simple sandwiches for younger tastes (even peanut butter and jelly). As with most lobster pounds, the less complicated and sophisticated your meal is here, the better the odds you'll be satisfied.

✪ **Primo.** 2 South Main St. (Route 173), Rockland. ☎ **207/596-0770.** www.primorestaurant.com. Reservations strongly suggested. Main courses, $16–$28. AE, DC, DISC, MC, V. Thurs–Mon 5:30–9:30pm; call for dates/hours in off-season. MEDITERRANEAN/NEW AMERICAN.

Primo opened in April 2000 and quickly developed New York–sized buzz, and with good reason. The restaurant, owned by executive chef Melissa Kelly and pastry chef Price Kushner, occupies two deftly decorated floors of a century-old home a short drive south of downtown Rockland (no views to speak of). The surprisingly delicate rustic fare ranges from wood-fired pizzas with a matzoh-thin crust to more ambitious offerings. You might choose from grilled duckling breast on a bed of mashed sweet potatoes with braised cabbage and a caramelized apple jus, or pepper-crusted venison with roasted beets and a pecan wild rice. It's hard to get a table during the peak summer season, but you can order off the menu from the cozy upstairs bar.

The Waterworks. Lindsey St., Rockland. ☎ **207/596-7950.** Reservations for parties of 6 or more only. Lunch $4–$8.95; dinner $8–$14.50. DISC, MC, V. Daily 11am–10pm (open at noon Sun). Closed Sun–Mon in winter. PUB FARE.

Set a half-block off Rockland's Main Street in the brick garage of the former waterworks (naturally), The Waterworks has the informal, comfortable feel of a brew pub without the brewery. The restaurant is divided into two spacious sections (where the sun streams through the room's tall windows during long, lazy afternoons). Turn left when you enter for the pub side, which is open and airy, with wooden floors and long oak tables where customers can be indelicate with their pints. To the right is the dining room, which is carpeted and quieter. Expect pub fare and "comfort food" (so billed) that includes roast turkey, pork loin, and meat loaf.

2 Camden

Camden is the quintessential coastal Maine village. Set at the foot of the wooded Camden Hills on a picturesque harbor that no Hollywood movie set could improve, the affluent village of Camden has attracted the gentry of the eastern seaboard for more than a century. The elaborate mansions of the moneyed set still dominate the shady side streets (many have been converted into bed-and-breakfasts), and Camden is possessed of a grace and sophistication that eludes many other coastal towns.

Nor have Camden's charms gone unnoticed. The village and the surrounding communities have become a haven for retired U.S. Foreign Service and CIA personnel, and has attracted its share of summering corporate bigwigs, including former Apple Computer C.E.O. John Sculley. More recently, the town received an economic injection from the rapid growth of MBNA, a national credit card company that has restored historic buildings and contributed significantly to Camden's current prosperity (this explains the high number of clean-cut young men in white shirts and ties you may see in and around town).

The best way to enjoy Camden is to park your car as soon as you can—which may mean driving a block or two off Route 1. The village is of a perfect scale to reconnoiter on foot, which allows a leisurely browse of boutiques and galleries. Don't miss the hidden town park (look behind the library), which was designed by the landscape firm of Frederick Law Olmsted, the nation's most lauded landscape architect.

On the downside: All this attention and Camden's growing appeal to bus tours is having a deleterious impact, say some longtime visitors. The merchandise at the shops seems to be trending downward to appeal to a lower common denominator, and the constant summer congestion distracts somewhat from the village's inherent charm. If you don't come expecting a pristine and undiscovered village, you're likely to enjoy the place all the more.

ESSENTIALS
GETTING THERE

Camden is on Route 1. Coming from the south, travelers can shave a few minutes off their trip by turning left on Route 90 six miles past Waldoboro, bypassing Rockland. The most traffic-free route from southern Maine is to Augusta via the Maine Turnpike, then via Route 17 to Route 90 to Route 1. **Concord Trailways** (☎ **800/639-3317**) offers bus service to and from Bangor and Portland.

VISITOR INFORMATION

The **Rockport-Camden-Lincolnville Chamber of Commerce,** P.O. Box 919, Camden, ME 04843 (☎ **800/223-5459** or 207/236-4404), dispenses helpful information from its center at the Public Landing in Camden, where there's also free parking. although spaces are scare in summer. The chamber is open year-round weekdays from 9am to 5pm and Saturdays 10am to 5pm. In summer, it's also open Sundays 10am to 4pm.

EXPLORING CAMDEN

Camden Hills State Park (☎ **207/236-3109**) is located about a mile north of the village center on Route 1. This 6,500-acre park features an oceanside picnic area, camping at 112 sites, a winding toll road up 800-foot Mt. Battie with spectacular views from the summit, and a variety of well-marked hiking trails. The day-use fee is $2 adult, 50¢ children 5 to 11.

One hike I'd recommend is an ascent to the ledges of **Mount Megunticook,** preferably early in the morning before the crowds have amassed and when the mist still lingers in the valleys. Leave from near the campground and follow the well-maintained trail to these open ledges, which requires only about a 30- to 45-minute exertion. Spectacular, almost improbable, views of the harbor await, as well as glimpses inland to the gentle vales. Depending on your stamina and desires, you can continue on the park's trail network to Mount Battie, or into the less-trammeled woodlands on the east side of the Camden Hills.

The Camden is wonderful to explore by bike. A pleasant loop, several miles long, takes you from the town of Camden into the village of Rockport—which has an equally scenic harbor and lighter tourist traffic. Bike rentals ($15 per day, $9 half-day), maps, and local riding advice are available at **Brown Dog Bikes** (☎ **207/236-6664**) at 53 Chestnut St. in Camden.

Try this bike route: Take Bayview Street from the center of town out along the bay, passing by opulent seaside estates. The road soon narrows and becomes quiet and pastoral, overarched with leafy trees. At the stop sign just past the cemetery, turn left and follow this route into Rockport. Along the way, you'll pass the local version of "landscape with cows": in this case, a small herd of belted Galloways. In Rockport, snoop around the historic harbor, then stop by **Maine Coast Artists,** Russell Avenue (☎ **207/236-2875**), a stately gallery that offers rotating exhibits of local painters, sculptors, and crafts people. Admission is free.

The Camden-Rockport Historical Society has prepared a 9-mile bike (or car) tour with brief descriptions of some of the historic properties along the way. The brochure describing the tour is free; check for it at the chamber of commerce at Camden public landing (see above), or ask for one at the Whitehall Inn (see below). The brochure also includes a two-mile walking tour of downtown Camden.

What to do in the evening? Besides quaffing a lager or ale at the Sea Dog Brewing Co. (see below), you might take in a foreign or art film at the **Bayview Street Cinema,** 10 Bayview St (☎ **207/236-8722**), on the second floor just off Camden's central intersection. The theater boasts a superb sound system, and there's an excellent line-up of frequently changing films throughout the year.

Come winter, there's skiing at the **Camden Snow Bowl** (☎ **207/236-3438**) just outside of town on Hosmer's Pond Road. This small, family-oriented ski area has a handful of trails and a modest vertical drop of 950 feet, but it also has good views of the open ocean and an exhilarating toboggan run. Toboggans are available for rent, or you can bring your own.

ON THE WATER

Several sailing ships make Camden their home base, and it's a rare treat to come and go from this harbor, which is considered by many to be the most beautiful in the state.

The 57-foot windjammer *Surprise* (☎ **207/236-4687**), was launched in 1918, and today takes a maximum of 18 passengers on two-hour non-smoking cruises from the Camden Public Landing. Fruit juices and cookies are served on board; children 12 and older only. Four excursions ($25) are offered daily in July and August, three daily in June, September, and October; reservations are helpful.

The *Schooner Lazy Jack* (☎ **207/230-0602**), has been plying the waters since 1947, and is modeled after the Gloucester fishing schooners of the late 19th century. There's a maximum of 13 passengers; children must be 10 or older. The two-hour tours are $20 per person; snacks are available on board, and you can BYOB.

For a more intimate view of the harbor, **Maine Sports Outfitters** (☎ **800/722-0826** or 207/236-8797) offers sea-kayaking tours of Camden's scenic harbor. The standard tour lasts two hours, costs $35, and takes paddlers out to

Curtis Island at the outer edge of the harbor. This beginner's tour is offered three times daily and is an easy, delightful way to get a taste of the area's maritime culture. Longer trips and instruction are also available. The outfitter's main shop, located on Route 1 in Rockport (a few minute's drive south of Camden), has a good selection of outdoor gear and is worth a stop for outdoor enthusiasts gearing up for local adventures or heading on to Acadia. Sign up for the tours either at the store or at the boathouse, which is located at the head of the harbor (near the town park).

WHERE TO STAY

Camden vies with Kennebunkport and Manchester, Vermont, for the title of bed-and-breakfast capital of New England. They're everywhere. Route 1 north of the village center— locally called High Street—is a virtual bed-and-breakfast alley, with many handsome homes converted to lodgings. Others are tucked on side streets.

Despite the preponderance of B&Bs, the total number of guest rooms (only about 300) is limited relative to the number of visitors, and during peak season lodging is tight. It's best to reserve well in advance. You might also try **Camden Accommodations and Reservations** (☎ **800/344-4830** or 207/236-6090), which offers assistance with everything from booking rooms at local B&Bs to finding cottages for seasonal rental.

If the inns and B&Bs listed below are unavailable or out of your budget, a handful of area motels and hotels may be able to accommodate you. South of the village center are the **Cedar Crest Motel,** 115 Elm St. (☎ **800/422-4964** or 207/236-4839), a handsome compound with coffee shop and a shuttle-bus connection downtown (closed winter; peak season rates $109 to $132); and long-time mainstay **Towne Motel,** 68 Elm St. (☎ **207/236-3377**), which is within walking distance of the village (open year-round; $99 to $115 double). Also right in town, just across the footbridge, is the modern if generic **Best Western Camden Riverhouse Hotel,** 11 Tannery Lane (☎ **800/755-7483** or 207/236-0500), which has an indoor pool and fitness center (open year-round; peak season $159 to $209).

One warning: High Street is a-rumble with cars and RVs during the summer months, and you may find the steady hum of traffic diminishes the small-town charm of the establishments that flank this otherwise stately, shady road. Restless sleepers should request rooms at the rear of the property.

Finally, there's camping at **Camden Hills State Park** (see "Exploring Camden," above).

The Belmont. 6 Belmont St., Camden, ME 04843. ☎ **800/238-8053** or 207/236-8053. www.thebelmontinn.com. E-mail: belmont@midcoast.com. 6 units. Peak season $115–$175 double; off-season $85–$125. Rates include full breakfast. AE, MC, V. From south on Rte. 1: Turn right at first stop sign in Camden; continue straight for 1 block; inn is on your left. From north: after passing through town on Rte. 1, turn left at blinking yellow light; continue straight for 1 block; inn is on your left. Children 12 and older are welcome.

The Belmont is in a handsome, shingle-style 1890s home with a wraparound porch set in a quiet residential neighborhood of unpretentious homes away from Route 1. The Belmont has a sense of understated, light-Victorian style throughout—the décor is more targeted toward repose than ostentation. The inn features numerous floral prints by Maine artist Jo Spiller, and there's a large guest room with great morning light named after her. All the guest rooms have polished wood floors and are furnished simply with eclectic antiques. Downstairs, there's an elegant common room with a fireplace alcove and two built-in benches; adjacent is a cozy bar with full liquor license.

Dining: The Marquis at the Belmont dining room is operated independently from the inn. Diners can choose from innovative international cuisine such as udon noodles with a gingered curry-coconut sauce, horseradish-marinated pork tenderloin with maple-glazed onions, and grilled halibut with a mango-scallion butter (entrees $16 to $24). Open for dinner daily except Sunday in summer; call for days and hours in the off-season.

Camden Harbour Inn. 83 Bayview St., Camden, ME 04843. ☎ **800/236-4266** or 207/236-4200. Fax 207/236-7063. www.camdenharbourinn.com. 22 units. TEL. Peak season $195–$255 double, including full breakfast. Off-season $105–$195, including continental breakfast. 2-night minimum in peak season. AE, DISC, MC, V. Children 12 and older are welcome. Pets OK on ground floor only.

The 1871 Camden Harbour Inn sits in a quiet neighborhood on a rise with a view of the sea and mountains beyond. It's one of the few old-fashioned Victorian-era hotels in town that hasn't been massively refurbished, and still retains something of a creaky, seaside holiday feel with lots of floral wallpaper, a mix of simple antiques and ill-advised modern furnishings, and thin towels. (Happily, the place isn't threadbare.) All rooms have private baths, most rooms have views, eight have balconies or terraces, six have wood-burning fireplaces. It's within walking distance of downtown Camden and its restaurants. The inn's first-floor restaurant was closed in 2000, but may reopen by 2001.

Camden Windward House. 6 High St., Camden, ME 04843. ☎ **207/ 236-9656.** Fax 207/230-0433. E-mail bnb@windwardhouse.com. 8 units. A/C TV TEL. Peak season $160–$230 double; off-season $99–$160 (priced $10 less midweek). All rates include full breakfast. AE, MC, V. Children 12 and older are welcome.

One of the frequent complaints about travelers staying in B&Bs on Camden's High Street is the noise from passing traffic. The Windward solved that problem in 1999 by adding a sound-muffling facade across the front of this historic 1854 house (you can't tell it's there), and installing double windows to further dampen the drone (all rooms are air-conditioned). As a result, when you walk in this historic house and close the door behind you, it feels as if you're miles away. The welcoming common rooms are decorated with a light Victorian touch, and feature a great collection of cranberry glass; in the library you'll find a guest refrigerator, icemaker, and afternoon refreshment. The guest rooms are varied in size, but all have televisions and phones with data ports. Four rooms have gas fireplaces; in 2000 the innkeepers added a two-bedroom suite with private balcony, cathedral ceiling, and a jacuzzi. Guests chose from seven or eight breakfast entrees, which are served in a pleasant dining room furnished with four maple tables.

Cedarholm Garden Bay. Route 1, Lincolnville Beach, ME 04849. ☎ **207/ 236-3886.** www.cedarholm.com. 6 units (includes 3 two-bedroom cottages). TV. Two-bedroom oceanfront cottage $250–$295 double; one-bedroom oceanfront cottage $235–$275; oceanview cottage $85–$145 double. Rates include breakfast. 2-night minimum in some cottages. Closed Dec–late Apr. MC, V.

Joyce and Barry Jobson—the daughter of the former owner and her husband—took over the inn in 1995, built a road down to the 460 feet of dramatic cobblestone shoreline, and constructed two modern, steeply gabled cedar cottages, each with two bedrooms. These are uniquely wonderful places, with great detailing like pocket doors, cobblestone fireplaces, handsome kitchenettes, and jacuzzis. They're easily among the region's most quiet and peaceful retreats. In 2001, the Jobsons added two smaller, simpler waterfront cottages suitable for couples; these lack the kitchens, fireplaces, and jacuzzis, but have microwaves and great views. Guests staying up the hill in the smaller, older cottages can still wander down to the shore and lounge on the common deck overlooking the upper reaches of Penobscot Bay. It's somewhat noisier up above, where it's closer to Route 1, and the prices reflect that.

Inn at Sunrise Point. Route 1 (P.O. Box 1344), Camden, ME 04843. ☎ **800/435-6278** or 207/236-7716. Fax 207/236-0820. www.sunrisepoint. com. E-mail: info@sunrisepoint.com. 7 units (4 in cottages). TV TEL. $195–$225 rooms; $275–$375 cottages. Rates include a full breakfast. AE, MC, V. Closed Nov–late May. No children.

This peaceful, private sanctuary 4 miles north of Camden Harbor seems a world apart from the bustling town. The service is crisp and helpful, and the setting can't be beat. Situated on the edge of Penobscot Bay down a long, tree-lined gravel road, the Inn at Sunrise Point consists of a cluster of contemporary yet classic shingled buildings set amid a nicely landscaped yard. The predominant sounds here are of birds and waves lapping at the cobblestone shore. A granite bench and Adirondack chairs on the front lawn allow guests to enjoy the bay view; breakfasts are served in a sunny conservatory. Guest rooms are spacious and comfortable and full of amenities, including fireplaces, VCRs, and individual heat controls. The cottages are at the deluxe end of the scale, and all feature double jacuzzis, fireplaces, wet bars, and private decks.

✪ **Maine Stay.** 22 High St., Camden, ME 04843. ☎ **207/236-9636.** www.mainestay.com. E-mail innkeeper@mainestay.com. 8 units. $80–$150 double including breakfast. AE, MC, V. Children over age 10 welcome.

The Maine Stay is Camden's premier bed-and-breakfast. Located in a home dating to 1802 but expanded in Greek Revival style in 1840, the Maine Stay is a classic slate-roofed New England homestead set in a shady yard within walking distance of both downtown and Camden Hills State Park. The eight guest rooms on three floors all have ceiling fans and are distinctively furnished with antiques and special decorative touches. Our favorite: the downstairs "Carriage House Room," which is away from the buzz of traffic on Route 1 and boasts its own stone patio.

The downstairs common rooms are perfect for unwinding, and the country kitchen is open to guests at all times. Hikers can set out on trails right from the yard into the Camden Hills. Perhaps the most memorable part of a stay here, however, will be the hospitality of the three hosts—Peter Smith, his wife Donny, and her twin sister, Diana Robson. The trio is genuinely interested in their guests' well-being, and they offer dozens of day trip suggestions, which are conveniently printed out from the inn's computer for guests to take with them. Of note to families is the "Stichery Suite," which occupies the whole of the third floor.

✪ **Norumbega.** 61 High St., Camden, ME 04843. ☎ **207/236-4646.** Fax 207/236-0824. www.norumbegainn.com. E-mail norumbega@acadia.net. 13 units. TEL. July–mid-Oct $160–$475 double; mid-May–June and late Oct, $125–375; Nov–mid-May $99–$295. All rates include full breakfast and evening refreshments. 2-night minimum in summer, weekends, and holidays. AE, DISC, MC, V. Children age 7 and older welcome.

You'll have no problem finding Norumbega. Just head north of the village and look for travelers pulled over taking photos of this Victorian-era stone castle overlooking the bay. The 1886 structure is both wonderfully eccentric and finely built, full of wondrous curves and angles throughout. There's extravagant carved-oak woodwork in the lobby, and a stunning oak and mahogany inlaid floor. The downstairs billiards room is the place to pretend you're a 19th-century railroad baron. (Or an information-age baron—the home was owned for a time by Hodding Carter III.)

Guest rooms have been meticulously restored and furnished with antiques. Five of the rooms have fireplaces, and the three "garden level rooms" (they're off the downstairs billiards room) have private decks. Most (not all) have televisions. Two rooms rank among the finest in New England—the "Library Suite," housed in the original two-story library with interior balcony, and the sprawling "Penthouse," with its superlative views. The inn is big enough to ensure privacy, but also intimate enough for you to get to know the other guests—mingling often occurs at breakfast, at the optional evening social hour, and in the afternoon, when the inn puts out its famous fresh-baked cookies.

Sunrise Motor Court. Rte. 1 (RR 3, Box 545), Lincolnville Beach, ME 04849. ☎ **207/236-3191.** 13 cottages (all shower only). TV. Peak season $49–$75 double. Rates include continental breakfast. DISC, MC, V. Closed Columbus Day–Memorial Day weekend. Located 4.5 miles north of Camden.

The Sunrise Motor Court, about 10 minutes north of Camden on Route 1, is a vintage 1950s-era establishment with excellent views of Penobscot Bay—though these views are regrettably across Route 1 and through a latticework of utility lines. Yet the place boasts a time-worn comfort, like a favorite old sweatshirt. The 13 cozy cottages are arrayed along a grassy hillside at the edge of a wood, and all are simply furnished with a bed and maybe a chair or two. All boast small decks and outdoor chairs, allowing guests to relax and enjoy the view. (Note that two cabins behind the manager's house lack a view.) This is a good bet for budget-conscious travelers who want to spend some time in the Camden area, yet not spend a small fortune doing so.

Whitehall Inn. 52 High St., Camden, ME 04843. ☎ **800/789-6565** or 207/236-3391. Fax 207/236-4427. www.whitehall-inn.com. E-mail stay@whitehall-inn.com. 50 units (8 units share 4 bathrooms). July–late Oct $165–$190 double with private bathroom, including breakfast and dinner ($150 with breakfast only); $140 shared bathroom, including breakfast and dinner ($105 breakfast only). Discounts in late May and June. AE, MC, V. Closed late Oct–late May.

The Whitehall is a venerable Camden establishment, the sort of place you half expect to find the young Cary Grant in a blue blazer tickling the ivories on the 1904 Steinway in the lobby. Set at the edge of town on Route 1 in a structure that dates to 1834, this three-story inn has a striking architectural integrity with its columns, gables, and long roofline. This is the place you think of when you think of the classic New England summer inn. The only downside is its location on Route 1—the traffic noise tends to persist through the evening then start up early in the morning. (Ask for a room away from the road.)

Inside, the antique furnishings—including the handsome Seth Thomas clock, oriental carpets, and cane-seated rockers on the front porch—are impeccably well cared for. Guest rooms are simple but appealing; only some rooms have phones. The Whitehall also occupies a minor footnote in the annals of American literature—a young local poet recited her poems here for guests in 1912, stunning the audience with her eloquence. Her name? Edna St. Vincent Millay.

Dining: The Whitehall's dining room boasts a slightly faded glory and service that occasionally limps along, but remains a good destination for reliable New England fare like scallops with basil and cherry tomatoes, and grilled lamb loin with rosemary and caramelized garlic (entrees $15.75 to $18.) Of course, there's always boiled Maine lobster.

Amenities: Tennis court, tour desk, nature trails, conference rooms, baby-sitting, guest safe, afternoon tea.

WHERE TO DINE

Atlantica. 1 Bayview Landing. ☎ **207/236-6011.** Reservations suggested. Main courses, $16–$28. AE, MC, V. Tues–Sat 5:30–9pm (open Sun also June–Aug). SEAFOOD/ECLECTIC.

Atlantica gets high marks for its innovative seafood menu and its consistently well-prepared fare under new management; executive chef Ken Paquin is a graduate of the Culinary Institute of America, and has been executive chef at a number of larger establishments, including the Equinox in Vermont. Located on the waterfront with a small indoor seating area and an equally small deck, Atlantica features subtly creative fare like pan-seared tuna with artichoke and smoked tomatoes, and scallops glazed with ginger and brown sugar. Our recommendation: start with a cup or bowl of the lobster-corn chowder. The restaurant may reopen for lunch in 2001; it's worth calling ahead to check.

Cappy's Chowder House. 1 Main St. ☎ **207/236-2254.** Main courses, lunch and dinner $5.95–$13.95. MC, V. Daily 7:30am–midnight. SEAFOOD/AMERICAN.

"People always remember their meal here," say fans of Cappy's, a local institution smack in the middle of Camden. Travelers—especially families—tend to drift in here more to drink up the atmosphere than to sample rarified cuisine. Prime rib is served every day, there's a hearty seafood stew flavored with kielbasa, and there's also the famous chowder (it's been noted by *Gourmet* magazine). "Old-time sodas" are also a specialty, and often a favorite with kids. The Crow's Nest upstairs is a bit quieter and offers glimpses of the harbor. Cappy's is well worth a stop if you're looking for a reasonably priced and filling meal, and you don't expect to be treated like a member of the House of Windsor.

Cork Restaurant. 51 Bayview St. ☎ **207/230-0533.** Reservations recommended. Main courses $16–$24. AE, DISC, MC, V. Summer daily 5:30–9pm; off-season closed Sun–Tues. WINE BAR.

Cork is hidden down at the far end of Bayview Street, but it's worth the walk. The two-story restaurant—a sort of blue-jeans-and-sports-coats-on-men kind of place—has a welcoming lounge on the first floor, and a dramatic upstairs dining room with bold colors, a soaring ceiling, and contemporary art on the walls. The menu leaves behind the standard seafood fare more typical of Camden; self-taught chef Aimee Ricca features dishes like lobster risotto, ostrich fillet with grilled red onions, and herb-crusted rack of lamb. Cork is on the high end of the price scale for the area; if you've budgeted for just one big night out, I'd opt for a drive to Primo in Rockland, about 20 minutes south (see p. 122).

Marriner's Restaurant. 35 Main St., Camden. ☎ **207/236-2647.** Breakfast $3.75–$5.95; lunch $4.25–$11.95 (mostly under $7). MC, V. Mon–Sat 6am–3pm. LUNCHEONETTE.

"The last local luncheonette" is how Marriner's sums itself up, along with the legend "Down Home, Down East, No Ferns, No Quiche." As you might guess, this is a fairly small and simple affair, done up in a not-very-subtle nautical theme with pine booths and vinyl seats, some of which are held together with duct tape. (Another sign: "Come on in, the locals will enjoy your accent.") Marriner's has been dishing up filling breakfasts and lunch since 1942, and it's the place for early risers to get a quick start on the day—those getting here later in summer will likely find themselves facing a wait. Lunches are basic and good, and include burgers, franks, egg salad sandwiches, and homemade clam and fish chowders. The lobster and crab rolls are both superb, as are the homemade pies.

Peter Ott's. 16 Bayview St., Camden. ☎ **207/236-4032.** Main courses $13.95–$22.95. MC, V. Daily 5:30–9:30pm. AMERICAN.

Peter Ott's has attracted a steady stream of satisfied local customers and repeat-visitor yachtsmen since it opened smack in the middle of Camden in 1974. While it poses as a steak house with its simple wooden tables and chairs and its manly meat dishes (like charbroiled Black Angus with mushrooms and onions, and sirloin steak dijonaise), it's grown beyond that to satisfy more diverse tastes. In fact, the restaurant offers some of the better prepared seafood in town, including a pan-blackened seafood sampler and grilled salmon served with a lemon caper sauce. Be sure to leave room for the specialty coffees and notable desserts, including a lemon-almond crumb tart.

Sea Dog Brewing Co. 43 Mechanic St., Camden. ☎ **207/236-6863.** Main courses $6.95–$12.95. AE, DISC, MC, V. Daily 11:30am–9pm (kitchen closed 2–5pm off-season). Located at Knox Mill one block west of Elm St. PUB FARE.

This is one of a handful of brew pubs that have found quick acceptance in Maine, and it makes a reasonable destination for quick pub food like nachos or hamburgers. It won't set your taste buds dancing, but it will satisfy basic cravings. On the ground floor of an old woolen mill that's been renovated by MBNA (a national credit card company), the restaurant has a pleasing, comfortable atmosphere with its booths, handsome bar, and views through tall windows of the old millrace. The beers are consistently excellent, especially the Hazelnut Porter.

The Waterfront. Bayview St. on Camden Harbor. ☎ **207/236-3747.** Main courses, lunch $6.95–$13.95; dinner $12.95–$22.95. AE, MC, V. Daily 11:30am–2:30pm and 5–10pm. Closes earlier in off-season. SEAFOOD.

The Waterfront disproves the restaurant rule of thumb that "the better the view, the worse the food." Here you can watch multimillion-dollar yachts and handsome windjammers come and go (angle for a harborside seat on the deck), yet still be pleasantly surprised by the food. The house specialty is fresh seafood of all kinds. Lunch and dinner menus are an enterprising mix of old-favorites and creative originals. On the old-favorites side are fried clams, crab cakes, boiled lobster, and a fisherman's platter piled with fried seafood. On the more adventurous side, is black sesame shrimp salad (served on noodles with a Thai vinaigrette), or seafood linguini with shrimp, mussels, squid, and caramelized balsamic onions. More earthbound fare for non-seafood eaters includes burgers, pitas, and strip steaks. A lighter pub menu is available between 2:30 and 5pm.

3 Belfast to Bucksport

The northerly stretch of Penobscot Bay is rich in history, especially maritime history. In the mid–19th century, Belfast and Searsport produced more than their share of ships, along with the captains to pilot them on trading ventures around the globe. In 1856 alone, 24 ships of more than 1,000 tons were launched from Belfast. The now-sleepy village of Searsport once had 17 active shipyards, which turned out some 200 ships over the years.

When shipbuilding died out, the Belfast area was sustained by a thriving poultry industry. Alas, that too declined as the industry moved south. In recent decades, the area has attracted artisans of various stripes, who sell their wares at various shops. Tourists tend to pass through the region quickly, en route from the tourist enclave of Camden to the tourist enclave of Bar Harbor. It's worth slowing down for.

ESSENTIALS
GETTING THERE
Route 1 connects Belfast, Searsport, and Bucksport.

VISITOR INFORMATION
The **Belfast Area Chamber of Commerce,** P.O. Box 58, Belfast, ME 04915 (☎ **207/338-5900**), staffs an information booth at 17 Main St. near the waterfront park that's open May to November daily, 10am to 6pm. Further north, try the **Bucksport Bay Area Chamber of Commerce,** 263 Main St. (P.O. Box 1880), Bucksport, ME 04416 (☎ **207/469-6818**). Self-serve information is available 24 hours a day; the office is staffed three days weekly (days vary).

EXPLORING THE REGION
En route from Camden to Belfast on Route 1, you'll drive through the community of Lincolnville Beach. There's a popular roadside lobster restaurant just off the beach; a short drive off the highway is the **Kelmscott Rare Breeds Foundation** (☎ **207/763-4088;** www.kelmscott.org). The nonprofit foundation is devoted to conserving endangered livestock breeds, like Gloucestershire old spots pigs and Cotswold sheep. Learn more about these and other animals (poultry, goats, and ponies, among them) during a visit to the information center and farm. The farm is open to the public daily except Monday. Hours from May to October are 10am to 5pm; from November to April it's open 10am to 3pm. Admission is $5 for adults, $3 for children 4 to 15, free for children under 4.

To reach the farm, head west on Route 173 from Lincolnville Beach and continue to Lincolnville Center; turn right on Route 52 and drive for about two miles to Van Cycle road; turn left and follow signs.

In Belfast, splendid historic homes may be viewed by veering off Route 1 and approaching downtown via High Street (look for the first "Downtown Belfast" sign). The **Primrose Hill District** along High Street was the most fashionable place for prosperous merchants to settle during the early and mid-19th century, and their stately homes reflect an era when stature was equal to both the size of one's home and the care one took in designing and embellishing it. Downtown Belfast also has some superb examples of historic brick commercial architecture, including the elaborate High Victorian Gothic–style building on Main Street that formerly housed the Belfast National Bank.

Near Belfast's small waterfront park you can take a diverting excursion on the scenic **Belfast and Moosehead Lake Railroad** (☎ 800/392-5500 or 207/948-5500). The railroad was chartered in 1867 and financed primarily by the town; in fact, until 1991 the B&ML railroad was the only railroad in the nation owned by a municipality. (It was also then locally called the "Broken and Mended.") The rail line was subsequently purchased by entrepreneurs, who have spruced it up considerably. The fleet features 11 vintage rail cars from Sweden, including a 1913 steam locomotive, and offers tours on the 33-mile rail line from both the village of Unity and downtown Belfast. (If you have your heart set on a steam locomotive, head to Unity; the Belfast train runs on diesel.)

The 1½-hour tour offers a wonderful glimpse of inland Maine and its thick forests and rich farmland. (The train also edges along Passagassawakeag River, a name which provokes considerable mirth in all but the most melancholy of children.) The Unity train features a dining car, where beer and wine may be purchased. Excursions run from mid-May to mid-October; call for hours and more information. The fare is $16 for adults, $12 for teens (12 to 17), and $8 for children (3 to 12), free for children under 3.

If you'd like to explore the Passagassawakeag by water, call Harvey Schiller at **Belfast Kayak Tours** (☎ 207/382-6204), or just show up at the Belfast City Pier boat ramp. With a great deal of charm and even more enthusiasm, Harvey will provide paddle instruction and take you out for a guided tour. Trips last 1½ hours; cost $25 for adults, $15 for kids 12 and under; and are available from 9am to 6pm daily except Wednesdays from July to Labor Day. Call for off-season hours, prices on longer tours, and group rates.

At the northern tip of Penobscot Bay, the Penobscot River squeezes through a dramatic gorge near Verona Island, which Route 1 spans on an attractive suspension bridge. This easily defended pinch in the river was perceived to be of strategic importance in the 1840s, when solid and imposing **Fort Knox** was constructed. While it was never attacked, the fort was manned during the Civil and Spanish-American wars, and today is run as a state park (☎ **207/469-7719**). It's an impressive edifice to explore, with graceful granite staircases and subterranean chambers that produce wonderful echoes. Admission is $2 for adults, 50¢ for children under 12.

Across the river from Fort Knox in the paper mill town of Bucksport is **Northeast Historic Film** (☎ **800/639-1636** or 207/469-0924), an organization founded in 1986 and dedicated to preserving and showing early films related to New England. In 1992 the group bought Bucksport's Alamo Theatre, which was built in 1916 and closed (after a showing of *Godzilla*) in 1956. Films are shown weekends in the renovated theater; call or check the group's website (www. oldfilm.org) to see what's coming up. Visitors can also stop by the store at the front of the theater (open Monday to Friday 9am to 4pm) to browse through videos and other items.

THE SEAFARING LIFE

✪ **Penobscot Marine Museum.** Church St. at Rte. 1, Searsport. ☎ **207/548-2529.** Adults $6, seniors $5, children 7–15 $2. Memorial Day–mid-Oct Mon–Sat 10am–5pm, Sun noon–5pm. Last ticket sold at 4pm.

The Penobscot Marine Museum is one of the best small museums in New England. Housed in a cluster of eight historic buildings atop a gentle rise in tiny downtown Searsport, the museum does a deft job in educating visitors about the vitality of the local shipbuilding industry, the essential role of international trade to daily life in the 19th century, and the hazards of life at sea. The exhibits are uncommonly well organized, and wandering from building to building induces a keen sense of wonderment at the vast enterprise that was Maine's maritime trade.

Among the more intriguing exhibits is a wide selection of dramatic marine paintings (including one stunning rendition of whaling in the Arctic), black and white photographs of many of the 286 weathered sea captains who once called Searsport home, exceptional photographs of a 1902 voyage to Argentina, and an early home decorated in the style of a sea captain, complete with lacquered furniture and accessories hauled back from trade missions to the Orient. Throughout, the curators do a fine job of both educating and entertaining visitors. It's well worth the price if you're the least interested in Maine's rich culture of the sea.

WHERE TO STAY

✪ **The White House.** 1 Church St., Belfast. ☎ **888/290-1901** or 207/338-1901. Fax 207/338-5161. www.mainebb.com. E-mail: whitehouse@mainebb.com. 6 units (1 with private hall bathroom). TEL. Peak season $90–$150 double including full breakfast. DISC, MC, V.

This architecturally stunning Greek Revival home is just a 10-minute walk from downtown Belfast, and offers more B&B than you might expect for the rates, which are rather average. Originally built as a sea captain's home in the 1840s and topped with a striking eight-sided cupola, the James P. White House was exquisitely refurnished, painted, wallpapered, by the three innkeepers. Downstairs, guests have the run of a library, an elegant parlor area, and a dining room where the hearty breakfasts are served. Few guests won't feel as if they're living large here. All bedrooms (two with TVs) have private bathrooms with hair dryer and gorgeously soft Egyptian cotton towels and robes. One of the nicest (and also the priciest) is the "Belfast Bay," an over-the-top Louis XVI–style room, with fireplace, whirlpool, and water views. Less fancy but no less appealing is the "Copperbeech Suite," located at the back of the house and featuring a sitting room and old pumpkin pine floors.

WHERE TO DINE

Darby's. 155 High St., Belfast. ☎ **207/338-2339.** Reservations suggested after 7pm. Main courses $3.95–$8.95 lunch, $5.75–$13.95 dinner. AE, DC, DISC, MC. V. Mon–Sat 11:30am–3:30pm, and 5–9pm; Sun 12–3:30pm and 5–8:30pm. AMERICAN/ECLECTIC.

Located in a Civil War–era pub with attractive stamped tin ceilings and a beautiful back bar with Corinthian columns, Darby's is a popular local hangout that boasts a comfortable, neighborhood-y feel. Order up a Maine microbrew or a single-malt whisky while you peruse the menu, which is more creative than you might expect for the pubby surroundings. Darby's not only serves up basic bar favorites like burgers and Cajun chicken on a bulkie roll, but also inventive dishes like mahogany duck and a steak and crispy onion sandwich. The desserts are all homemade and tend toward the basic, with cheesecake, pies, and a decidedly undietetic Scottish toffee pudding cake. If you like the artwork on the wall, ask about it. It's probably painted by a local artist, and it's probably for sale.

MacLeod's. Main St., Bucksport. ☎ **207/469-3963.** Reservations recommended on weekends and in summer. Main courses $4.95–$10.95 lunch, $8.95–$14.95 dinner. AE, DC, MC, V. Mon–Fri 11:30am–9pm, Sat–Sun 5–9pm (closed Sun evenings in off-season). ECLECTIC HOMESTYLE.

MacLeod's is a comfortable, pubby place in downtown Bucksport that teems on weekends with Bucksport residents—from workers at the pulp mill to local businessmen. With its simple wood tables, Windsor chairs, and relentlessly upbeat background music, MacLeod's won't be confused with a place for fancy dining, but it does offer good meals, sizable portions, and consistent quality. For dinner, entrees include grilled lamb shish kabob, raspberry chicken, baked sea scallops, or a unique "lasagne al pescatore," made with shrimp, scallops, and crabmeat with a rich lobster sauce.

The Rhumb Line. 200 East Main St. (Rte. 1), Searsport. ☎ **207/548-2600.** Reservations suggested. Main courses $18–$24. MC, V. Open year-round, daily in summer 6–9pm; call for off-season hours. NEW AMERICAN.

The Rhumb Line features locally grown ingredients—the tomatoes and basil in a mozzarella salad had just been picked from the garden in back of the inn, and the tender horseradish-crusted salmon (served with a remoulade) was farmed in nearby Ellsworth. If you're not in the mood to start with one of the fresh salads, try the wonderful smoky-flavored lentil and chicken soup. As far as entrees go, avoid the cream-laden pasta dishes, which can be on the heavy side, and stick with favorites like grilled rack of lamb with blackberry mint vinegar, or the sautéed fillet of haddock with roasted garlic, basil oil, and olives.

Twilight Cafe. Route 1, East Belfast (across from Perry's Nut House). ☎ **207/338-0937.** Sunday brunch $9–$12; dinner entrees $16–$25. AE, DISC, MC, V. Mon–Sat 5–9pm; Sun 11am–3pm. Closed Oct 15–May 15. NEW AMERICAN.

It's easy to zip by the well-regarded Twilight Cafe when cruising up Route 1—it looks more like a hamburger joint than one of northern Penobscot Bay's more sophisticated eateries. The interior of the restaurant, which opened in April 2000, is small, basic, and unexceptional. The food, however, sings and has attracted a happy repeat clientele. The dinner offerings are eclectic, and few will fail to find something that appeals— pecan-crusted lobster cakes with crème fraîche, Caribbean jerk shrimp with citrus linguini, or lamb chops with shallots, mustard, and mint. There's a small wine list.

6

Blue Hill Peninsula

*T*he Blue Hill Peninsula is a back roads paradise. If you're of a mind to get lost on country lanes that suddenly dead-end at the sea or inexplicably start to loop back on themselves, this is the place. In contrast to the western shores of Penobscot Bay, the Blue Hill Peninsula attracts few tourists, and has more of a lost-in-time character. The roads are hilly, winding, and narrow, passing through leafy forests, along venerable saltwater farms, and touching on the edge of an azure inlet here or there. By and large it's overlooked by the majority of Maine's tourists, especially those who like their itineraries well-structured and their destinations clear and simple.

1 Castine & Environs

Castine gets my vote for the most gracious village in Maine. It's not so much the stunningly handsome, meticulously maintained mid-19th-century homes that fill the side streets. Nor is it the location on a quiet peninsula, 16 miles south of tourist-clotted Route 1. No, what lends Castine most of its charm are the splendid, towering elm trees, which still overarch many of the village streets. Before Dutch elm disease ravaged the nation's tree-lined streets, much of America once looked like this, and it's easy to slip into a debilitating nostalgia for this most graceful tree, even if you're too young to remember the America of the elms. Through perseverance and a measure of luck, Castine has managed to keep several hundred elms alive, and it's worth the drive here for this alone.

For American history buffs, Castine offers more than trees. This outpost served as a strategic town in various battles among British, Dutch, French, and feisty colonials in the centuries following its settlement in 1613. It was occupied by each of those groups at some point, and historical personages like Miles Standish and Paul Revere passed through during one epoch or another. The town has a dignified, aristocratic bearing, and it somehow seems appropriate that

Tory-dominated Castine welcomed the British with open arms during the Revolution.

An excellent brief history of Castine by Elizabeth J. Duff is published in brochure form by the Castine Merchant's Association. The brochure, which also includes a walking tour of Castine, is entitled "Welcome to Castine" and is available at several shops in town, at the town hall, and at most state information centers.

Castine is most likely to appeal to those who can entertain themselves. It's a peaceful place to sit and read, or take an afternoon walk. If it's outlet shopping or cute boutiques you're looking for, you're better off moving on. "This is not Bar Harbor," one local innkeeper noted dryly.

ESSENTIALS
GETTING THERE

Castine is located 16 miles south of Route 1. Turn south on Route 175 in Orland (east of Bucksport) and follow this to Route 166, which winds its way to Castine. Route 166A offers an alternate route along Penobscot Bay.

VISITOR INFORMATION

Castine lacks a formal information center, but the clerk at the **Town Office** (☎ **207/326-4502**) is often helpful with local questions.

EXPLORING CASTINE

One of the town's more intriguing attractions is the **Wilson Museum** (days, ☎ **207/326-8753,** or between 5 and 9pm call the curator at ☎ **207/326-8545**) on Perkins St., an appealing and quirky anthropological museum constructed in 1921. This small museum contains the collections of John Howard Wilson, an archeologist and collector of prehistoric artifacts from around the globe. His gleanings are neatly arranged in a staid, classical arrangement of the sort that proliferated in the late 19th and early 20th centuries. The museum is open from end of May to the end of September daily except Monday 2 to 5pm; admission is free.

Next door is the **John Perkins House,** Castine's oldest home. It was occupied by the British during the Revolution and the War of 1812, and a tour features demonstrations of old-fashioned cooking techniques. The Perkins House is open

July and August on Wednesday and Sunday only from 2 to 5pm. Admission is $2.

Castine is also home to the **Maine Maritime Academy** (☎ 207/326-4311), which trains sailors for the rigors of life at sea with the merchant marine. The campus is on the western edge of the village, and the 498-foot vessel *T.V. State of Maine,* the hulking gray training ship, is often docked in Castine, all but overwhelming the village. Free half-hour tours of the ship are offered in summer (assuming the ship is in port) from 10am to noon, and 1 to 4pm.

Also worth exploring is **Dyce's Head Light** at the extreme western end of Battle Avenue. While the 1828 light itself is no longer operating and not open to the public, it's well worth scrambling down the trail to the rocky shoreline along the Penobscot River just beneath the lighthouse. A small sign indicates the start of the public trail.

ON THE WATER

This is a lovely, open harbor, with open land and forest edging the watery expanse. A couple of options exists for cruising on the water.

Castine Kayak Adventures (☎ 207/326-9045; www.castinekayak.com), offers six-hour ($105) and three-hour ($55) sea kayak tours departing from Dennett's Wharf restaurant. Both trips are appropriate for those without experience; a brief intro will get you started with this graceful and often meditative sport. You'll often spot wildlife, like bald eagles, harbor seals, and ospreys. The six-hour tour includes a bag lunch. Ask also about the two-hour sunset tours ($40), and the nighttime paddles ($45), when you can watch the bioluminescence trail behind your boat like the Milky Way.

Smoke on the water? That's likely to be the 30-foot *Laurie Ellen,* which claims to be "the nation's only wood-powered, steam-driven passenger launch inspected and approved by the U.S. Coast Guard." It was launched in 1999 by Capt. Randy Flood, who's the guy behind the **Castine Steamboat Co.** The unique boat has a striped canopy and will hold up to 18 passengers. Tours of the harbor run one-hour and are offered five times daily from late June to Labor Day, sailing from Dennett's Wharf, next to the town landing. Tickets are $17.50 adult, $10 children. Call ☎ 207/374-2536 (or contact Randy via his cell phone aboard the boat during the summer: **207/266-2841**). Randy's web site is www.castinesteamboat. com.

A TOUR OF CAPE ROSIER

Across the Bagaduce River from Castine is Cape Rosier, one of Maine's better-kept secrets. The bad news is, to reach the cape you need to backtrack to Route 175, head south toward Deer Isle, then follow Route 176 to the turnoff to Cape Rosier— about 18 miles of driving to cross 1 mile of water. As a dead-end peninsula, there's no through traffic and roads suddenly turn to dirt in sections. The cape still has a wild, unkempt flavor with salty views of Penobscot Bay; it's not hard to imagine that you're back in Maine of the 1940s.

A loop of 15 miles or so around the cape starting on Goose Falls Road is suitable for travel by mountain bike or as a leisurely car trip. The views are uncommonly beautiful, with a mix of blueberry barrens, boreal forest, farmsteads, summer estate houses, and coves dotted with yachts and lobster boats. There's virtually no commercial development of any sort. It's no accident that Helen and Scott Nearing, the late back-to-the-land gurus and authors of *Living the Good Life,* chose to settle here when Vermont became too developed for their tastes. A number of Nearing acolytes continue to live on Cape Rosier.

If the weather's agreeable, stop for a walk on the state-owned **Holbrook Island Wildlife Sanctuary,** a 1,200-acre preserve laced with trails and abandoned roads. The sanctuary is located at the northern end of the cape (look for signs). Among the choices: the Backshore Trail passes along open meadows to the shoreline; and the Summit Trail is all mossy, mushroomy, and medieval, with teasing glimpses of the water from the top.

WHERE TO STAY

Castine Harbor Lodge. Perkins St (P.O. Box 215), Castine, ME 04421. ☎ **207/326-4335.** www.castinemaine.com. E-mail: chl@acadia.net. 9 units (2 share 1 bathroom; 1 with private hall bathroom). $75–$150 double. Rates include continental breakfast. DC, DISC, MC, V. Pets allowed ($10 per night).

This is a great spot for families. Housed in a grand 1893 mansion (the only inn on the water in Castine), it's run with an informal good cheer that allows kids to feel at home amid the regal architecture. The main parlor is dominated by a pool table, and there's Scrabble and Nintendo for the asking. The spacious rooms are eclectically furnished, with some antiques and some modern. Two of the guest rooms share an adjoining bathroom—of note to traveling families. The family dog is welcome. And if you're not traveling with a family? It's still a great spot if you prefer a well-worn comfort to high-end elegance. Last word: the bathrooms have the best views of any in the state.

Castine Inn. Main St. (P.O. Box 41), Castine, ME 04421. ☎ **207/326-4365.** Fax 207/326-4570. www.castineinn.com. E-mail: relax@castineinn.com. 19 units. $85–$135 double ($210 suite). Rates include full breakfast. 2-night minimum in July and Aug. MC, V. Closed mid-Dec–May. Children 8 and older are welcome.

The Castine Inn is a Maine Coast rarity—a hotel that was originally built as a hotel (not as a residence), in this case in 1898. This handsome cream-colored village inn, designed in an eclectic Georgian-Federal–revival style, has a fine front porch and attractive gardens. Inside, the lobby takes its cue from the 1940s, with wingback chairs and loveseats and a fireplace in the parlor. There's also an intimate, dark lounge decked out in rich green hues, reminiscent of an Irish pub. The guest rooms on the two upper floors are attractively if unevenly furnished in early-American style—the innkeepers are revamping the rooms one by one to an even gloss, even adding luxe touches. Until they're all renovated, it may be wise to ask to view the available rooms before you sign in.

Dining: The elegant dining room serves up Castine's best fare, and some of the best food in the state. The Chef/owner, Tom Gutow, served stints at Bouley and Verbena in New York. The menu changes nightly with ingredients varying by the season, but you might expect to find dishes such as lobster with vanilla butter, mango mayonnaise and tropical fruit salsa, or lamb loin with eggplant, green lentils, tomatoes, and rosemary jus. Entrees range from $15 to $26. One night each week they offer a buffet; you're better off that night heading to Dennett's Wharf (see below).

Pentagöet Inn. Main St. (P.O. Box 4), Castine, ME 04421. ☎ **800/845-1701** or 207/326-8616. Fax 207/326-9382. www.pentagoet.com. E-mail: pentagoet@hypernet.com. 16 units (2 with private hallway bathrooms). $80–$150 double, including full breakfast. MC, V. Closed Mar–Apr. Pets by reservation. Suitable for older children only.

Here's the big activity at the Pentagöet: Sit on the wraparound front porch on cane-seated rockers and watch the slow-paced activity on Main Street. That's not likely to be overly appealing to those looking for a fast-paced vacation, but it's the perfect salve for someone seeking respite from urban life. This quirky yellow and green 1894 structure with its prominent turret is tastefully furnished downstairs with hardwood floors, oval braided rugs, and a wood stove. It's comfortable without being overly fussy, professional without being chilly, personal without being overly intimate. The rooms on the upper two floors of the main house are furnished eclectically, with a mix of antiques and collectibles. The five guest rooms in the adjacent Perkins Street building—a more austere Federal-era house—are furnished simply and feature painted floors. There's no air conditioning, but all rooms have ceiling or window fans.

Dining: The inn's first floor features the cozy Passports Pub and a dining room with delightful outdoor seating in summer. Meals are a mix of the regional and global—chicken pot pie and Spanish seafood stew, for example. The restaurant is open daily in summer, limited days during the off-season. Entrees are priced from $9.95 to $19.95.

WHERE TO DINE

The best dinner in town is at the Castine Inn (see above). For lunch or more informal dinner fare, try the following.

Dennett's Wharf. Sea St. (next to the Town Dock). ☎ **207/326-9045.** Reservations recommended in summer and for parties of 6 or more. Lunch $5.50–$17.95; dinner $8.95–$17.95. AE, DISC, MC, V. Daily 11am–midnight. Closed mid-Oct–Apr 30. PUB FARE.

Located in a soaring waterfront sail loft with dollar bills tacked all over the high ceiling, Dennett's Wharf offers upscale bar food amid a lively setting leavened with a good selection of microbrews. If the weather's decent, there's outside dining under a bright yellow awning with superb harbor views. Look for grilled sandwiches, roll-ups, and salads at lunch; dinner includes lobster, stir-fry, and steak teriyaki. And how did all those bills get on the ceiling? Ask your server. It will cost you exactly $1 to find out.

2 Deer Isle

Deer Isle is well off the beaten path, but worth the long detour off Route 1 if your tastes run to pastoral countryside with a nautical edge. Loopy, winding roads cross through forest and farmland, and travelers are rewarded with sudden glimpses of the sun-dappled ocean and mint-green coves. An occasional settlement crops up now and again.

Deer Isle doesn't cater exclusively to tourists, as many coastal regions do. It's still occupied by fifth-generation fishermen, farmers, longtime rusticators, and artists who prize their seclusion. The village of Deer Isle has a handful of inns and galleries, but its primary focus is to serve locals and summer residents, not transients. The village of Stonington, on the southern tip, is a rough-hewn sea town. Despite serious incursions the past five years by galleries and enterprises dependent on seasonal tourism, it remains dominated in spirit by fishermen and the occasional quarry worker.

ESSENTIALS
GETTING THERE

Deer Isle is accessible via several winding country roads from Route 1. Coming from the west, head south on Route 175 off Route 1 in Orland, then connect to Route 15 to Deer Isle. From the east, head south on Route 172 to Blue Hill, where you can pick up Route 15. Deer Isle is connected to the mainland via a high, narrow, and graceful suspension bridge, built in 1938, which can be somewhat harrowing to cross in high winds.

VISITOR INFORMATION

The **Deer Isle-Stonington Chamber of Commerce** (☎ 207/ 348-6124) staffs a seasonal information booth just beyond the bridge on Little Deer Isle. The booth is open daily in summer from 10am to 4pm, depending on volunteer availability.

EXPLORING DEER ISLE

Deer Isle, with its network of narrow roads to nowhere, is ideal for perfunctory rambling. It's a pleasure to explore by car, and is also inviting to travel by bike, although hasty and careening fishermen in pickups can make this unnerving at times. Especially tranquil is the narrow road between Deer Isle and Sunshine to the east. Plan to stop and explore the rocky coves and inlets along the way. To get here, head toward Stonington on Route 15. Just south of the village of Deer Isle, turn east toward Stinson Neck and continue along this scenic byway for about 10 miles over bridges and causeways.

Along this road, watch for the **Haystack Mountain School of Crafts** (☎ 207/348-2306). The campus of this respected summer crafts school is stunning. Designed in the early 1960s by Edward Larrabee Barnes, the campus is set on a steep hillside overlooking the cerulean waters of Jericho Bay. Barnes cleverly managed to play up the views while respecting the delicate landscape by building a series of small buildings on pilings that seem to float above the earth. The classrooms and studios are linked by boardwalks, many of which are connected to a wide central staircase, ending at the "Flag Deck," a sort of open-air commons just above the shoreline.

The buildings and classrooms are closed to the public, but summer visitors are welcome to walk to the Flag Deck and stroll the nature trail adjacent to the campus. There's also one public tour weekly June to August Wednesdays at 1pm, during which you can catch glimpses of the studios. Donations are appreciated. Call for further information.

Stonington, at the very southern tip of Deer Isle, consists of one commercial street that wraps along the harbor's edge. While bed-and-breakfasts and boutiques have made some inroads here, it's still mostly a rough-and-tumble waterfront town with strong links to the sea, and you're likely to observe lots of activity in the harbor as lobster boats come and go. If you hear industrial sounds emanating from just offshore, that's probably the stone quarry on Crotch Island, which has been supplying architectural granite to builders nationwide for more than a century.

You can learn more about the stone industry at the **Deer Isle Granite Museum** on Main Street (☎ **207/367-6331**). The museum features some historical artifacts from the quarry's golden years, but the real draw is a working diorama (8 by 15 feet) of Crotch Island as it would have appeared around 1900. It features a little railroad, little boats, and little cranes moving little stones around. Kids under 10 years old find it endlessly fascinating. The museum is open from late May to August daily 10am to 5pm. (Sunday it opens at 1pm.) Donations are requested.

A DAY TRIP TO ISLE AU HAUT

Rocky and remote Isle au Haut offers the most unusual hiking and camping experience in northern New England. This 6- by 3-mile island, located 6 miles south of Stonington, was originally named Ille Haut—or High Island—in 1604 by French explorer Samuel de Champlain. The name and its pronunciation evolved—today, it's generally pronounced "aisle-a-ho"—but the island itself has remained steadfastly unchanged over the centuries.

About half of the island is owned by the National Park Service and maintained as an outpost of Acadia National Park (see chapter 7). A 60-passenger "mailboat" makes a stop in the morning and late afternoon at Duck Harbor, allowing for a solid day of hiking while still returning to Stonington by nightfall. At Duck Harbor the NPS also maintains a cluster of five Adirondack-style lean-tos, which are available for overnight camping. Advance reservations are essential: Contact **Acadia National Park,** Bar Harbor, ME 04609, or call ☎ **207-288-3338.** The park doesn't charge a fee to explore its island holdings.

One-half of the island is privately owned, some by fishermen who can trace their island ancestry back three centuries, and some by summer rusticators whose forebears discovered the bucolic splendor of Isle au Haut in the 1880s. The summer population of the island is about 300, with about 50 die-hards remaining year-round. The mailboat also stops at the small harborside village, which has a few old homes, a handsome church, and tiny schoolhouse, post office, and store. Day-trippers will be better served ferrying straight to Duck Harbor.

The **Isle au Haut Boat Company** operates a ferry (☎ **207/367-6516;** www.isleauhaut.com) to the island, which leaves from the pier at the end of Sea Breeze Avenue in Stonington. In summer (mid-June to mid-September), the *Miss Lizzie* departs for the village of Isle au Haut daily at 7am, 11:30am, and 4:30pm; the *Mink* departs for Duck Harbor daily at 10am and 4:30pm. (Limited trips go to Isle au Haut the remainder of the year.) The round-trip boat fare to either village or Duck Harbor is $26 for adults and $12 for Children under 12. The crossing takes about 45 minutes to the village, one hour to Duck Harbor. Reservations are not accepted; it's best to arrive at least a half an hour before departure. The ferry has been working to set up online reservations; check the company's web site (www.isleauhaut.com) for the status.

SEA KAYAKING & BOATING ALONG "MERCHANT'S ROW"

Peer southward from Stonington and you'll see dozens of spruce-studded islands between the mainland and the dark, distant ridges of Isle au Haut. These islands, ringed with salmon-pink granite, are collectively called Merchant's Row, and they're invariably ranked by experienced coastal boaters as among the most beautiful in the state. Thanks to these exceptional islands, Stonington is among Maine's most popular destinations for sea kayaking. Many of the islands are open to day visitors and overnight camping, and one of the Nature Conservancy islands even hosts a flock of sheep. Experienced kayakers should contact the **Maine Island Trail Association** (☎ **207/596-6456** or 207/761-8225) for more information about paddling here; several of the islands are open only to association members.

Old Quarry Charters (☎ **207/367-8977**), just outside the village of Stonington, offers guided kayak tours, as well as kayaks for rent. (Old Quarry will rent only to those with prior experience, so it's best to call ahead to discuss your needs.) Tours range from two hours ($27) to a full day, seven-hour tour that weaves out through the islands and includes a stop for a swim at an abandoned quarry ($100). Overnight camping trips are also offered. Other services: parking and a launch site for those who've brought their own boats ($5 per boat), sailboat tours and lessons, charter tours aboard a 38-foot lobster boat, a three-suite bed-and-breakfast ($160 to $200), and camping ($20 per couple). For more information, visit the web: www.oldquarrycharters.com.

Outfitters based outside the region that offer guided overnight kayak trips around Merchant's Row include **Maine Island Kayak Co.** (☎ **800/796-2373** or 207/766-2373; www.maineislandkayak.com) or **Maine Sports Outfitters** (☎ **207/236-8797**).

WHERE TO STAY

Located on the island side of the bridge from the mainland is **Eggemoggin Landing,** Rte. 15 (☎ **207/348-6115**), a recommended lodging option on the island for those looking to spend less than charged at the inns below. It's a standard motel with basic rooms, but features a great location on the shores of Eggemoggin Reach with good views of the bridge. It's open from May to October, with rates of $69 to $75 in season, $10 less in spring and fall. Pets are allowed spring and fall only ($10 extra charge). A restaurant serves three meals on the premises; the motel also offers kayaks, bike rentals, and sailboat cruises.

⭘ **Goose Cove Lodge.** Goose Cove Rd. (P.O. Box 40), Sunset, ME 04683. ☎ **207/348-2508.** Fax 207/348-2624. www.goosecovelodge.com. E-mail: goosecove@goosecovelodge.com. 23 units. Open mid-May–mid-Oct; July and Aug 2-night minimum (one week min in cottages). High season $140–$300 double; low season $120–$274. Rates include full breakfast. Ask about low-season packages. Some units have 3-person minimum during high season. MC, V.

A rustic compound adjacent to a nature preserve on a remote coastal point, Goose Cove Lodge is a superb destination for families and lovers of the outdoors. Exploring the grounds offers an adventure every day. You can hike out at low tide to salty Barred Island, or take a guided nature hike on any of five trails. You can mess around in boats in the cove (the inn has kayaks and canoes), or borrow one of the inn's bikes for an excursion. Twenty of the rooms offer fireplaces or Franklin stoves; two recently built (1997), architecturally designed modern cottages sleep six, and are available through the winter. Our favorites? "Elm" and "Linnea," cozy cabins tucked privately in the woods on a rise overlooking the beach.

Dining: Each evening begins with a cocktail hour at 5:30 in the lodge, followed by dinner. Guests sit family style and dine while enjoying views of the cove and distant islands. There's always a vegetarian option at dinner, along with other creative entrees, like roasted baby pheasant with beets, white truffle oil, grilled fennel, and sweet cumin glacé; or a grilled beef tenderloin served with beans, beet greens, and roasted pears. The dining room is open to the public (reservations mandatory); come for lunch on the deck, or for dinner as space permits (entrees $18 to $26).

Inn on the Harbor. Main St. (P.O. Box 69), Stonington, ME 04681. ☎ **800/942-2420** or 207/367-2420. Fax 207/367-5165. www.innontheharbor.com. E-mail webmaster@innontheharbor.com. 13 units. TV TEL. $100–$130 double. Rates include continental breakfast. AE, DISC, MC, V. Closed Jan–mid-Apr. Children 12 and older welcome.

This appealingly quirky waterfront inn has the best location in town—perched over the harbor and right on the main street. After a major makeover a few years ago, the guest rooms (10 of which overlook the harbor) are now nicely appointed with antiques and sisal carpets. Swap notes about your room with other guests over complimentary sherry and wine served in the reception room or on the expansive deck in late afternoon. This is a great location for resting up before or after a kayak expedition, or a good base for a day trip out to Isle au Haut. All rooms except the suite, located across town in the innkeeper's home, feature in-room phones. Breakfast includes homebaked muffins and breads. The inn also operates a restaurant a short walk away called the Cafe Atlantic (☎ **207/367-6373**), which features seafood, pasta, and beef (prime rib on weekends) with entrees priced at $12 to $18. Parking is on the street or at nearby lots and can be inconvenient during busy times.

Oakland House Seaside Resort/Shore Oaks. 435 Herrick Rd., Brooksville, ME 04617. ☎ **800/359-7352** or 207/359-8521. www.oaklandhouse.com. E-mail: jim@oaklandhouse.com. 10 inn units plus 15 cottages (3 inn units share 1 bathroom). Inn: summer $139–$239 double including breakfast and dinner; off-season $75–$115 including breakfast. Cottages: $1,195–$1,573 double per week including breakfast and dinner. 2-night minimum for inn on weekends. MC, V. Closed mid-Oct–early May. Children age 14 and up welcome in inn; children welcome in all cottages.

Located on the mainland just north of the bridge to Deer Isle, Oakland House is a classic summer resort that's been in the same family since the American Revolution. For the past half-century the main draw has been the cluster of shoreside cottages, tucked among 50 acres and half-mile of shorefront with extraordinary views of Eggemoggin Reach. These are mostly set aside for week-long stays (Saturday to Saturday). The cottages are of varying vintages but most have fireplaces with wood delivered daily. For shorter visits, a grand 1907 shorefront home has been converted to a 10-room inn called Shore Oaks; innkeepers Jim and Sally Littlefield have been making it over in recent years in an Arts and Crafts–inspired style. In peak season, guests take their meals at the old 1889 hotel, with tasty options ranging from the simple (broiled swordfish) to the more extravagant (crab and panko crusted salmon with a lobster cream reduction).

Activities on the grounds include hiking trails (be sure to hike the Blue Dot Trail to Lookout Rock), dubbing around in rowboats, swimming in the frigid saltwater, hiking to a (warmer) lake for swimming (shared with a kid's summer camp), and watching videos in the barn after dinner. Boat charters and a lobster bake are options in the summer.

Pilgrim's Inn. Deer Isle, ME 04627. ☎ **207/348-6615.** Fax 207/348-7769. www.pilgrimsinn.com. 13 units, 2 cottages (3 rooms with shared bathroom). $165 double with shared bathroom, $190 with private bathroom; cottages $220. Rates include breakfast and dinner. MC, V. Closed mid-Oct–mid-May (cottages open year-round). Pets allowed in cottages only. Children 10 and older are welcome.

Set just off a town road and between an open bay and a millpond, this is a historic, handsomely renovated inn. The inn was built in 1793 by Ignatius Haskell, a prosperous sawmill owner. His granddaughter opened the home to boarders, and it's been housing summer guests ever since. The interior is tastefully decorated in a style that's informed by early Americana, but not beholden to historic authenticity. The guest rooms are well appointed with antiques and painted in muted colonial colors; especially intriguing are the rooms on the top floor with impressive diagonal beams. Two nearby cottages are also available. Activities include strolling around the village, using the inn's bikes, and taking scenic drives.

Dining: Dinners start with cocktails and hors d'oeuvres in the common room at 6pm, followed by one seating at 7pm in the adjacent barn dining room. Several entrees are offered, and the creative American cuisine is not likely to disappoint. You might feast on tenderloin of pork in phyllo with local shiitake mushrooms, or roasted ratatouille napoleon with a lemon balsamic vinaigrette and grilled spring onions. Dinner is open to the public by reservation at a fixed price of $32.50.

WHERE TO DINE

For fine dining, check out Goose Cove Lodge or the Pilgrim's Inn (see "Where to Stay," above).

Fisherman's Friend. School St., Stonington. ☎ **207/367-2442.** Reservations recommended peak season and weekends. Sandwiches $2.50–$6.50; dinner entrees $6.95–$15.95. DISC, MC, V. July–Aug daily 11am–9pm; June and Sept–Oct daily 11am–8pm; Apr–May Tues–Sun 11am–8pm. Closed Nov–Mar. Directions: Located up the hill from the harbor past the Opera House. SEAFOOD.

This is a great local-eats place. Lively and boisterous, it's usually as crowded as it is unpretentious. The menu features basic homecooked meals, and typically includes a wide range of fresh fish prepared in a variety of styles, including charbroiled. If you find yourself beset with a fierce craving for lobster, do yourself a favor and bypass the usual; instead, order up a bowl of the lobster stew, which is brimming with meaty lobster chunks. It's not a light meal, but travelers often find themselves making excuses to linger in Stonington another day to indulge in a second bowl of stew. Dessert selections, including berry pies and shortcake, are extensive and traditional New England; $2 will buy a hearty serving of Grapenut pudding with real whipped cream. BYOB.

3   Blue Hill

Blue Hill, pop. 1,900, is fairly easy to find—just look for gently domed Blue Hill Mountain, which lords it over the northern end of Blue Hill Bay. Set between the mountain and the bay is the quiet and historic town of Blue Hill, clustering along the bay shore and a burbling stream. There's never much going on, and that seems to be exactly what attracts summer visitors back time and again—and may explain why two excellent bookstores are located here. Many old-money families maintain retreats set along the water or in the rolling inland hills, but Blue Hill offers several excellent choices for lodging if you're not well endowed with local relatives. It's a good destination for an escape, and will especially appeal to those deft at crafting their own entertainment.

When in the area, be sure to tune into the local community radio station, WERU at 89.9 FM. It was started some years back by Noel Paul Stookey (the Paul in Peter, Paul & Mary) in a chicken coop. The idea was to spread around good music and provocative ideas. It's become slicker and more professional in recent years, but still maintains a pleasantly homespun flavor.

ESSENTIALS
GETTING THERE
Blue Hill is southeast of Ellsworth on Route 172. Coming from the west, head south on Route 15 five miles east of Bucksport (it's well marked with road signs).

VISITOR INFORMATION
Blue Hill does not maintain a visitor information booth. Look for the "Blue Hill, Maine" brochure and map at state information centers, or write the **Blue Hill Chamber of Commerce,** P.O. Box 520, Blue Hill, ME 04614. The staffs at area inns and restaurants are usually able to answer any questions you might have.

SPECIAL EVENTS
The **Blue Hill Fair** (☎ **207/374-9976** for information) is a traditional country fair with livestock competitions, displays of vegetables, and carnival rides. The fair takes place at the fairgrounds northwest of the village on Route 172 on Labor Day weekend.

EXPLORING BLUE HILL

A good way to start your exploration is to ascend the open summit of **Blue Hill Mountain,** from which you'll have superb views of the azure bay and the rocky balds on nearby Mount Desert Island. To reach the trailhead from the village, drive north on Route 172, then turn west (left) on Mountain Road at the Blue Hill Fairgrounds. Drive 8 mile and look for the well-marked trail. An ascent of the "mountain" (elevation 940 feet) is about a mile, and requires about 45 minutes. Bring a picnic lunch and enjoy the vistas.

Blue Hill has traditionally attracted more than its fair share of artists, especially, it seems, potters. On Union Street, stop by **Rowantrees Pottery** (☎ 207/374-5535), which has been a Blue Hill institution for more than half a century. The shop was founded by Adelaide Pearson, who was inspired to pursue pottery as a career after a conversation with Mahatma Gandhi in India. Rowantrees' pottery is richly hued, and the potters who've succeeded Pearson continue to use glazes made from local resources.

Another inventive shop, the family-run **Rackliffe Pottery** on Ellsworth Road (☎ 207/374-2297), uses native clay and lead-free glazes, and the bowls, vases, and plates produced here have a lustrous, silky feel. Visitors are welcome to watch the potters at work. Both shops are open year-round.

Even if you're not given to swooning over historic homes, you owe yourself a visit to the intriguing **Parson Fisher House** (contact Eric Linnell, ☎ 207/374-2339, for information), located on Routes 176 & 15, one-half mile west of the village. Fisher, Blue Hill's first permanent minister, was a rustic version of a Renaissance man when he settled here in 1796. Educated at Harvard, Fisher not only delivered sermons in six different languages, including Aramaic, but was a writer, painter, and minor inventor whose energy was evidently boundless. On a tour of his home, which he built in 1814, you can see a clock with wooden works he made, and samples of the books he not only wrote but published and bound himself.

Parson Fisher House is open from July to mid-September daily except Sunday from 2 to 5pm. Admission is $2 adults, free for children under 12.

If you're an ardent antique hunter or bibliophile, it's worth your while to detour to the **Big Chicken Barn** (☎ 207/667-7308) on Route 1 between Ellsworth and Bucksport (it's

9 miles west of Ellsworth, 11 miles east of Bucksport). This sprawling antiques mall and bookstore is of nearly shopping mall proportions—more than 21,000 square feet of stuff in an old poultry barn.

WHERE TO STAY

Blue Hill Farm Country Inn. Rte. 15 (P.O. Box 437), Blue Hill, ME 04614. ☎ **207/374-5126.** 14 units (7 with shared bathroom). June–Oct $80–$95 double; off-season $70–$80 double (no shared bathroom in off-season). All rates include continental breakfast. AE, MC, V.

Comfortably situated on 48 acres 2 miles north of the village of Blue Hill, the Blue Hill Country Farm Inn offers some of the most relaxing and comfortable common areas you'll find anywhere. The first floor of a vast barn has been converted to a spacious living room for guests, with a handful of sitting areas arrayed such that you can opt for privacy or the company of others. Or, in an adjoining old farmhouse, you can curl up in the cozy, intimate common room which is amply stocked with a good selection of books. There's also the old kitchen, no longer used for cooking, but now a fine place to linger.

It's fortunate that the common areas are so exceptionally well done, because you're not likely to spend much time in the guest rooms, which tend to be small and lightly furnished. The more modern rooms are upstairs in the barn loft and are nicely decorated in a country farmhouse style, but these are a bit motel-like, with rooms set off a central hallway. The three older rooms in the farmhouse have more character and share a single bathroom with a small tub and hand-held shower.

Blue Hill Inn. Union St. (P.O. Box 403), Blue Hill, ME 04614. ☎ **207/374-2844.** Fax 207/374-2829. www.bluehillinn.com. E-mail: bluhilin@downeast.net. 12 units. $108–$175 double; $210–$2,345 suite. Rates include breakfast. 2-night minimum in summer. DISC, MC, V. Closed Dec–mid-May. Children 13 and older are welcome.

The Blue Hill Inn has been hosting travelers since 1840. Situated on one of Blue Hill's main thoroughfares and within walking distance of most everything, this Federal-style inn features a convincing colonial American motif throughout, with the authenticity enhanced by creaky floors and door jambs slightly out of true. The innkeepers have furnished all the rooms pleasantly with antiques and down comforters; four rooms feature wood-burning fireplaces. A more contemporary luxury suite is located in an adjacent building, which features cathedral ceiling, fireplace, kitchen, and deck. Ask about packages that include kayaking, hiking, or sailing.

Dining: Meals are made chiefly with local, organic ingredients; among the creative dishes are lobster with a vanilla beurre blanc and roast duck with green peppercorn sauce. The wine selection is excellent. Dinner is served Wednesday to Friday and is open to the public; reservations are required.

WHERE TO DINE

Jean-Paul's Bistro. Main St., Blue Hill. ☎ **207/374-5852.** Lunch $6.95–$8.95. MC, V. Daily 11am–5pm. Closed mid-Sept—June 30. Located at the intersection of rtes. 172 and 15. UPSCALE SANDWICHES.

You get a lot of mileage for a moderate price at Jean-Paul's, which serves up lunch and tea during its brief summer season (it's open in July, August, and early September only). This is the place to head when the sun's shining overhead and summer blazes in its full glory. Behind this old farmhouse in the village center are stone terraces and a lawn that slopes down to the head of Blue Hill Bay. Choose either a table on the terraces, or plop yourself into one of the wide-armed Adirondack chairs on the lawn overlooking the water. (The lawn is a popular spot for solo diners who prefer to eat in the company of a good book.) Lunches tend toward quiche, croissant sandwiches, and salads. The walnut tarragon chicken salad is tasty; the delicious desserts make liberal use of local blueberries.

Jonathan's. Main St., Blue Hill. ☎ **207/374-5226.** Reservations recommended. Main courses, $14–$18. MC, V. Mon–Sat 5–9:30pm. BISTRO.

Located in the middle of Blue Hill, Jonathan's appeals to almost everyone—from the younger local crowd to the old-money summer denizens. The background music is jazz or light rock, the service brisk and professional, and the wine list extensive and creative. Guests choose between the barn-like back room with its comfortable knotty-pine feel, or the less elegant front room facing Main Street. The menu changes every five weeks, and the kitchen emphasizes locally raised and seasonal dishes— think of it as Maine-meets-Europe, with updated versions of regional classics, and reinterpretations of European fare using Maine ingredients. Look for entrees like the popular braised lamb shank with maple barbecue sauce; mixed grill of quail, rabbit, and venison sausage; and poached salmon with dill sauce. Appetizers run along the lines of warm smoked mussel and chèvre salad, or pear salad with Maine cheeses.

7

Mount Desert Island & Acadia National Park

*M*ount Desert Island is home to spectacular Acadia National Park, and for many visitors the two places are one and the same. Yes, tourism drives the island economy, and the presence of tourists defines the summer spirit of Maine's largest island. And the park does contain the most dramatic coastal real estate on the eastern seaboard.

Yet the park holdings are only part of the appeal of this immensely popular island, which is connected to the mainland via a short, two-lane causeway. Beyond the parklands are scenic harborside villages and remote backcountry roads, quaint B&Bs and fine restaurants, oversized 19th-century summer "cottages" and the unrepentant tourist trap of Bar Harbor. Those who arrive on the island expecting untamed wilderness invariably leave disappointed. Those who understand that Acadia National Park is but one chapter (albeit a very large one) in the intriguing story of Mount Desert Island will enjoy their visit thoroughly.

Mount Desert (pronounced "de-*sert*") is divided into two lobes separated by Somes Sound, the only legitimate fjord in the continental U.S. (A fjord is a valley carved by a glacier that subsequently filled with rising ocean water.) Those with a poetic imagination see Mount Desert shaped as a lobster, with one large claw and one small. Most of the parkland is on the meatier east claw, although large swaths of park exist on the leaner west claw as well. The eastern side is more developed, with Bar Harbor the center of commerce and entertainment. The western side has a more quiet, settled air, and teems more with wildlife than tourists. The island isn't huge—it's only about 15 miles from the causeway to the southernmost tip at Bass Harbor Head—yet visitors can do a lot of adventuring in such a compact space. The best plan is to take it slow, exploring whenever possible by foot, bicycle, canoe, or kayak.

1   Acadia National Park

It's not hard to fathom why Acadia is consistently one of the biggest draws in the U.S. national park system. The park's landscape is a rich tapestry of rugged cliffs, restless ocean, and deep, silent woods. Acadia's landscape, like so much of the rest of northern New England, was carved by glaciers some 18,000 years ago. A mile-high ice-sheet shaped the land by scouring valleys into their distinctive U shapes, rounding many of the once-jagged peaks, and depositing huge boulders about the landscape, such as the famous 10-foot-high "Bubble Rock," which appears to be perched precariously on the side of South Bubble Mountain.

The park's more recent roots can be traced back to the 1840s, when noted Hudson River School painter Thomas Cole packed his sketchbooks and easels for a trip to this remote island, then home to a small number of fishermen and boatbuilders. His stunning renditions of the surging surf pounding against coastal granite were later displayed in New York and triggered an early tourism boom as urbanites flocked to the island to "rusticate." By 1872, national magazines were touting Eden (Bar Harbor's name until 1919) as a desirable summer resort. It attracted the attention of wealthy industrialists, and soon became summer home to Carnegies, Rockefellers, Astors, and Vanderbilts, who built massive summer cottages with literally dozens of rooms. (One "cottage" even boasted 28 bathrooms.) More recently, lifestyle doyenne Martha Stewart occupied a multi-million-dollar hilltop compound in Seal Harbor originally built for Edsel Ford.

By the early 1900s, the huge popularity and growing development of the island began to concern its most ardent supporters. Boston textile heir and conservationist George Dorr and Harvard president Charles Eliot, aided by the largesse of John D. Rockefeller Jr., started acquiring large tracts for the public's enjoyment. These parcels were eventually donated to the federal government, and in 1919 the public land was designated Lafayette National Park, the first national park east of the Mississippi. Renamed Acadia in 1929, the park has grown to encompass nearly half the island, with holdings scattered about piecemeal here and there.

Rockefeller purchased and donated about 11,000 acres—about one-third of the park. He's also responsible for one of the park's most extraordinary features. Around 1905 a dispute

Mount Desert Island/Acadia National Park

erupted over whether to allow noisy new motorcars on to the island. Resident islanders wanted these new conveniences to boost their mobility; John D. Rockefeller Jr., whose fortune was from the oil industry (students of irony take note), strenuously objected, preferring the tranquility of the car-free island. Rockefeller went down to defeat on this issue, and the island was opened to cars in 1913. In response, the multimillionaire set about building an elaborate 57-mile system of private carriage roads, featuring a dozen gracefully handcrafted stone bridges. These roads, open today only to pedestrians, bicyclists, and equestrians, are concentrated most densely around Jordan Pond, but also ascend to some of the most scenic open peaks and wind through sylvan valleys.

ESSENTIALS
GETTING THERE

Acadia National Park is reached from the town of Ellsworth via Route 3. If you're coming from southern Maine, you can avoid the coastal congestion along Route 1 by taking the Maine

Turnpike to Bangor, picking up I-395 to Route 1A, then continuing south on Route 1A to Ellsworth. While this looks longer on the map, it's by far the quickest route in summer.

Daily flights from Boston to the airport in Trenton, just across the causeway from Mt. Desert Island, are offered year-round by Continental affiliate **Colgan Air** (☎ **800/523-3273** or 207/667-7171).

In summer, **Concord Trailways** (☎ **888/741-8686** or 207/942-8686) offers van service among Bangor (including an airport stop), Ellsworth, and Bar Harbor between late May and mid-September. Reservations are required.

GETTING AROUND

A free ✪ **islandwide bus shuttle service** was inaugurated in 1999 as part of an effort to reduce the number of cars on the island's roads. The propane-powered buses, which are equipped with racks for bikes, serve six routes that cover nearly the entire island, and will stop anywhere you request outside the village centers, including trailheads, ferries, small villages, and campgrounds. All routes begin or end at the Village Green in Bar Harbor, but you're encouraged to pick up the bus wherever you're staying, whether motel or campground, to avoid parking hassles in town. Route no. 3 goes from Bar Harbor along much of the Park Loop, offering easy access to some of the park's best hiking trails. The buses operate from late June to early September; ask for a schedule at any of the island information centers.

GUIDED TOURS

Acadia National Park Tours (☎ **207/288-3327**) offers two-and-a-half-hour park tours departing twice daily (10am and 2pm) from downtown Bar Harbor. The bus tour includes three stops (Sieur De Monts Springs, Thunder Hole, and Cadillac Mountain) and plenty of park trivia courtesy of the driver. This is an easy way for first-time visitors to get a quick introduction to the park before setting out on their own. Tickets are available at Testa's Restaurant, 53 Main St., Bar Harbor; $20 adult, $7.50 children under 14.

ENTRY POINTS & FEES

A one-week park pass, which includes unlimited trips on Park Loop Road, costs $10 per car; no additional charge per passenger. (No daily pass is available.) The main point of entry to Park Loop Road, the park's most scenic byway, is at the visitor center at **Hulls Cove.** Mount Desert Island consists of an interwoven network of park and town roads, allowing visitors to enter the park at numerous points. A glance at a park map (available free at the visitor center) will make these access points self-evident. The entry fee is collected at a toll-booth on Park Loop Road one-half mile north of Sand Beach.

VISITOR CENTERS

Acadia staffs two visitor centers. The **Thompson Island Information Center** (☎ 207/288-3411) on Route 3 is the first you'll pass as you enter Mount Desert Island. This center is maintained by the local chambers of commerce, but park personnel are often on hand to answer inquiries. It's open May to mid-October, and is a good stop for general lodging and restaurant information.

If you're interested primarily in information about the park itself, continue on Route 3 to the National Park Service's **Hulls Cove Visitor Center** about 7.5 miles beyond Thompson Island. This attractive stone-walled center includes profession-ally prepared park service displays, such as a large relief map of the island, natural history exhibits, and a short introductory film. You can also request free brochures about hiking trails and the carriage roads, or purchase postcards and more detailed guidebooks. The center is open mid-April to October. Information is also available year-round, by phone or in person, from the park's **headquarters** (☎ 207/288-3338) on Route 233 between Bar Harbor and Somesville.

Your questions might also be answered in advance on the park's web page at **www.nps.gov/acad.**

PARK ACCOMMODATIONS

The national park itself offers no overnight accommodations other than two campgrounds (see below). But visitors don't have to go far to find a room. That's especially true for Bar Harbor, which is teeming with motels and inns. The rest of the island also has a good, if scattered, selection of places to spend the night. See "Where to Stay" on page 186 under the Exploring the Rest of the Island section.

SEASONS

Visit Acadia in September if you can. Between Labor Day and the foliage season of early October, the days are often warm and clear, the nights have a crisp northerly tang, and you can avoid the hassles of congestion, crowds, and pesky insects. Not that the park is empty in September. Bus tours seem to proliferate at that time, which results in crowds at the most popular sites. Not to worry: If you walk just a minute or two off the road you can find solitude and an agreeable peacefulness. Hikers and bikers have the trails and carriage roads to themselves.

Summer, of course, is peak season at Acadia. Weather is perfect for just about any outdoor activity in July and August. Most days are warm (in the 70s or 80s), with afternoons frequently cooler than mornings owing to ocean breezes. While sun seems to be the norm, come prepared for rain and fog, both frequent visitors to the Maine coast. And once or twice each summer a heat wave will settle into the area, producing temperatures in the 90s, dense haze, and stifling humidity, but this rarely lasts more than two or three days. Soon enough, a brisk north wind will blow in from the Canadian Arctic, churning up the waters and forcing visitors into sweaters at night. Sometime during the last two weeks of August, a cold wind will blow through at night and you'll smell the approach of autumn, with winter not far behind.

Winter is increasingly popular among travelers who enjoy cross-country skiing on the carriage roads. Be aware, though, that snow is inconsistent and services are very much limited in the off-season.

REGULATIONS

The usual national park rules apply. Guns may not be used in the park; if you have a gun, it must be "cased, broken down, or otherwise packaged against use." Fires and camping are allowed only at designated areas. Pets must be on leashes at all times. Seat belts must be worn in the national park (this is a federal law). Don't remove anything from the park, either man-made or natural; this includes cobblestones from the shore.

RANGER PROGRAMS

Frequent ranger programs are offered throughout the year. These include talks at campground amphitheaters and tours of various locations around the island. Examples are the Otter Point nature hike, Mr. Rockefeller's bridges walk, a Frenchman Bay cruise (rangers provide commentary on commercial trips; make reservations with commercial tour boat owners), and a discussion of changes in Acadia's landscape. Ask for a schedule of events or more information at either of the two visitor centers or campgrounds.

ENJOYING THE PARK

Try to allow three or four days at a minimum for visiting the park. If you're passing through just briefly, try to work in at least three of the four following activities.

One minor, motherly tip: When you set out to explore the park, pack a picnic lunch and keep it handy. Once you're in the park, there are few places to stop for lunch or snacks. Having drinks and a bite to eat at hand will prevent breaking up your day with time-wasting backtracking into Bar Harbor or elsewhere in a desperate effort to fend off starvation. The more food you bring with you, the more your options for the day will expand.

DRIVE THE PARK LOOP ROAD

This almost goes without saying, since it's the park's premier attraction. This 20-mile road runs along the island's eastern shore, then loops inland along Jordan Pond and Eagle Lake. The road runs high along the shoulders of dramatic coastal mountains, then dips down along the boulder-strewn coastlines. The dark granite is broken by the spires of spruce and fir, and the earthy tones contrast sharply with the frothy white surf and the steely, azure sea. The two-lane road is one-way along the coastal stretches; the right-hand lane is set aside for parking, so it's easy to make frequent stops to admire the vistas.

Ideally, visitors will make at least two trips on the loop road. The first is for the sheer exhilaration and to suss out the lay of the land. On the second trip, plan to stop frequently, leaving your car behind while you set off on trails and wander down to the coastline.

Attractions along the coastal loop include scenic **Sand Beach,** the only sand beach on the island; **Thunder Hole,** a shallow oceanside cavern into which the surf surges, compresses, and bursts out with an explosive force and a concussive sound (young kids seem to be endlessly mesmerized by this); and **Cadillac Mountain,** the highest point on the island at 1,530 feet, and the place in the United States first touched by the sun during much of the year. The mountaintop is accessible by car along an early (now upgraded) carriage road, but the parking lot at the summit is often crowded and drivers are often testy. You're better off hiking to the top, or scaling a more remote peak.

✪ BIKE THE CARRIAGE ROADS

The 57 miles of carriage road built by John D. Rockefeller Jr. are among the park's most extraordinary treasures. After Rockefeller's death in 1960, the roads became somewhat shaggy and overgrown until a major restoration effort brought them back a decade ago. Today, these roads are superbly restored and maintained, and though built for horse and carriage, they are ideal for cruising by mountain bike and offer some of the most scenic, relaxing biking found anywhere in the United States. Park near Jordan Pond and plumb the tree-shrouded lanes that lace the area, taking time to admire the stonework on the uncommonly fine bridges. Afterwards, stop for tea and popovers at the **Jordan Pond House,** which has been a popular island destination for over a century, although it's unlikely as much Lycra was in evidence 100 years ago.

A decent map of the carriage roads is available free at the park's visitor center. (Where the carriage roads cross private land—generally between Seal Harbor and Northeast Harbor—the roads are closed to mountain bikes.) More detailed guidebooks are sold at area bookstores.

Mountain bikes may be rented along Cottage Street in Bar Harbor, with rates around $15 to $17 for a full day, $10 to $12 for a half-day. Most bike shops include locks and helmets as basic equipment, but ask what's included before you rent. Also ask about closing times, since you'll be able to get a couple extra hours in with a later-closing shop. **Bar Harbor Bicycle Shop** (☎ **207/288-3886**), at 141 Cottage St., gets our vote for the most convenient and friendliest; you might also try **Acadia Outfitters** (☎ **207/288-8118**), at 106 Cottage St., or **Acadia Bike & Coastal Kayak** (☎ **207/288-9605**), at 48 Cottage St.

CANOE A LAKE

Mount Desert's several ponds offer scenic if limited canoeing, and most have public boat access. Canoe rentals are available at the north end of Long Pond in Somesville from **National Park Canoe Rentals** (☎ **207/244-5854**). The cost is $22 for 4 hours. Long Pond is the largest of the island ponds, and offers good exploring. Pack a picnic and spend a few hours reconnoitering the pond's 3-mile length. Much of the west shore and the southern tip lie within Acadia National Park. Jet Skis, incidentally, are banned in the national park.

HIKE A MOUNTAIN

This quintessential Acadia experience shouldn't be missed. The park is studded with low "mountains" (they'd be called hills elsewhere) that offer superb views over the island and the open ocean. The trails weren't simply hacked out of the hillside; many were crafted by experienced stonemasons and others with high aesthetic intent. The routes aren't the most direct, nor were they the easiest to build. But they're often the most scenic, taking advantage of fractures in the rocks, picturesque ledges, and sudden vistas.

Acadia National Park has 120 miles of hiking trails in addition to the carriage roads. The Hulls Cove Visitor Center offers a one-page chart of area hikes; combined with the park map, this is all you'll need since the trails are well maintained and well marked. It's not hard to cobble together loop hikes to make your trips more varied. Coordinate your hiking with the weather; if it's damp or foggy, you'll stay drier and warmer strolling the carriage roads. If it's clear and dry, head for the highest peaks with the best views.

Among my favorite trails is the **Dorr Ladder Trail,** which departs from Route 3 near The Tarn just south of the Sieur de Monts entrance to the Loop Road. This trail begins with a series of massive stone steps ascending along the base of a vast slab of granite, and then passes through crevasses (not for the wide of girth) and up ladders affixed to the granite. The views east and south are superb.

An easy lowland hike is around **Jordan Pond,** with the northward leg along the pond's east shore on a hiking trail, and the return via carriage road. It's mostly level, with the total loop measuring just over 3 miles. At the north end of Jordan Pond, consider heading up the prominent, oddly symmetrical mounds called **The Bubbles.** These detours shouldn't take much more than 20 minutes each; look for signs off the Jordan Pond Shore Trail.

On the western side of the island, an ascent of **Acadia Mountain** and return takes about an hour and a half, but hikers should schedule in some time for lingering while they enjoy the view of Somes Sound and the smaller islands off Mount Desert's southern shores. This 2.5-mile loop hike begins off Route 102 at a trailhead 3 miles south of Somesville. Head eastward through rolling mixed forest, then begin an ascent over ledgy terrain. Be sure to visit both the east and west peaks (the east peak has the better views), and look for hidden balds in the summit forest that open up to unexpected vistas.

Enjoy a Carriage Ride

Carriage rides are offered by **Wildwood Stables** (☎ 207/ 276-3622), a national park concessioner located a half-mile south of Jordan Pond House. The 1-hour Day Mountain trip departs three times daily, yields wonderful views, and costs $13.50 for adults, $7 for children 6 to 12, and $4 for children 2 to 5. Longer tours and charters are also available, as is a special carriage designed to accommodate passengers with disabilities; reservations are encouraged.

Climb a Cliff

Many of the oceanside rock faces attract experienced rock climbers, as much for the beauty of the climbing areas as the challenge of the climbs and the high-grade quality of the rock. For novices or experienced climbers, **Acadia Mountain Guides** (☎ 207/288-8186; www.acadiamountainguides. com) offers rock-climbing lessons and guide services, ranging from a half-day introduction to rock climbing to intensive workshops on self-rescue and instruction on how to lead climbs. The Bar Harbor shop is located at 198 Main St., at the corner of Mt. Desert Street.

Paddle a Sea Kayak

Experienced sea kayakers flock to Acadia to test their paddling skills along the surf at the base of rocky cliffs, to venture out to the offshore islands, and to probe the still, silent waters of Somes Sound. Novice sea kayakers also come to Acadia to try their hand with guided tours, which are offered by several outfitters. Many new paddlers have found their inaugural experiences gratifying; others have complained that the quantity of paddlers taken out on quick tours during peak season makes the experience a little too much like a cattle drive to truly enjoy. (Insider tip: rainy days can be magical on the water and surprisingly dry once you're sealed inside a kayak; with fewer crowds, you're also likely to have a more private experience.)

You can turn up a variety of tours, ranging from a 2½-hour harbor tour to a 7-hour full-day excursion, by contacting the following guide services, all of which are located on Cottage Street: **Acadia Outfitters** (☎ **207/288-8118**), at 106 Cottage St.; **Coastal Kayaking Tours** (☎ **800/526-8615** or 207/288-9605), at 48 Cottage St.; **National Park Sea Kayak Tours** (☎ **800/347-0940** or 207/288-0342), at 39 Cottage St.; and **Island Adventure Kayak Tours & Rentals** (☎ **207/288-3886**), at 137 Cottage St. Rates range from approximately $35 to $45 per person for a 2- to 3-hour harbor or sunset tour, $75 for a full-day excursion.

Sea kayak rentals are available from Loon Bay Kayaks, located summers at Barcadia Campground, at the junction of Route 3 and Route 102 (☎ **888/786-0676** or 207/288-0099), which will deliver a boat to you, and from National Park Canoe Rental, 1 West St., Bar Harbor (☎ **207/288-0007**). Solo kayaks rent for $32 to $35 per day.

CAMPING

The National Park Service maintains two campgrounds within Acadia National Park. Both are extremely popular; during July and August expect both to fill by early to mid-morning.

The more popular of the two is **Blackwoods** (☎ **207/288-3274**), located on the island's eastern side. Access is from Route 3, 5 miles south of Bar Harbor. Bikers and pedestrians have easy access to the loop road from the campground via a short trail. The campground has no public showers, but an enterprising business just outside the campground entrance offers clean showers for a modest fee. Camping fees are $18 per night and reservations are accepted; **reservations** may be made up to five months in advance by calling ☎ **800/365-2267.** (This is to a national reservation service, whose contract is revisited from time to time by the park service; if it's nonworking, call the campground directly to ask for the current toll-free reservation number.) Reservations may also be made on the web between 10am and 10pm only at reservations.nps.gov.

Seawall (☎ **207/244-3600**) is on the quieter, western half of the island near the fishing village of Bass Harbor. This is a good base for road biking, and several short coastal hikes are within easy striking distance. Many of the sites are walk-ins, which require carrying your gear a hundred yards or so to the site. The campground is open late May to September on a first-come, first-served basis. In general, if you get here by 9 or 10am, you'll be pretty much assured of a campsite, especially if you're a tent camper. There are no showers, but they're available nearby. Camping fees are $12 to $18 per night.

Private campgrounds handle the overflow. The region from Ellsworth south boasts 14 private campgrounds, which offer varying amenities. The **Thompson Island Information Center** (☎ 207/288-3411) posts up-to-the-minute information on which campgrounds still have vacancies; it's a good first stop for those arriving without camping reservations.

Two private campgrounds stand above the rest. **Bar Harbor Campground,** Route 3, Salisbury Cove (☎ 207/288-5185), on the main route between the causeway and Bar Harbor doesn't take reservations, and you can often find a good selection of sites if you arrive before noon, even during the peak season. Some of its 300 sites are set in piney woods; others are on an open hillside edged with blueberry barrens. The wooded sites are quite private. There's a pool for campers, uncommonly clean bathhouses, and campers always get to pick their own sites rather than be arbitrarily assigned one. Rates range from $18 for a basic, no-services site to $25 for all hookups.

At the head of Somes Sound is **Mount Desert Campground,** Route 198 (☎ 207/244-3710), which is especially well suited for campers (RVs to a maximum of 20 feet only). This heavily wooded campground has very few undesirable sites, and a great many desirable ones, including some walk-in sites right at the water's edge. The rate is $22 per night. (*Note:* This campground should not be confused with the Mount Desert Narrows Campground, which is more RV-oriented and located closer to the causeway.)

Another option is **Lamoine State Park** (☎ 207/667-4778), which faces Mount Desert from the mainland across the cold waters of northernmost Frenchman Bay. This is an exceptionally pleasant, quiet park with private sites, a shower house, and a small beach about a half-hour's drive from the action at Bar Harbor. The campground has been belatedly discovered by travelers in the last half-dozen years, but still rarely fills to capacity.

2 Bar Harbor

Bar Harbor has historical roots in the grand resort era of the late 19th century. The region was discovered by wealthy

Bar Harbor

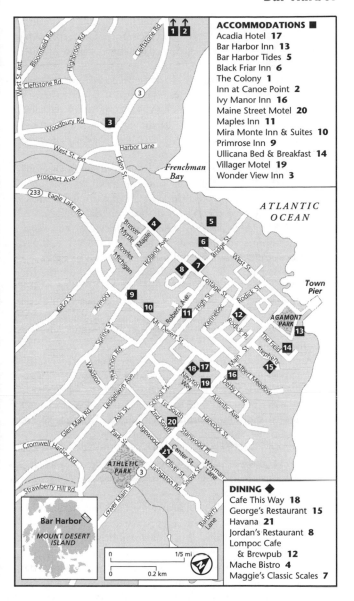

ACCOMMODATIONS ■
Acadia Hotel **17**
Bar Harbor Inn **13**
Bar Harbor Tides **5**
Black Friar Inn **6**
The Colony **1**
Inn at Canoe Point **2**
Ivy Manor Inn **16**
Maine Street Motel **20**
Maples Inn **11**
Mira Monte Inn & Suites **10**
Primrose Inn **9**
Ullicana Bed & Breakfast **14**
Villager Motel **19**
Wonder View Inn **3**

ATLANTIC OCEAN

Frenchman Bay

Town Pier

AGAMONT PARK

ATHLETIC PARK

Bar Harbor
MOUNT DESERT ISLAND

0   1/5 mi
0   0.2 km

DINING ◆
Cafe This Way **18**
George's Restaurant **15**
Havana **21**
Jordan's Restaurant **8**
Lompoc Cafe
 & Brewpub **12**
Mache Bistro **4**
Maggie's Classic Scales **7**

rusticators, drawn by the mid-19th-century landscape paintings that were exhibited in Boston and New York. Later, sprawling hotels and boarding houses cluttered the shores and hillsides as the newly affluent middle class flocked here in summer by steamboat and rail from Eastern Seaboard cities. When the resort was at its zenith near the turn of the last century, Bar Harbor had rooms enough to accommodate some 5,000 visitors. Along with the hotels and guest houses, hundreds of cottages were built by the wealthiest rusticators who came here season after season.

The tourist business continued to grow through the early part of the 1900s, then all but collapsed as the Great Depression and the growing popularity of automobile travel doomed the era of the extended vacation. Bar Harbor was dealt a further blow in 1947 when a fire fueled by an unusually dry summer and fierce northwest winds leveled many of the most opulent cottages and much of the rest of the town. (To this day, no one knows with any certainty how the fire started.) The fire destroyed five hotels, 67 grand cottages, and 170 homes. In all, some 17,000 acres of the island were burned. Downtown Bar Harbor was spared, and many of the in-town mansions along the oceanfront were missed by the conflagration.

After a period of quiet slumber (some storefronts were still boarded up as late as the 1970s), Bar Harbor has been rejuvenated and rediscovered in recent years as tourists have poured in, followed by entrepreneurs who have opened dozens of restaurants, shops, and boutiques. The less charitable regard Bar Harbor as just another tacky tourist mecca—the downtown hosts a proliferation of T-shirt vendors, ice-cream cone shops, and souvenir palaces. Crowds spill off the sidewalk and into the street in midsummer, and the traffic and congestion can be truly appalling.

Yet Bar Harbor's vibrant history, distinguished architecture, and beautiful location along Frenchman Bay allow it to rise above its station as mild diversion for tourists. Most of the island's inns, motels, and B&Bs are located here, as are dozens of fine restaurants, making it a desirable base of operations. Bar Harbor is also the best destination for supplies and services; there's a decent grocery story and laundromat, and you can stock up on other necessities of life.

As for the congestion, it's fortunate that Bar Harbor is compact enough that once you find a parking space or a room for the night, the whole town can be navigated on foot. Arriving here early in the morning also considerably improves your odds of securing parking within easy striking distance of the town center. *Suggestion:* Explore Bar Harbor before and after breakfast, then set off for the hills, woods, and coast the rest of the day.

ESSENTIALS
GETTING THERE

Bar Harbor is located on Route 3 about 10 miles southeast of the causeway. Seasonal bus service is available in summer; for schedules contact **Concord Trailways** (☎ **800/639-3317**). Concord Trailways also operates a seasonal four-times daily van shuttle between Bar Harbor and the Bangor International Airport; call ☎ **888/741-8686.**

VISITOR INFORMATION

The **Bar Harbor Chamber of Commerce,** P.O. Box 158, Bar Harbor, ME 04609 (☎ **207/288-5103;** e-mail: bhcc@ acadia.net) stockpiles a huge arsenal of information about local attractions at its offices at 93 Cottage Street. Write, call, or e-mail in advance for a directory of area lodging and attractions. The chamber's web site (www.acadia.net/bhcc) is chock full of information and helpful links.

EXPLORING BAR HARBOR

Wandering the compact downtown on foot is a good way to get a taste of the town. Among the best views in town are those from the foot of Main Street at grassy **Agamont Park,** which overlooks the town pier and Frenchman Bay. From here, set off past the Bar Harbor Inn on the **Shore Path,** a winding, wide trail that follows the shoreline for a short distance along a public right of way. The pathway passes in front of many of the elegant summer homes (some converted to inns), offering a superb vantage point to view the area's architecture.

From the path, you'll also have an open view of **The Porcupines,** a cluster of spruce-studded islands just offshore. This is a good spot to witness the powerful force of glacial action. The south-moving glacier ground away at the islands, creating a gentle slope facing north. On the south shore, away from the glacial push (glaciers simply melted when they retreated north), is a more abrupt, cliff-like shore. The resulting islands look like a small group of porcupines migrating southward—or so early visitors imagined.

A short stroll from the Village Green is the **Bar Harbor Historical Society,** 33 Ledgelawn Ave. (☎ **207/288-0000** or 207/288-3807). The society moved into this handsome 1918 former convent in 1997, where they've showcased artifacts of life in the old days—dishware and photos from the grand old hotels, and exhibits on noted landscape architect Beatrix Farrand. Leave enough time to spend a few minutes thumbing through the scrapbooks about the devastating 1947 fire. The museum is open mid-June to mid-October Monday to Saturday from 1 to 4pm; admission is free.

Located on the grounds of one of Bar Harbor's more magnificent summer estates is the **College of the Atlantic** (☎ **207/288-5015**), a school founded in 1969 with a strong emphasis on environmental education. The campus, with its old and new buildings, is uncommonly picturesque (great views of Frenchman Bay!). The school's Museum of Natural History, 105 Eden St. (☎ **207/288-5395**), features exhibits prepared by current and former students that focus on the interaction between island residents, including the two-legged, the four-legged, the finned, and the furred. The building housing the museum was originally the Acadia National Park headquarters, and was moved and expanded prior to its opening in June 2000.

The museum is open daily mid-June to Labor Day 10am to 5pm; the rest of the year it's open Thursday and Friday 1 to 4pm, Saturday 10am to 4pm, and Sunday 1 to 4pm. Admission is $3.50 adults, $2.50 seniors, $1.50 teens, and $1 children 12 and under.

One of downtown's less obvious attractions is the **Criterion Theater** (☎ **207/288-3441**), a movie house built in 1932 in a classic art deco style and which so far has avoided the degradation of multiplexification. The 900-seat theater, located on Cottage Street, shows first-run movies in summer and is worth the price of admission for the fantastic if somewhat faded interiors; the movie is secondary. As once was the case at most movie palaces, it still costs extra to sit in the more exclusive loges upstairs.

ON THE WATER

Bar Harbor is a base for several ocean endeavors, including whale-watching tours. Operators offer excursions in search of humpbacks, finbacks, minkes, and the infrequently seen endangered right whale. The sleekest is the *Friendship V* (☎ **800/942-5374** or 207/288-2386), which operates from the municipal pier in downtown Bar Harbor. Tours are on a fast, twin-hulled three-level excursion boat that can hold 200 passengers in two heated cabins. The tours run three hours plus; the cost is $35 per adult. A puffin- and whale-watch tour is offered for $39 per adult. There's free on-site parking, and a money-back guarantee that you'll see whales.

For a more intimate excursion, **Acadian Whale Watcher Co.,** 52 West St. (☎ **800/421-3307** or 207/288-9794), offers trips on a smaller boat with two observation decks (free parking). Ask also about puffin and whale combo tours. Rates are comparable to or slightly less than the *Friendship V.*

WHERE TO STAY

EXPENSIVE

The Bar Harbor Inn. Newport Drive (P.O. Box 7), Bar Harbor, ME 04609. ☎ **800/248-3351** or 207/288-3351. www.barharborinn.com. 153 units. A/C TV TEL. Peak season $155–$289 double; spring and late fall $85–$219. Rates include continental breakfast. AE, DISC, MC, V. Closed Dec–late Mar.

The Bar Harbor Inn, located just off Agamont Park, nicely mixes traditional and contemporary. Situated on shady waterfront grounds just a minute's stroll from downtown boutiques (it's also at the start of the Shore Path), the inn offers convenience and gracious charm. The main shingled inn, which dates back to the turn of the 19th century, has a settled, old-money feel, with its semi-circular dining room with ocean views, and the button-down elegance of the lobby. The guest rooms, located in the main inn and two additional structures, are decidedly more contemporary. Guest rooms in the Oceanfront Lodge and Main Inn both offer spectacular views of the bay, and many have private balconies; the less expensive Newport building lacks views but is comfortable and up-to-date.

Dining: The inn's semi-formal dining room serves up resort fare along with the best ocean view in town. Entrees include grilled vegetable ravioli, filet mignon, and grilled strip steak ($16.95 to $28.95). The Terrace Grille, serving simpler fare like chowders, salads, and boiled lobster ($9.95 to $14.95), is downstairs; it also overlooks the bay, features outdoor seating in good weather, and is open daily for lunch and dinner.

Amenities: Heated outdoor pool, hot tub, morning newspaper, conference space, limited room service, afternoon coffee and cookies.

Bar Harbor Tides. 119 West St., Bar Harbor, ME 04609. ☎ **207/288-4968.** www.barharbortides.com. E-mail: info@barharbortides.com. 4 units. TV. $175–$325 double, including full breakfast. DISC, MC, V. Closed Nov–mid-June.

The Bar Harbor Tides features just four guest rooms in a wonderful sprawling 1887 cream-colored mansion. It's located at the head of a long, lush lawn that descends to the water's edge, all on 1½ acres in a neighborhood of imposing homes within easy strolling distance of the village center. When you first enter, it feels as though you're visiting someone's great aunt—someone's very, very rich great aunt. But soon enough it feels like home, as you unwind in one of the two spacious living rooms (one upstairs and one down) or, more likely, on the verandah, which has a unique outdoor fireplace. Breakfast is served on the porch in good weather; otherwise it's enjoyed in the regal dining room with polished wood floors and views out to Bar Island.

Inn at Canoe Point. Rte. 3, Bar Harbor, ME 04609. ☎ **207/288-9511.** www.innatcanoepoint.com. E-mail: canoe.point@juno.com. 5 units. Peak season $160–$265 double; off season $80–$160. Rates include breakfast. DISC, MC, V. Children 16 and over accepted.

The Inn at Canoe Point boasts the best deck on the island— it virtually hangs over the ocean tucked away in a rocky cove, with great views across the northern bay. There's even a cluster of Adirondack chairs arrayed for sprawling. The inn itself is equally magical, built in 1889 in a style that might best be described as "storybook Tudor." Guests arrive down a short, winding road through an attractive stand of pines. Although the inn is just 75 yards or so off bustling Route 3, you might as well be on an island far away. The interior is sleekly contemporary and comfortable. The guests' living room has a stunning modern stone fireplace, superb views, and a great selection of reading material. Rooms vary, but all are attractively appointed. The "Garret Suite" occupies the whole third floor and is quite spacious; the tiny "Garden Room" makes up for its relatively diminutive size with wonderful windows on three sides. The main trick here is actually getting a room;

they tend to be booked up weeks in advance, so reserve well ahead (or come in the off-season).

Ivy Manor Inn. 194 Main St., Bar Harbor, ME 04609. ☎ **888/670-1997** or 207/288-2138. www.ivymanor.com. E-mail: ivymanor@acadia.net. 7 units. A/C TV TEL. Peak season $175–$350; off-peak $95–$200. Rates include full breakfast. 2-night minimum on holiday weekends. AE, DISC, MC, V. Closed late Oct–early May. Children over 12 welcome.

The Ivy Manor quickly proved a welcome addition to Bar Harbor's upscale lodging pool when it opened in 1997. Located in a 1940s-era Tudor-style house that was once home and office of a doctor, the Ivy Manor was thoroughly done over in an understated French Victorian style, mostly in lush, rich colors including burgundy. The rooms are larger than average; most are carpeted and furnished with attractive, tasteful antiques from the innkeeper's collection. Some rooms have antique clawfoot tubs; others have small outdoor sitting decks (none with views to speak of). Among our favorite rooms: no. 6, a small suite with a private sitting room and small fireplace, and no. 1, the honeymoon room with an imposing walnut headboard and matching armoire. All rooms have small TVs. Leave time for a cocktail in the cozy first-floor lounge after you return from your day's outing.

Dining: See Michelle's, in "Where to Dine," below.

✪ **Sunset on West**. 115 West St., Bar Harbor, ME 04609. ☎ **207/288-4242.** Fax 207/288-4545. www.sunsetonwest.com. E-mail: sunsetonwest@gwi.net. 4 units. Peak season $175–$275; off season $150–$235. Rates include full breakfast. MC, V. Closed Nov–Mar. Children 16 and older welcome.

This gracious bed-and-breakfast opened in 1999 and instantly became one of our favorite small places in Bar Harbor for its great location, bold decor, attention to detail, and over-the-top breakfasts. The newly renovated 1910 shingled cottage is located on elegant West Street, with views of the water (but no waterfront property) and four guest rooms. Guests have run of much of the downstairs, including a music room with a baby grand piano and a wood-burning fireplace, and a pantry with a guest refrigerator, stemware, and a selection of teas. All guestrooms feature the plushest towels I've come across, Hammacher Schlemmer robes, down comforters and pillows, and VCRs (you can choose from 200 films in the collection of innkeepers Nancy and Mel Johnson). "Morning Glory" is the smallest of the rooms and doesn't face the water, but is still bright and cheerful and has a clawfoot tub. The "Sunset Suite" has a sitting room with gas fireplace and a porch with a water view; "Nocturne" is a spacious suite that's perfect for those seeking a getaway; it also has a porch along and a sitting room. Breakfasts are elaborate, with choices like ricotta hotcakes with blueberries, and crème fraîche scrambled eggs in dill crepes with smoked salmon.

MODERATE

Black Friar Inn. 10 Summer St., Bar Harbor, ME 04609. ☎ **207/288-5091.** Fax 207/288-4197. www.blackfriar.com. E-mail: blackfriar@blackfriar.com. 7 units (3 with private hall bathrooms). A/C. $90–$150 double, including full breakfast. 2-night minimum mid-June–mid-Oct. DISC, MC, V. Closed Dec–May. Children 12 and older welcome.

The Black Friar Inn, tucked on a side street overlooking the municipal building parking lot, is easily overlooked. But this yellow-shingled structure with quirky pediments and a some-what eccentric air offers good value for Bar Harbor. A former owner "collected" interiors and installed them throughout the house. Among them is a replica of the namesake Black Friar Pub in London, complete with elaborate carved-wood paneling (it's now a common room), stamped tin walls in the breakfast room, and a doctor's office (now a guest room). The Black Friar's rooms are carpeted and furnished with a mix of antiques, and most are rather small. The least expensive are the two garret rooms on the third floor, which each have a detached private bathroom down the hall.

Maples Inn. 16 Roberts Ave., Bar Harbor, ME 04609. ☎ **207/288-3443.** www.maplesinn.com. E-mail: maplesinn@acadia.net. 6 units (1 with private hall bathroom). Mid-June–mid-Oct $90–$150 double; off-season $60–$95. Rates include full breakfast. 2-night minimum on holiday weekends. DISC, MC, V. No small children.

The Maples is a popular destination among those attracted to outdoor activities. You'll often find guests swapping stories of the day's adventure on the handsome front porch, or lingering over breakfast to compare notes about the best hiking trails. The rather modest (by Bar Harbor standards) yellow farmhouse-style home is tucked away on a leafy side street among other B&Bs; it's an easy walk downtown to a movie or dinner. The innkeepers have a good way of making guests comfortable, with board games and paperbacks scattered about, and down comforters in all rooms. The rooms aren't huge, but you're not likely to feel cramped either. The two-room "White Birch" has a fireplace and is the largest;

"White Oak" has a private deck with plastic patio furniture. Breakfasts—including dishes like Bananas Holland America—are appropriately filling for a full day outdoors.

Mira Monte Inn. 69 Mt. Desert St., Bar Harbor, ME 04609. ☎ **800/ 553-5109** or 207/288-4263. Fax 207/288-3115. E-mail: mburns@acadia.net. 12 units. A/C TV TEL. Summer $145–$225 double; off-season $85–$130. Rates include breakfast. 2-night minimum stay in midsummer. AE, DC, DISC, MC, V. Closed Nov–May.

A stay at this impressive grayish-green Italianate mansion, built in 1864, feels a bit like a trip to grandmother's house—a grandmother who inherited most of her furniture from *her* grandmother. The antiques are more intriguing than elegant, and the common rooms are furnished in a pleasant country Victorian style. The 2-acre grounds, located within a few minutes' walk of Bar Harbor's restaurants and attractions, are attractively landscaped and include a cutting garden to keep the house in flowers. There's a nice brick terrace away from the street, which makes a fine place to enjoy breakfast on warm summer mornings. The guest rooms are blessed with a profusion of balconies and fireplaces—most rooms have one or the other or both. The room styles vary widely; some are heavy on the Victorian, others have the feel of a country farmhouse. If you're a light sleeper, avoid the rooms facing Mt. Desert Street; those facing the gardens in the rear are far more peaceful. Families should inquire about the suites in the adjacent outbuilding.

Primrose Inn. 73 Mount Desert St., Bar Harbor, ME 04609. ☎ **877/ 846-3424** or 207/288-4031. www.primroseinn.com. E-mail: primrose@ acadia.net. 10 units plus 5 efficiencies. TV TEL. Peak season $90–$175 double, shoulder seasons $75–$124 double; efficiencies $700–$950 per week. Daily rates include breakfast. DISC, MC, V. Closed late Oct–Apr. Pets allowed ($75 fee; call first).

This handsome pale-green and maroon Victorian stick-style inn, originally built in 1878, is one of the more notable properties on mansion row along Mount Desert Street. Its distinctive architecture has been not only preserved, but even improved upon with an addition in 1987 that added 10 rooms with private baths, and resulted in a number of balconies being added. The inn is comfortable and furnished with "functional antiques" and more modern reproductions, and many rooms have a floral theme and thick carpets. It's not a stuffy place—it has a distinctly informal air that encourages guests to mingle and relax in the common room, decorated in a light country Victorian style complete with piano. Two guest rooms feature whirlpools or fireplaces. The suites in the rear are spacious and comfortable, and the efficiencies make sense for families who could benefit from a kitchen (for rent by the week only).

Ullikana Bed & Breakfast. 16 The Field, Bar Harbor, ME 04609. ☎ **207/ 288-9552.** www.ullikana.com. 10 units (2 with detached bathroom), plus 6 across street in Yellow House. $135–$235 double ($185 in Yellow House). All rates include full breakfast. MC, V. Closed mid-Oct–early May. Children age 8 and up are welcome.

This Tudor cottage dates from 1885, and is tucked on a quiet side street near Agamont Park and the Bar Harbor Inn (the owners report that its name has long been shrouded in mystery). The 10-bedroom "cottage" is solidly built, and the downstairs with its oak trim and wainscotting is heavy and dark in English gentleman's club kind of way. The guest rooms are varied in size, but all are spacious and nicely decorated in a country Victorian mode, some with iron or brass cottage beds. "Audrey's Room" has a pleasant, storybook feel to it, with pastel colors, high ceilings, and a cozy bathroom with a clawfoot tub. Summery Room no. 6 has a deck with glimpses of the bay, along with a sofa and clawfoot tub for relaxing. Across the lane is the attractive "Yellow House," which has six additional rooms. The house and rooms are both simpler in style than the main cottage, and it boasts its own large common area on the first floor. Especially appealing here are the porch rockers with views of the whimsical sculpture on the grounds.

INEXPENSIVE

Acadia Hotel. 20 Mt. Desert St., Bar Harbor, ME 04609. ☎ **888/876-2463** or 207/288-5721. www.acadiahotel.com. E-mail: acadiahotel@acadia.net. 10 units. A/C TV. Peak season $75–$150 double; off-season $45–$135. MC, V.

The Acadia Hotel is nicely situated overlooking the Village Green, easily accessible to in-town activities and free shuttles to elsewhere on the island. This handsome, simple home dating from the late 19th century has a wraparound porch and guest rooms decorated in a busy country-floral motif that some might find rather frilly. The rooms vary widely in size and amenities; two have whirlpools, two have phones, and one has a kitchenette. Ask for the specifics when you book. The smaller rooms offer good value for those who don't plan to spend much time inside.

The Colony. Route 3 (P.O. Box 56), Hulls Cove, ME 04644. ☎ **800/ 524-1159** or 207/288-3383. E-mail: thecolony@acadia.net. 55 units. A/C TV TEL. $65–$105 double (discounts in Oct). Closed mid-Oct–early June. AE, DC, DISC, MC, V.

The Colony is a vintage motor court consisting of a handful of motel rooms (starting at $95) and a battery of cottages arrayed around a long green. It will be most appreciated by those with a taste for the authentically retro; others might decide to look for accommodation more lavishly appointed. The rooms are furnished in a simple '70s style that won't win any awards for decor, but all are comfortable; many have kitchenettes. It's situated just across Route 3 from a cobblestone beach, and a 10-minute drive from Bar Harbor. The Colony offers one of the better values on the island.

WHERE TO DINE

If you're looking for a low-key sweet after a meal at one of the restaurants reviewed below, head over to **Ben & Bill's Chocolate Emporium,** 66 Main St. (☎ **207/288-3281**), for a tasty and generous ice cream cone. In the evenings, you may have to join in the line spilling out the door. Visitors are often tempted to try their novelty, lobster ice cream. Visitors often regret giving into that temptation.

EXPENSIVE

George's. 7 Stephens Lane. ☎ **207/288-4505.** www.georgesbarharbor. com. Reservations recommended. Entrees $25; appetizer, entree, and dessert packages $37–$40. AE, DISC, MC, V. Daily 5:30–10pm; shorter hours after Labor Day. Closed Nov–early May. CONTEMPORARY MEDITERRANEAN.

George's takes some sleuthing to find, but it's worth the effort. This is a Bar Harbor classic, offering fine dining in classy but informal surroundings for more than two decades. (It's located in the small clapboard cottage behind Main Street's First National Bank.) George's captures the joyous feel of summer nicely with four smallish dining rooms (and plenty of open windows) and additional seating on the terrace outside, which is the best place to watch the gentle dusk settle over town. The service is upbeat and the meals wonderfully prepared. All entrees sell for one price ($25), and include salad, vegetable, and potato or rice. Offerings change with the season and availability. You won't go wrong with basic choices, like steamed lobster or roast chicken, but you're better off opting for the more adventurous fare like lobster strudel or the "To Die For" mustard shrimp (also offered as an appetizer). The house specialty is lamb in its many incarnations, including chargrilled lamb tenderloin with a rosemary-infused three-bean ragout. The restaurant consistently receives the annual *Wine Spectator* award of excellence.

✪ **Havana.** 318 Main St. ☎ **207/288-2822.** Reservations recommended. Main courses $12–$28. AE, DC, DISC, MC, V. Daily 5:30–10pm. Closed Jan–Mar. LATINO/FUSION.

Havana established a new creative standard for restaurants when it opened in 1999 in this town of fried fish and baked stuffed haddock. The spare but sparkling decor in the old storefront is as classy as you'll find in Boston or Washington, D.C., and the menu could compete in any urban area as well. Owner Michael Boland says his menu is inspired by Latino fare, which he melds nicely with New American ideas. While the offerings change weekly, expect items like appetizers of crab and roasted corn cakes with a cilantro sour cream, or sweet potato ravioli with a crabmeat-chipotle béchamel sauce. Recent entrees included ale-roasted rack of lamb, grilled tuna served with a tequila, lime and habanero glaze, and baked snapper with a mango-chili sauce served over coconut rice. The wine list is small and basic, but won't offend anyone.

Mache Bistro. 135 Cottage St. ☎ **207/288-0447.** Reservations recommended. Main courses $16–$22. AE, MC, V. Daily 6–10pm. Closed Apr–Jan 1. BISTRO.

Newly opened in 2000, Mache developed a devoted following among those who know quality food and preparation. The small restaurant (nine tables) with soothing but plain decor hides a sophisticated kitchen. (For instance, one wouldn't expect an imported cheese course offered in a place with plywood floors. Yet there you have it.) The menu changes monthly; appetizers could include a salad with bleu cheese, apples, and truffle oil; or a smoked-lobster bisque. Main courses recently featured a seared steak with black trumpet infused jus, and a Brittany fisherman's soup made with local seafood. Duck is often on the menu, and it's often a good choice.

Michelle's. 194 Main St. ☎ **207/288-0038.** Reservations required during peak season. Main courses $22–$42. Daily 6–9pm. Closed late Oct–early May. FRENCH.

Michelle's is located in the graceful Ivy Manor Inn (see above), and caught the attention of the state's epicures when it opened in 1997. The three dining rooms are elegant and set out with fresh roses and candles (there's outside seating when the weather's good). The extensive menu elaborates on traditional French cuisine with subtle New England twists. The appetizers include smoked salmon layered with a chervil mousse, and foie gras with black truffle. Main courses are elaborate affairs, with dishes like chateaubriand for two carved at the table, and Michelle's bouillabaisse for two, which includes lobster, mussels, clams, scallops and the fresh catch of the day. Appropriately for Bar Harbor, the seafood selection is extensive.

MODERATE

Café This Way. 14½ Mt. Desert St. ☎ **207/288-4483.** Reservations recommended for dinner. Main courses, breakfast $3.25–$5.95, dinner $12–$19. MC, V. Summer daily 7–11am (8am–1pm Sun), and Mon–Sat 6–9pm. NEW AMERICAN.

This is the kind of place we love, where they know how to do wonderful things with relatively simple ingredients. Café This Way has the feel of a casually hip coffee house, and is much more airy than one might guess upon first looking at this cozy cottage tucked on a side street down from the village green. Bookshelves line one wall, and there's a small bar tucked in a nook. The breakfasts are excellent and mildly sinful, with offerings like eggs Benedict with spinach, artichoke, and tomato. The red-skinned potatoes are crispy and delicious; the robust coffee requires two creamers to lighten it. Dinners are equally appetizing, with tasty dishes like butternut squash ravioli, crab cakes with a tequila-lime sauce, and filet mignon grilled with fresh basil.

Elaine's Starlight Oasis. 78 West St. ☎ **207/288-3287.** Reservations not accepted. Main courses $6.95–$12.95. Wed–Mon 5–9:30pm (closes earlier in off-season). Closed Nov–May 1. VEGETARIAN.

Bar Harbor's only fully vegetarian restaurant, Elaine's opened in 1998 and has been happily embraced by herbivorous visitors. Located near the waterfront on West Street in a cozy, contemporary space, the menu includes house specialties "beef" burgundy (made with seitan), and a Jamaican jerk tofu served with herb-roasted vegetables. Other offerings on the menu include salads, mushroom lasagna, eggplant casserole, and tempeh Parmesan. Deserts are rich and tasty, especially the homemade cheesecake.

Maggie's Classic Scales. 6 Summer St. ☎ **207/288-9007.** Reservations recommended in July and Aug. Main courses $14.95–$20.95. DISC, MC, V. Daily 5–10pm; closed mid-Oct–mid-June. SEAFOOD.

The slogan for Maggie's is "notably fresh seafood," and the place invariably delivers on that understated promise. (Only locally caught fish is used.) It's a casually elegant spot tucked off Cottage Street, good for a romantic evening with soothing music and attentive service. Appetizers include smoked salmon, lobster spring rolls, and steamed oysters with a saffron hollandaise. Main courses range from basic boiled lobster and simple grilled salmon, to more innovative offerings like Maine seafood provençal, and sautéed halibut with lime butter and heirloom beans. Desserts are homemade and worth leaving room for.

INEXPENSIVE

Jordan's Restaurant. 80 Cottage St. ☎ **207/288-3586.** Breakfast $2.95–$6.75; lunch $2.25–$8.25. MC, V. Daily 5am–2pm. Closed Feb and Mar. DINER.

This unpretentious breakfast and lunch joint has been dishing up filling fare since 1976, and it offers a glimpse of old Bar Harbor before the local economy was dominated by T-shirt shops. It's a popular haunt of working folks in town on one errand or another, but the staff is also genuinely friendly to tourists. Diners can settle into one of the pine booths or at a laminated table and order off the placemat menu, choosing from basic fare like grilled cheese with tomato or a slight but serviceable hamburger that's just $3.25. The soups and chowders are all homemade. Breakfast is the specialty here, with a broad selection of three-egg omelets, along with muffins and pancakes made with wild Maine blueberries.

Lompoc Cafe and Brewpub. 36 Rodick St. ☎ **207/288-9392.** Reservations not accepted. Sandwiches $4.50–$6.50; dinner $8.95–$15.95. MC, V. May–Nov daily 11:30am–1am. Closed Dec–Apr. AMERICAN/ECLECTIC.

The Lompoc Cafe has a well-worn, neighborhood bar feel to it—little wonder since waiters and other workers from around Bar Harbor congregate here after hours. The cafe consists of three sections—there's the original bar, a tidy beer garden just outside (try your hand at bocce), and a small and open barn-like structure at the garden's edge to handle the overflow. The

Lobster by the Pound

The ingredients for a proper feed at a local lobster pound are a pot of boiling water, a tank of lobsters, some well-worn picnic tables, a good view, and a six-pack of Maine beer—no pretensions, no frills.

One of the best destinations for lobster is **Beal's Lobster Pier** (☎ 207/244-7178) in Southwest Harbor, one of the oldest pounds in the area. **Thurston's Lobster Pound** (☎ 207/244-7600) in tiny Bernard (across the water from Bass Harbor) was atmospheric enough to be used as a backdrop for the Stephen King miniseries "Storm of the Century"; it's a fine place to linger toward dusk. **Abel's Lobster Pound** (☎ 207/276-5827), on Route 198 five miles north of Northeast Harbor, overlooks the deep blue waters of Somes Sound; eat at picnic tables under the pines or indoors at the restaurant. It's quite a bit pricier than other lobster restaurants at first glance, but they don't charge for the extras like many other lobster joints, and some visitors claim that the lobsters here are more succulent.

On the mainland just north of the causeway is the wonderful **Oak Point Lobster Pound** (☎ 207/667-6998). This is off the beaten path (although still popular and often crowded), where you can enjoy your lobster with a sensational view of the island's rocky hills. To get here, turn west off Route 3 onto Route 230 before crossing to Mt. Desert, then continue 4 miles to the restaurant.

brewery next door produces several unique beers, including a blueberry ale (intriguing concept, but ask for a sample before ordering a full glass), and the smooth Coal Porter. Bar menus are usually yawn-inducing, but this one has some pleasant surprises, like the Persian plate (hummus and grape leaves), Szechuan eggplant wrap, and crab and shrimp cakes. Vegetarians will also find a decent selection. Alas, the kitchen's aspirations don't always live up to its execution. Live music is offered some evenings, when there's a small cover charge.

3 Elsewhere on Mount Desert Island

There's plenty to explore outside of Acadia National Park and Bar Harbor. Quiet fishing villages, deep woodlands, and

unexpected ocean views are among the jewels that turn up
when one peers beyond the usual places.

ESSENTIALS
GETTING AROUND

The east half of the island is best navigated on Route 3, which
forms the better part of a loop from Bar Harbor through Seal
Harbor and past Northeast Harbor before returning up the
eastern shore of Somes Sound. Route 102 and Route 102A
provide access to the island's western half. See information on
the **free islandwide shuttle service** in "Getting Around" Acadia National Park section on page 160.

VISITOR INFORMATION

The best source of information on the island is at the **Thomp-
son Island Information Center** (☎ 207/288-3411) on
Route 3 just south of the causeway connecting Mount Desert
Island with the mainland. Another source of local information
is **Mount Desert Chamber of Commerce,** P.O. Box 675,
Northeast Harbor, ME 04662 (☎ 207/276-5040).

EXPLORING THE REST OF THE ISLAND

On the tip of the eastern lobe of Mount Desert Island is the
staid, prosperous community of **Northeast Harbor,** long one
of the favored retreats among the Eastern Seaboard's upper
crust. Those without personal invitations to come as house
guests will need to be satisfied with glimpses of the shingled
palaces set in the fragrant spruce forests and along the rocky
shore. But the village itself is worth investigating. Situated on
a scenic, narrow harbor, with the once-grand Asticou Inn at its
head, Northeast Harbor is possessed of a refined sense of elegance that's best appreciated by finding a vantage point, then
sitting and admiring.

One of the best, least publicized places for enjoying views
of the harbor is from the understatedly spectacular ✪ **Asticou
Terraces** (☎ 207/276-5130). Finding the parking lot can be
tricky: Head one-half mile east (toward Seal Harbor) on
Route 3 from the junction with Route 198, and look for the
small gravel lot on the water side of the road with a sign reading ASTICOU TERRACES. Park here, cross the road on foot, and
set off up a magnificent path made of local rock that ascends
the sheer hillside with expanding views of the harbor and the
town. This pathway, with its precise stonework and the

occasional bench and gazebo, is one of the nation's hidden marvels of landscape architecture. Created by Boston landscape architect Joseph Curtis, who summered here for many years prior to his death in 1928, the pathway seems to blend in almost preternaturally with its spruce-and-fir surroundings, as if it were created by an act of God rather than of man. Curtis donated the property to the public for quiet enjoyment.

Continue on the trail at the top of the hillside and you'll soon arrive at Curtis's cabin (open to the public daily in summer), behind which lies the formal **Thuya Gardens,** which are as manicured as the terraces are natural. These wonderfully maintained gardens, designed by noted landscape architect Charles K. Savage, attract flower enthusiasts, students of landscape architecture, and local folks looking for a quiet place to rest. It's well worth the trip. A donation of $2 is requested of visitors to the garden; admission to the terraces is free.

From the harbor visitors can depart on a seaward trip to the beguilingly remote **Cranberry Islands.** You have a couple of options: either travel with a national park guide to Baker Island, the most distant of this small cluster of low islands, and explore the natural terrain; or hop one of the ferries to either Great or Little Cranberry Island and explore on your own. On Little Cranberry there's a small historical museum run by the National Park Service that's worth a few minutes. Both islands feature a sense of being well away from it all, but neither offers much in the way of shelter or tourist amenities, so travelers should head out prepared for the possibility of shifting weather. For ferry information, contact **Beal & Bunker** (☎ 207/244-3575), which departs from Northeast Harbor ($10 round-trip adults, $5 children under 12).

When leaving Northeast Harbor, plan to drive out via **Sargent Drive.** This one-way route runs through Acadia National Park along the shore of Somes Sound, affording superb views of this glacially carved inlet.

On the far side of Somes Sound, there's good hiking (see p. 165, "Hike a Mountain," under the Enjoying the Park section.), and the towns of Southwest Harbor and Bass Harbor. These are both home to fishermen and boatbuilders, and are rather more humble than the settlements of the landed gentry at Northeast and Seal harbors across the way.

In Southwest Harbor, look for the intriguing **Wendell Gilley Museum of Bird Carving** (☎ 207/244-7555) on

Route 102 just north of town. Housed in a new building constructed specifically to display the woodcarvings, the museum contains the masterwork of Wendell Gilley, a plumber who took up carving birds as a hobby in 1930. His creations, ranging from regal bald eagles to delicate chickadees, are startlingly lifelike and beautiful. The museum offers woodcarving classes for those inspired by the displays, and a gift shop sells fine woodcarving. It's open Tuesday to Sunday 10am to 4pm, June to October, Friday to Sunday in May, November, and December. The museum is closed January to April. Admission is $3.25 adults, $1 children 5 to 12.

WHERE TO STAY

Asticou Inn. Rte. 3, Northeast Harbor, ME 04662. ☎ **800/258-3373** or 207/276-3344. www.asticou.com. E-mail: asticou@acadia.net. 47 units. TEL. Summer $302–$392 double, including continental breakfast and dinner (from $250 with breakfast only); spring and fall $140–$210 double, with breakfast. MC, V. Closed Nov–mid-May. Children 6 and older welcome.

The once-grand Asticou Inn, which dates to 1883, occupies a prime location at the head of Northeast Harbor. Its weathered gray shingles and profusion of overhanging eaves give it a stern demeanor, but it also has elements of eccentricity. The Asticou is more elegant on the exterior and in its location than in the interior, although a $500,000 renovation in 1999 spruced things up a bit. Despite some incipient shabbiness, a wonderful Old World gentility seems to arise from the creaking floorboards and through the thin guest-room walls. The rooms are furnished in a simple summer-home style, as if a more opulent décor was somehow too ostentatious.

Dining: Recent wholesale changes have improved the dining room, where longtime guests had noted a decline in quality. The dinner dance and elaborate "grand buffet" on Thursday nights in summer remain hallowed island traditions and worth checking out. (Expect smoked seafood, lobster Newburg, salads and relishes, a dessert tray, and more.) Seatings are on the hour; jackets are requested for men in the evening.

Amenities: Outdoor heated pool, one clay tennis court, concierge, limited room service, laundry, turndown service, baby-sitting, valet parking, safe deposit boxes, business center, conference rooms.

✪ **Claremont.** P.O. Box 137, Southwest Harbor, ME 04679. ☎ **800/ 244-5036** or 207/244-5036. www.theclaremonthotel.com. clmhotel@ acadia.net. 30 inn rooms, 12 cottages. TEL. Inn rooms: July–Labor Day $150 double including breakfast, $225 including breakfast and dinner; off-season $89 double including breakfast, $190 including breakfast and dinner. Cottages: July–Labor Day $165–$185; off-season $100–$150. 3-day minimum on cottages. No credit cards. Closed mid-Oct–early June.

Early prints of the 1884 Claremont show an austere four-story wooden building with a single gable overlooking Somes Sound from a grassy rise. And the place hasn't changed all that much since. The Claremont offers nothing fancy or elaborate, just simple, classic New England grace. It's wildly appropriate that the state's most high-profile and combative croquet tournament takes place here annually in early August; all those folks in their whites seem right at home. The common areas and dining rooms are pleasantly appointed in an affable country style. There's a library with rockers, a fireplace, and jigsaw puzzles waiting to be assembled. Two other fireplaces in the lobby take the chill out of the morning air.

Most of the guest rooms are bright and airy, furnished with antiques and some old furniture that doesn't quite qualify as "antique." The bathrooms are modern. Guests opting for the full meal plan at the inn are given preference in reserving rooms overlooking the water; it's almost worth it, although dinners are lackluster. There's also a series of cottages, available for a three-day minimum. Some are set rustically in the piney woods; others offer pleasing views of the sound.

Dining: The dining room is open nightly. Meals are mainly reprises of American classics like salmon, grilled lamb, and steamed lobster; guests report being underwhelmed by the kitchen's flair. The dining room is open to the public; jackets and ties are requested on men. Entrees range from $18 to $24.

Amenities: One clay tennis court, rowboats, bicycles (free to guests), croquet court, baby-sitting arrangements.

Inn at Southwest. 371 Main St. (P.O. Box 593), Southwest Harbor, ME 04679. ☎ **207/244-3835.** www.innatsouthwest.com. E-mail innatsw@ acadia.net. 9 units (2 with private hall bathrooms). Summer and early fall $95–$145 double; off-season $65–$105. All rates include full breakfast. Closed Nov–Apr. DISC, MC, V.

There's a decidedly late-19th-century air to this mansard-roofed Victorian home, but it's restrained on the frills. The guest rooms are named after Maine lighthouses, and are furnished with both contemporary and antique furniture. All rooms have ceiling fans and down comforters. Among the most pleasant rooms is "Blue Hill Bay" on the third floor, with its large bathroom, sturdy oak bed and bureau, and glimpses of the scenic harbor. Breakfasts offer ample reason to rise and shine, featuring specialties like vanilla Belgian waffles with raspberry sauce, and crab potato bake.

✪ **Lindenwood Inn.** 118 Clark Point Rd. (P.O. Box 1328), Southwest Harbor, ME 04679. ☎ **207/244-5335.** www.lindenwood.com. 21 units (some with shower only), 2 suites. June–mid-Oct $95–$245 double; mid-Oct–June $75–$195. All rates include full breakfast. AE, MC, V.

The Lindenwood offers a refreshing change from the fusty, overly draperied inns that tend to proliferate along Maine's coast. Housed in a handsome 1902 Queen Anne–style home at the harbor's edge, the inn's rooms are modern and uncluttered, the colors simple and bold. The adornments are few (those that do exist are mostly from the innkeeper's collection of African and Pacific art and artifacts), but clean lines and bright natural light more than create a relaxing mood—you'll even begin to view the cobblestone doorstops as works of art. The spacious suite with its great harbor views is especially appealing. If you're on a budget, ask for a room in the annex, housed in an 1883 home just a minute's walk down the block. The rooms are somewhat smaller and unadorned, but still offer nice touches (like bright halogen reading lamps) and make a superb base from which to explore the area. Eight of the rooms feature fireplaces; most also have telephones, but ask when you book if this is important to you.

Amenities: Jacuzzi, heated outdoor pool, boat dock.

WHERE TO DINE

For a quick bite or a picnic lunch to go, don't overlook the informal **Docksider Restaurant,** hidden a block off the main commercial drag in Northeast Harbor, 14 Sea St (☎ **207/ 276-3965**). The crab rolls and lobster rolls are outstanding, made simply and perfectly. The small restaurant also features a host of other fare, including lobster dinners, sandwiches, chowder, fried seafood, and grilled salmon.

The Burning Tree. Rte. 3, Otter Creek. ☎ **207/288-9331.** Reservations recommended. Main courses $16–$22. Aug daily 5–9pm; Mid-June–July, early fall Wed–Mon 5–9pm. Closed Columbus Day–mid-June. REGIONAL/ORGANIC.

Located on busy Route 3 between Bar Harbor and Northeast Harbor, The Burning Tree is an easy restaurant to speed right by. But that's a mistake. This low-key restaurant, with its bright, open, and sometimes noisy dining room, serves up the freshest food in the area. Much of the produce and herbs comes from its own gardens, with the rest of the ingredients supplied locally wherever possible. Seafood is the specialty here, and it's consistently prepared with imagination and skill. The menu changes often to reflect local availability.

Jordan Pond House. Park Loop Rd., Acadia National Park (near Seal Harbor). ☎ 207/276-3316. Advance reservations not accepted; call before arriving to hold table. Lunch $6.50–$12.75; afternoon tea $6.25–$7.25; dinner $13–$18. AE, DISC, MC, V. Mid-May–late Oct daily 11:30am–8pm (until 9pm July–Aug). AMERICAN.

The secret to the Jordan Pond House? Location, location, location. The restaurant traces its roots back to 1847, when a farm was established on this picturesque property at the southern tip of Jordan Pond looking north toward The Bubbles, a picturesque pair of glacially sculpted mounds. It was popular during the mania for teahouses in the late 19th century. But tragedy struck in 1979 when the original structure and its birch-bark dining room was destroyed by fire. A more modern, two-level dining room was built in its place—it has less charm, but it still has the location. And the food. If the weather's agreeable, ask for a seat on the lawn with its unrivaled views. Afternoon tea with popovers is a hallowed Jordan Pond House tradition. Ladies-Who-Lunch sit next to Mountain-Bikers-Who-Wear-Lycra, and everyone feasts on the huge, tasty popovers and strawberry jam served with a choice of teas or fresh lemonade. The lobster and crab rolls are abundant and filling; the lobster stew is expensive but very, very good. Dinners include classic resort entrees like prime rib, steamed lobster, and baked scallops with a crumb topping.

Keenan's. Route 102A, Bass Harbor. ☎ 207/244-3403. Reservations suggested for parties of 5 or more. Sandwiches and main courses $5–$17. No credit cards. Summers 5–9pm daily; weekends only in off-season. SEAFOOD.

Boisterous, inelegant, and fun. That's the quickest description of this classic and informal seafood shack at a fork in the road. It's long been one of those local secrets that most travelers zip right by without a second thought. It's worth slowing down, pulling in, and ordering up some of the best seafood value for your money on the island. The fried clams are well prepared, and the spicy gumbo packs a kick. If you're of a mind to gorge on seafood, go with the teeming seafood sampler, which includes lobster, crab, mussels, clams, and corn, all for under $20.

Redfield's. Main St., Northeast Harbor. ☎ **207/276-5283.** Reservations strongly recommended in summer. Main courses $18.95–$26.95. AE, MC, V. June–Oct Mon–Sat 6:30–9pm; Nov–May Fri–Sat only, 6:30–9pm. CONTEMPORARY.

Located in a storefront in Northeast Harbor's tiny downtown, this elegant restaurant is decorated with a subtle and restrained touch. Patrons can enjoy a libation at the wonderful marble bar (it was taken from an old soda fountain), then settle in and peruse the short but tempting menu, which draws its inspiration from cuisines around the world. Choices change frequently, but could include appetizers of Stilton cheese fondue over artichoke hearts, or smoked lobster with a sauce of corn, tomato, and serrano chilies; entrees are along the lines of sesame-dipped salmon fillet with ginger-tamari sauce, and venison with dried cranberry and port compote.

8

The Downeast Coast

*T*he term "Downeast" comes from the old sailing ship days. Ships heading east had the prevailing winds at their backs, making it an easy "downhill" run to the eastern ports. Heading the other way took more skill and determination.

Today, it's a rare traveler who gets far Downeast to explore the rugged coastline of Washington County. Few tourists venture beyond Acadia National Park, discouraged perhaps by the lack of services for visitors and the low number of high-marquee attractions. They may also be creeped out by the sometimes spooky remoteness of the region. But Downeast Maine has substantial appeal. There's an authenticity that's been lost in much of coastal Maine, and is only a distant memory in the rest of New England. Many longtime visitors to the state say that this is how all of Maine used to be back in the 1940s and 1950s, when writer E.B. White first arrived. Pad Thai, the *New York Times,* and designer coffee have not yet crossed the border into Washington County. Those seeking a glimpse of a rugged, hardscrabble way of life where independence is revered above all else aren't likely to go away disappointed.

Many residents still get by as their forebears did—by scratching a living from the land. Scalloping, lobstering, and fishing remain major sources of income, as do logging and other forest work. Grubbing for bloodworms in spring, picking wild blueberries in the barrens in late summer, and tipping fir trees for wreathmaking in late fall round out the income. In recent years, aquaculture has become an important part of the economy around Passamaquoddy and Cobscook bays; travelers will see vast floating pens, especially around Eastport and Lubec, where salmon are raised for markets worldwide.

1 Essentials

GETTING THERE

Downeast Maine is most commonly reached via Route 1 from Ellsworth. Those heading directly to Washington County in summer can take a more direct, less congested route via Rte. 9 from Brewer (across the river from Bangor), connecting south to Route 1 via Rte. 193 or Rte. 192.

VISITOR INFORMATION

The **Machias Bay Area Chamber of Commerce,** P.O. Box 606, Machias, ME 04654 (☎ 207/255-4402), provides tourist information from its offices at 23 E. Main St. (Route 1). The offices are open 9am to 5pm Tuesday to Saturday (also open Monday in summer).

EVENTS

Eastport celebrates **Fourth of July** in extravagant hometown style each year, a tradition that began in 1820 after the British gave up possession of the city (they captured it during the War of 1812). Some 15,000 people come to this city of 1,900 during the four-day event, which includes vendors, games, and contests, and culminates with a grand parade on the afternoon of the Fourth.

The **Machias Wild Blueberry Festival** celebrates the local cash crop in mid-August each year. Events include a blueberry pancake breakfast (of course!), a blueberry pie-eating contest, performances, and the sales of blueberry-themed gift items. Contact the Chamber of Commerce (☎ 207/255-4402) for the exact dates.

2 Exploring Downeast Maine

Below are some of the highlights of the region, described from west to east. The driving time direct from Ellsworth to Lubec via Routes 1 and 189 is about two hours with no stops. Allow considerably more time for visiting the sites mentioned below, and just plain snooping around.

Burnham Tavern. Main St. (Rte 192), Machias. ☎ **207/255-4432.** $2 adult, 25¢ children. Mid-June–Labor Day Mon–Fri 9am-5pm.

In June 1775, a month after the Battle of Lexington in Massachusetts, a group of patriots hatched a plan at the gambrel-roofed Burnham Tavern that led to the first naval battle of the Revolutionary War. The armed schooner *Margaretta* was in Machias harbor to obtain wood for British barracks. The patriots didn't think much of this idea, and attacked the ship using much smaller boats they had commandeered, along

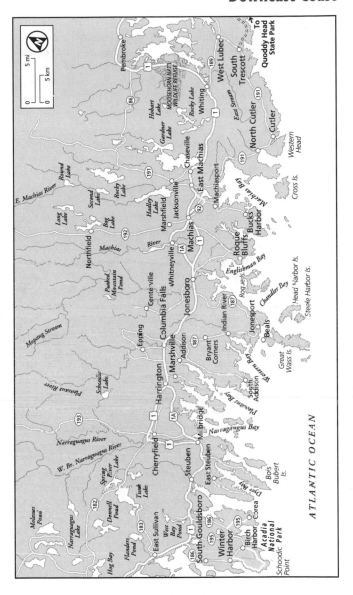

with muskets, swords, axes, and pitchforks. The patriots prevailed, killing the captain of the *Margaretta* in the process.

Visitors can learn all about this episode during a tour of the tavern, which was built on a rise overlooking the river in 1770. On display are booty taken from the British ship, along with the original tap table and other historic furniture and ephemera. The tours lasts around 1 hour.

✪ **Cutler Coastal Trail.** Rte. 191, Cutler. Contact Maine Bureau of Park and Recreation ☎ **207/287-3821**. Free admission. Always open. Directions: from the village of Cutler: head northeast on Rte. 191; approx. 4.5 miles outside of town look for parking lot and signs on right.

Marked by a sign at a small parking lot, this dramatic loop trail passes through diverse ecosystems, including bogs, barrens, and dark and tangled spruce forests. But the highlight of this trail, which traverses state-owned land, is the mile-long segment along the rocky headlands high above the restless ocean. Some of the most dramatic coastal views in the state are located along this isolated stretch, which overlooks dark-gray-to-black rocks and an often tumultuous sea. Visible on the horizon across the Bay of Fundy are the west-facing cliffs of the Canadian island of Grand Manan. Plan on at least 2 or 3 hours for the whole loop, although more time spent whiling away the afternoon hours on the rocks is well worth the while. If it's damp or foggy, rainpants are advised to fend off the moisture from the low brush along the trail.

Eastport Historic District. Water St., Eastport. Directions: From Rte. 1 in Perry, take Rte. 190 south for 7 miles.

In the 1880s the city of Eastport—three miles from Lubec by water but 50 minutes by car—had a population of nearly 5,000 and 18 bustling sardine plants. The population is now less than 2,000 and all the sardine plants are gone. But much of the handsome commercial brick architecture remains on downtown's Water St., a compact thoroughfare that also affords lovely views of Campobello Island and Passamaquoddy Bay. The majority of the buildings between the post office and the library are on the National Register of Historic Places. Here you'll find the nation's oldest operating ship chandlery (S.L. Wadsworth & Son, 42 Water St., ☎ **207/853-4343**), and the Quoddy Maritime Museum, Water Street (☎ **207/ 853-4297**), where you can view a 14 foot by 16 foot model of the proposed Passamaquoddy Tidal Power Project, a FDR-era attempt to harness the 25-foot tides to produce hydroelectric power.

Just north of Eastport is the Old Sow, said to be the largest whirlpool in the western hemisphere. It's a bit finicky and is impressive only during the highest tides; the best way to see it is to take a seasonal ferry to Deer Island (in New Brunswick, Canada) and back. There's a nominal fee for passengers, and you don't have to go through the cursory Canadian customs check if you don't want to disembark. The ferry departs from behind the Eastport Fish and Lobster House at 167 Water St.

Great Wass Preserve. Black Duck Cove Rd., Great Wass Island, Jonesport. Contact Nature Conservancy ☎ **207/729-5181.** Free admission. Open daylight hours. Directions: From Jonesport cross bridge to Beals Island (signs); continue across causeway to Great Wass Island. Bear right at next fork; pavement ends; continue past lobster pound to a small parking lot on the left marked by Nature Conservancy logo (oak leaf).

This exceptional 1,524-acre parcel, acquired by the Nature Conservancy in 1978, contains an excellent 5-mile loop hike covering a wide cross-section of native terrain, including bogs, heath, rocky coastline, and forests of twisted jack pines. Maps and a birding checklist are found in a stand at the parking lot. Follow one fork of the trail to the shoreline; work your way along the storm-tossed boulders to the other fork, then make your way back to your car. If a heavy fog has settled into the area, as often happens, don't let that deter your hike. The dense mist creates a medieval tableau that makes for magical hiking.

Roosevelt Campobello International Park. Rte. 774, Campobello Island, New Brunswick. ☎ **506/752-2922.** Free admission. Daily 10am–6pm. Closed mid-Oct–late May.

Take a brief excursion out of the country and across the time zone. The U.S. and Canada maintain a joint national park here, celebrating the life of Franklin D. Roosevelt, who summered here with his family in the early 1900s. Like other affluent Americans, the Roosevelt family made an annual trek to the prosperous colony at Campobello Island. The island lured folks from the sultry cities with a promise of cool air and a salubrious effect on the circulatory system. ("The extensive forests of balsamic firs seem to affect the atmosphere of this region, causing a quiet of the nervous system and inviting sleep," read an 1890 real estate brochure.) The future U.S. president came to this island every summer between

1883—the year after he was born—and 1921, when he was suddenly stricken with polio. Franklin and his siblings spent those summers exploring the coves and sailing around the bay, and he always recalled his time here fondly. (It was his "beloved island," he said, coining a phrase that gets no rest in local promotional brochures.)

You'll learn much about Roosevelt and his early life at the visitor center, where you can view a brief film, and during a self-guided tour of the elaborate mansion, covered in cranberry-colored shingles. For a "cottage" this huge, it is surprisingly comfortable and intimate. The park is truly an international park—run by a commission with representatives from both the U.S. and Canada, making it like none other in the world. U.S. citizens won't need more than a driver's license to cross the border and return.

Leave some time to explore farther afield in the 2,800-acre park, which offers scenic coastline and 8.5 miles of walking trails. Maps and walk suggestions are available at the visitor center.

Ruggles House. Main St., Columbia Falls. ☎ **207/483-4637.** $3.50 adult, $2.50 children. June–mid-Oct Mon–Sat 9:30am–4pm, Sun 11am–4:30pm.

This fine Federal home dates from 1818, and was built for Thomas Ruggles, an early timber merchant and civic leader. The home is very grand and opulent, but in a curiously miniature sort of way. There's a flying staircase in the central hallway, pine doors hand-painted to resemble mahogany, and detailed wood carvings in the main parlor, done over the course of 3 years by an English craftsman equipped, legend says, with only a penknife. Locals once said his hand was guided by an angel. Tours last 20 minutes to a half-hour

Schoodic Point. Acadia National Park, Winter Harbor. ☎ **207/288-3338.** Free admission. Directions: drive east from Ellsworth on Rte. 1 for 17 miles to W. Gouldsboro, then turn south on Rte. 186 to Winter Harbor. Outside of Winter Harbor, look for the brown-and-white National Park signs.

This remote unit of Acadia National Park is just 7 miles from Mount Desert Island across Frenchman Bay, but it's a long 50-mile drive to get here via Ellsworth. A pleasing loop drive hooks around the tip of Schoodic Point. The one-way road (no park pass required) winds along the water and through forests of spruce and fir. Good views of the mountains of Acadia open up across Frenchman Bay; you'll also see buildings of a historic naval station housed on the point. Park near the tip of this isolated promontory and explore the salmon-colored rocks that plunge into the ocean. It's especially dramatic when the seas are agitated and the surf crashes loudly.

West Quoddy Head Light & Quoddy Head State Park. W. Quoddy Head Rd., Lubec. ☎ 207/733-0911. Lighthouse grounds: free admission. Park: $1 adult, 50¢ children 5–11. Open during daylight hours.

This famed red-and-white light (it's been likened to a barbershop pole and a candy cane) marks the easternmost point of the United States and ushers boats into the Lubec Channel between the U.S. and Canada. The light, operated by the Coast Guard, isn't open to the public, but visitors can walk the grounds near the light and along headlands at the adjacent state park. The park overlooks rocky shoals that are ceaselessly battered by high winds, pounding waves, and some of the most powerful tides in the world. Watch for fishing boats straining against the currents, or seals playing in the waves and sunning on the offshore rocks. The park consists of 480 acres of coastline and bog, and several trails wind through the dark conifer forest and crest the tops of rocky cliffs. Some of the most dramatic views are just a short walk down the path at the far end of the parking lot.

3   Where to Stay & Dine

Crocker House Country Inn. HC 77 (Box 171), Hancock Point, ME 04640. ☎ 207/422-6806. Fax 207/422-3105. www.acadia.net/crocker. E-mail: crocker@acadia.net. 11 units. TEL. Mid-June–mid-Oct $90–$130 double; off-season $70–$90. Rates include breakfast. AE, MC, V. Closed Jan–late Apr. Pets allowed with prior permission.

Built in 1884, this handsome, shingled inn is off the beaten track on picturesque Hancock Point, across Frenchmen Bay from Mount Desert Island. It's a cozy retreat, perfect for rest, relaxation, and quiet walks (it's about a 4-minute walk from the water's edge). The rooms are tastefully decorated with comfortable country decor. Two rooms are located in the adjacent carriage house. The common areas are more relaxed than fussy, like the living room of a friend who's always happy to see you. The inn has a few bikes for guests to explore the point; nearby are four clay tennis courts.

Dining: Dinner here is a highlight, with tremendous care taken with the meals, and a fun, convivial atmosphere, featuring live piano on weekends. The menu focuses on traditional favorites, including French onion soup, artichoke hearts with crabmeat, and oysters Rockefeller for starters. Entrees include a good selection of fresh seafood, such as scallops, salmon, and shrimp, all creatively prepared; non-seafood items include filet mignon and rack of lamb. The desserts and breads are home-made. There's a Sunday brunch during the peak summer months.

✪ **Le Domaine.** Rte. 1 (P.O. Box 496), Hancock, ME 04640. ☎ **800/554-8498** or 207/422-3395. www.ledomaine.com. E-mail: ledomaine@acadia.net. Fax 207/422-2316. 5 units. A/C TEL. $175 double, $260 suites. Rates include full breakfast. AE, DISC, MC, V. Closed mid-Oct–mid-June.

An epicure's delight, Le Domaine long ago established its repu-tation as one of the most elegant and delightful destinations in Maine. Set on Route 1 about 10 minutes east of Ellsworth, this inn has the continental flair of an impeccable French auberge. While the highway in front can be a bit noisy, the garden and woodland walks out back offer plenty of compen-sating serenity. The rooms are comfortable and tastefully appointed without being pretentious; a couple of years ago the innkeeper combined four rooms to create two suites, and added air conditioning and phones to all of the rooms. The guest rooms are on the second floor in the rear of the property; private terraces face the gardens and the 90 acres of forest owned by the inn. Rooms are loaded with extras, like Bose radios, fresh flowers, lighted make-up mirrors, wine glasses, and corkscrews.

Dining: The real draw here is the exquisite dining room, which is famed for its understated elegance. Chef Nicole Purslow carries on the tradition established when her French-immigrant mother opened the inn in 1946, offering superb country cooking in the handsome candle-lit dining room with pine-wood floors and sizable fireplace. The ever-changing meals still sing. My favorite appetizer? It's called "My mother's pâté of organic chicken livers that I cannot improve upon." Entrees might include baby grilled lamb chops in a house marinade, or lightly crusted sweetbreads with capers and lemon juice. Plan to check in by 5:30pm as dinner is served Tuesday to Saturday between 6pm and 9pm. Dinner is avail-able to non-guests; entrees are $24.50 to $29.

See also Accommodations and Restaurant indexes, below.

RESTAURANT INDEX